Sarabeth's Bakery

From My Hands to Yours

Sarabeth Levine

with Rick Rodgers · Photographs by Quentin Bacon

Foreword by Mimi Sheraton

RIZZOLI
NEW YORK

New York · Paris · London · Milan

I dedicate this book to the memory of
my beloved aunt, Ruth Margouleff, who shared *Grandmère's* secret
marmalade recipe, from her hands to mine.

·······························

First published in the United States of America in 2010 by Rizzoli International Publications, Inc. 300 Park Avenue South · New York, New York 10010 www.rizzoliusa.com Text copyright © 2010 Sarabeth Levine · written with Project Editor: Sandra Gilbert · Assistant Project Editor: Tracey Zabar · Design: Louise Fili Ltd. · Typesetting: 2 Eggs On A Roll 10 9 8 7 6 5 4 3 2 1 · Printed in China · ISBN: 978-0-8478-3408-2 · Library of Congress Control Number: 2010927318 Rick Rodgers · Photography copyright © 2010 Quentin Bacon · All rights reserved. No part of this publication may be reproduced, stored in a retrieval system, or transmitted in any form or by any means, electronic, mechanical, photocopying, recording, or otherwise, without prior consent of the publisher. 2010 2011 2012 2013

Contents

Chapter Five
Party Cakes and Company 139

Chapter Six
Pies and Tarts 171

Chapter Seven
Plain and Fancy Cookies 201

Chapter Eight
Spoon Desserts 227

Foreword

by Mimi Sheraton

·····························

YOU HAVE THE BOOK, NOW SIT BACK AND WAIT FOR THE MOVIE. CONSIDER AN APPEALINGLY WHOLESOME, INSPIRING STORY OF AN EARTHY, CHEER-ful career woman who began by simmering up tiny jars of marmalade in a New York City apartment kitchen. Despite all odds—juggling home, husband, and children and the prejudices against women as entrepreneurs—she went on to create seven restaurants and an award-winning, palate-winning line of jewel-like preserves and specialty foods. In fact, Sarabeth Levine looks so much the part, she could really play herself. She is much in the long tradition of the *cuisine de femme*, a woman chef who is a keeper of the flame and always reflects tradition, even when making subtle innovations. Or perhaps in this case, *patisserie de femme* would be more to the point.

Just a glance at the photograph facing the title page of this book shows us how the film should open: We see a starchy white smock tied with a neat bow on a trim, self-assured figure. Strong, obviously ca-pable hands generously offer an apronful of warm plump and knobby brioche, undoubtedly fresh from the oven and just as undoubtedly made by those same hands. One can almost sniff the pastries' sweet, buttery yeastiness and anticipate the joy of teeth sinking through the thin golden brown crust into the soft, sunny sponge inside.

In some ways, I may regret ever seeing this book. As though my life is not complicated enough, a new bug has bitten me. Now I want to bake, of all things. Of all things, because I am by nature much more a cook than a baker, preferring the comparatively loose discipline a cook usually can enjoy, in contrast to what seems to be the merciless exactitude required of the baker. Unless of course that baker really understands what's going on with each cookie and croissant and so can improvise and create varia-tions, or perhaps even save a batch of dough en route to disaster. Which is to say, unless that baker is someone as talented as Sarabeth Levine. Now with these delicious photographs and explicit recipes for a mouthwatering array of classic and original temptations, I'm beginning to think that baking may be simpler than I thought.

But then through the many years I have known Sarabeth, she has changed my mind about a lot of things. Never a lover of jams or other sweet fruit preserves, I first considered her orange-apricot marmalade an exception to my rule, as I do now with my new favorite—the rich and sophisticated sunset-tinged blood orange marmalade that I stir into plain yogurt, spread onto toasted, buttered

English muffins or hot waffles, and dab on top of vanilla ice cream or the sour cream that crowns my cheese blintzes.

Similarly I would never have imagined that I could be knocked out by cream of tomato soup or that salty, tired stand-by of Jewish kosher dairy restaurants, lox with eggs and onions. Yet about thirty years ago when I had my first brunch in Sarabeth's original tiny cafe on Amsterdam Avenue, I tasted her versions of those dishes, became addicted, and reorder them to this day, even fighting my desire to stray to her homey chicken pot pie at lunch or dinner. Almost overwhelming these savory dishes were the scrumptious breads and pastries that remain Sarabeth's real claim to fame and that are the subjects of this book.

Now one of my favorite ways to take my mandatory thirty-minute morning constitutional is to walk from my home in Greenwich Village to the Chelsea Market and back. Many mornings my halfway stop is Sarabeth's Bakery in that market, where I check out the activity in the huge, airy white and floury bake shop, wave hello to Sarabeth as she is often there at that hour, and then settle down in the cafe for an adorable puffy cheese Danish and a cup of really good steaming hot coffee. Before leaving I replenish my freezer supply of the best rugelach in New York and the best I have ever had this side of my grandmother's kitchen. Each one is crisply hand-tapered of light cream cheese dough, and crunchy with walnuts, a hint of cocoa, and caramelized cinnamon sugar; the little roll-ups held together with the thinnest glaze of jam, my preference being apricot over raspberry when I have the choice. Granted such activity does not add up to the most rigorous workout, to say nothing of the fact that the yeasty, gently sweet cheese Danish more than makes up for any calorie loss realized on my walk, but in this case just breaking even is winning.

As there are recipes for all of those luscious baked goods in this book, I may become self-sufficient, although I doubt it. Sarabeth has generously—and fearlessly—given the most exacting instructions for ingredients, utensils, and techniques, to say nothing of the recipes for all of her specialties. In some instances they even are annotated for professional bakers, a mark of her own justified self-confidence.

So where will I start my new life as an amateur baker? Choosing by photographs and my own taste, that would surely mean the brioche, the apple turnovers, the almost "tasteable" chocolate babka, currant scones, and the rosemary focaccia that would be delicious with chunks of Parmesan. Trying for richer effects, I surely would take a stab at the turban-shaped chocolate cake credited to Mrs. Stein and the incomparable, snowy vanilla-scented cheesecake. Not being a lover of rich layer cakes, I might skip that category in order to have more time for those wonderful rugelach and glorious berry and fruit tarts, not to forget lemon meringue tartlets and the pecan and bourbon tart. And maybe all of the cookies—so far my favorite things to bake and eat and have on hand for visits from my granddaughter. And maybe when she is expected for dinner, dessert will be the triple-chocolate chocolate pudding. Topped with whipped cream and chocolate shavings, how wrong could I go?

In the end, how many of these recipes I actually try will be obvious from the number of pages marked with butter, red berry, and chocolate fingerprints.

Stay tuned.

Introduction

....

IT'S AMAZING HOW A FAMILY RECIPE CHANGED MY LIFE COMPLETELY, INSPIR-ING A CAREER THAT CREATED A BAKERY, A JAM FACTORY, AND RESTAURANTS. It all started with *Grandmère's* marmalade.

Grandmère was my aunt Ruth's mother-in-law, who lived with Ruth and Uncle Jean in their beautiful home on Long Island. *Grandmère* was as French as a croissant and prided herself on her cooking. But her true métier was her orange-apricot marmalade, which she made in secrecy in her secluded basement kitchen. Only once did I have the chance to see her pot of glistening fruit and sugar. I walked down to the basement and there was *Grandmère* in her kitchen, watching over the pot. The aroma was irresistible. When I tried to sneak a taste as she was filling the glass jars, she looked at me through her rimless silver glasses, quickly moved the marmalade away from my fingers, and placed the lid on top. She never wrote down her recipe, cloaking the formula in deeper mystery. We all thought she had spirited the recipe away from France, clutched to her bosom. Recently, I uncovered the real story behind the origin of her marmalade: During the Depression, a neighbor in the Bronx had shared the secret recipe with her.

Years ago, my brother Mel came to New York and we decided to visit Aunt Ruth. She set her table for tea and we told her how much we missed the marmalade. To our surprise and delight, she reached for a pencil and paper and said, "Here is a list of what we need; go shopping and we will make some." Although *Grandmère* guarded the recipe with her life, Ruth clearly had paid attention when her mother-in-law wasn't looking. We could not believe our ears, and off we went to gather oranges, apricots, and everything else that was needed. We carefully observed the cooking process and I took detailed notes.

A few months later, I visited Mel at his home in Boulder, Colorado, and he asked me to bring the marmalade recipe. It was there that we made the first batch of fifty jars as holiday gifts for friends. I remember how proud we felt looking at those jars, lined up like a golden army.

Soon after, in 1980, I met Bill Levine at a party in Manhattan and a year later married the greatest guy alive. Bill, a general contractor, was building a dessert cafe with his partners. He asked me to help with the interior design and the menu planning. This was an opportunity to work on a creative project, and I happily accepted.

My days became very exciting and Bill and I loved working together. I had the idea to serve the marmalade at the cafe and made a small batch for him to sample. He thought it was fantastic. Opening day arrived, the marmalade was ready, and as you might have guessed, everyone loved it. It occurred to me that I could create my own business, the "golden" opportunity I had been waiting for.

With jars of the homemade marmalade in hand, I visited New York's upscale specialty food shops and met with their buyers. They loved it and said, "Never have we tasted anything like this—it is original and we must carry it." However, they didn't like the name of the marmalade (*Grandmère's*, of course) or the package design. Before long, my beloved marmalade, renamed Sarabeth's, with its redesigned label, made it to the shelves, only to disappear overnight.

Sarabeth's Orange-Apricot Marmalade had been born and soon was featured in *New York* magazine with a rave review. Our apartment kitchen turned into a madhouse as endless orders poured in. The windows were steamed from the constantly bubbling marmalade and the entire townhouse smelled like deliciously fragrant oranges. I bought bigger pots, more jars, and another stove. I had to line the kitchen floor with aluminum foil to protect the wood from the drips of hot marmalade. After school, my daughter Jennifer picked the seeds out of the orange slices, and in the evenings, Bill worked by my side, labeling and boxing the jars. We were one big sticky family.

It wasn't long before it became necessary to move the production out of our apartment. Bill sold his share of the cafe and enthusiastically offered to build a shop for the new business on what was then a distinctly inelegant Amsterdam Avenue on Manhattan's Upper West Side. The location was perfect, the rent was cheap, and I could walk the two blocks to work. Knowing I had to offer more than just preserves to our customers, we built a small bakery, equipped with a forty-gallon steam kettle for making the jams.

I dug out my treasured notebook, filled with recipes that I had collected over the years. The ones I loved most were from my mother-in-law, Margaret Firestone. She had opened her recipe box and taught me a million things about cooking and baking. It was Margaret, with her exotically spiced chicken paprikash and buttery cakes, who knew that a delicious meal was not complete without a simple dessert— a philosophy I champion to this day.

The storefront quickly became a small retail bakery and cafe with three tables, where we showcased our preserves and baked goods and began serving breakfast. We accomplished a great deal in that one-thousand-square-foot shop. Peggy Cullen, a talented baker, generously guided me as we baked together. Every day I jumped out of bed and rushed to the bakery. I learned by immersion. I loved it! Nothing discouraged me. Not the long hours or the physical labor. Not even the time Bill and I walked by the closed store and overheard a couple looking through the window: "A jam store in the middle of Manhattan? She'll never make it." We looked at each other and smiled.

We eventually opened our first restaurant on the Upper East Side. Next, we moved the West Side bakery and jam production across the street into a larger space, where we built a restaurant and served breakfast, lunch, and dinner. In those days, few places were making the morning meal with style, and my homey breakfast was a rarity. Like the aroma of freshly baked bread, word about Sarabeth's spread throughout Manhattan, and long lines began to form. People sighed over our pancakes, loved our omelettes and scones, and no one could resist the golden marmalade. Bill closed his construction company to join me in our expanding business.

Over the years, we opened new restaurants and eventually moved the bakery into the Chelsea Market, where I now spend much of my time. Bill oversees the sales, production, and distribution of our

Legendary Spreadable Fruits at our factory in the Bronx. We have come full circle: back to the very place where *Grandmère* learned to make the marmalade!

When I decided to write this book, I wanted it to be more than a collection of recipes. Sarabeth's is known for its perfect renditions of classic baking. Our pumpkin muffins and shortbread are beloved; our English muffins are like nothing you will buy at the supermarket; our croissants are flaky and light; and our buttery European-style coffee cakes are truly just like those our grandmothers made.

So what makes these recipes different from others you may have? Details. I want to teach you the tricks, tips, and techniques that I have learned from my mentors, or discovered myself. I have written recipes that share these important fine points, and accompanied them with photographs of my hands at work. The photos will clarify the directions, so that your home-baked goods will look and taste like the ones at the bakery.

Although there are plenty of simple recipes, elevate your baking by trying some of the more complex ones. Do not be put off when the recipe looks long—some desserts take time to make, and may require many ingredients and patience. Delight in the process of gently lifting a fragile pie shell and carefully moving it without breaking it. And if the mysteries of French layered dough, such as puff pastry, croissant, and Danish, have intimidated you, my precise explanations are sure to inspire the confidence you need to create impressive breakfast pastries. While you could bake the bread pudding in a large dish and spoon it into bowls, it is the elegant individual serving sizes that make the dessert extraordinary, and that is what I teach you.

Baking is about sharing. Each of us is influenced by someone—whether a mother or a master chef. Over the years, bakers have come to Sarabeth's to share and learn. Some have moved on to follow their dreams, some have stayed, and the desserts and pastries are the culmination of what we have learned from one another. Once you have mastered your favorites, honor the chemistry, play with the flavors and presentations, and make them your own. But most of all, share them with others in the spirit of discovery and creativity.

From My Hands to Yours,

Sarabeth

The Baker's Pantry

·····························

A T THE BAKERY IN CHELSEA MARKET, LARGE PLATE-GLASS WINDOWS ALLOW PASSERSBY TO SEE THE BAKERS AND ME AT WORK. I LIKE THE FACT THAT our actions are there for all to see. Observers easily discern from the sacks of flour and other dry goods that we use nothing but the best ingredients. Our utensils have a patina that bears witness to their many years of constant but careful use.

The home baker will find, just as we have at Sarabeth's, that there can be no compromises when it comes to quality. It is often said that great food starts with fine ingredients, an obvious statement if there ever was one. However, it is equally important to have excellent equipment and utensils.

We have all heard good cooks say that they aren't good bakers. When I press someone to find out what it is about baking that is confounding, it is usually that he or she has never taken the opportunity to learn the basics of baking and unknowingly settles for mediocre ingredients and equipment. There is a reason why there are many different types of flour at the supermarket, and switching one for the other can make serious trouble for a recipe. Use a flimsy half-sheet pan instead of a sturdy one, and your pastries could burn on the bottom. These common problems (and other baking quandaries) are easy fixes.

This section will explain the basic ingredients and equipment and tools that you need for making great baked goods.

INGREDIENTS

Flours and Meals The array of flours at the market can be confusing. Understanding the basics of flour is an important step toward being a good baker.

Wheat flour contains proteins, and when two of these proteins, glutenin and gliadin, are moistened, they combine to form gluten. This substance makes dough tender or tough, or as bakers say, weak or strong. The gluten strength is determined by the variety of wheat (red or white, distinguished by the color of the bran, the grain's outer coating), when it was grown (winter or spring), and the hardness of the kernel (hard or soft). The amount of protein in flour is important because it translates into the amount of potential gluten in the flour. (Depending on its gluten content, flour can be called weak or strong as well.) When the dough is kneaded or mixed, an invisible web of gluten forms in the dough. The dough expands from the carbon dioxide released by the leavening (or the steam expelled by the dough's liquid as it evaporates under the oven's heat), and the gluten web stretches, keeping the dough from collapsing. (Flours made from grains other than wheat, such as rye or buckwheat, have very little or no gluten, and must be mixed with wheat flour if the bread made from them is to rise at all.)

Whole wheat flour has been ground from the intact wheat kernels, including the indigestible bran, and is high-gluten flour with about 14 percent protein. White flour has had the bran removed, which reduces the amount of protein, and also makes the baked goods lighter in texture and color.

Bread flour (about 13 percent protein), also considered high gluten, is made from hard wheat, helping the dough hold its shape when the dough expands from the yeast's carbon dioxide.

All-purpose flour is made from a combination of winter and spring flours to give a moderate protein count of 9 to 12 percent, depending on the brand and how the flour is processed. When white flour is allowed to age, its color lightens naturally. Flour can also be chemically bleached, which reduces the gluten content and flavor. Most common bleached all-purpose flours contain about 9 percent protein.

Unbleached all-purpose flour, with a protein content of about 11 percent, is my personal choice for its versatility and flavor, and I use it for almost all of my baked goods. (You may see "unbromated" on the package label. Potassium bromate, a possible carcinogen, was a common additive to American flour as a gluten enhancer, but most producers have changed to ascorbic acid, which has similar properties.) I am not concerned about unbleached flour's relatively high protein content, as my sweet baked goods contain butter and sugar, two ingredients that act as tenderizers and compensate for the extra protein. The exact amount of protein varies from brand to brand and, in fact, from region to region.

Pastry flour is another favorite flour of mine. This unbleached white flour is milled from soft wheat; it has a low protein content of about 8 percent and makes wonderfully tender baked goods. It is not a common supermarket item, but it is easily available by mail order. Do not confuse this flour with whole wheat pastry flour, a staple at natural food stores. As you might not use pastry flour as often as other flours, freshness may be an issue. Store it in an airtight plastic bag in the freezer, where it will keep for a year. Be sure to let the flour come to room temperature before using.

Cake flour has a slightly lower protein content than unbleached pastry flour. I prefer pastry flour, but if it's not available, use cake flour. King Arthur Flour makes an unbleached cake flour that is especially good. Do not use self-rising cake flour. Store cake flour as for pastry flour.

Measuring Flour American home bakers usually use the volume measurement system, which requires measuring cups and spoons. The rest of the world weighs their ingredients on a scale. When it comes to the argument of volume measuring versus weighing, flour is especially problematic. During storage, flour settles, and when it is transferred to a measuring cup, it settles again. If the flour is packed into the cup, it will weigh more than if it is lightly spooned. The American volume measuring method with a cup is practical, but the European weight method wins hands-down for accuracy, and it's the one that all professional bakeries use. If you have a good kitchen scale, you may learn to prefer the scaling method, too. At the bakery, where we make huge batches of batter and dough, we must use the scaling system.

For measuring flour at home, I use the easy "dip-and-sweep" method. Using squat measuring cups designed for dry goods, dip the cup into the flour. Using a knife or the edge of a metal spatula, sweep the excess flour off the top so the flour is level with the edge of the cup. Never use a dry-measure metal cup to measure liquids, because the liquid can't reach the top (where the measurement is complete) without spilling. For liquids, use a glass measuring cup, checking the amount with the cup at eye level.

Butter Use Grade AA unsalted (sometimes called sweet) butter. Lesser grades have more water, making a softer butter that doesn't cream well. Professional bakers prefer unsalted butter for a couple of reasons. First, it allows the baker to control the amount of salt in the recipe. Salt will bring out the flavor in baked goods, but too much is a disaster. But the main reason is that unsalted butter is fresher than salted, because salt preserves the butter and prolongs its shelf life.

When a recipe calls for "cool" room-temperature butter, this means 65° to 70°F, no warmer. The butter should feel slightly cool and have a malleable texture, and not be soft or shiny. Butter at this temperature and texture will incorporate better during the creaming process, making your baked goods lighter. To reach this temperature, cut the butter into ½-inch cubes and place in the mixing bowl used to cream the butter and sugar. Let stand in a warm place in the kitchen (near the oven, for example) for about 15 minutes, about the time needed to preheat most ovens and gather the rest of the ingredients. Remember that there will be some heat created by the friction of beating the butter, so it is better to err on the side of having the butter too firm.

Dairy Products **Milk, sour cream, and buttermilk** are used to moisten batters and doughs, and also provide butterfat for tenderness. The acids in sour cream and buttermilk also react with the gluten to reduce its toughening properties. In these recipes, milk and sour cream are always full-fat. Do not substitute reduced-fat versions of these products, or you will reduce the total butterfat in the recipe, which will adversely affect the end result. Buttermilk is usually low-fat, so don't expect to find a full-fat brand.

Heavy cream is used in some doughs, batters, and custards, but can also be whipped and utilized as a topping or accompaniment for cakes, pies, and tarts. Search out pasteurized (not ultra-pasteurized) heavy cream, which is minimally processed and has an especially rich taste and thick body.

Eggs Use Grade A large eggs. To the naked eye, eggs may not seem to vary much from size to size, but you will get dramatically different results by substituting jumbo for large. Room-temperature eggs blend well in batters and beat with the most volume, so remove the eggs from the refrigerator 1 hour before using. Or, place uncracked eggs in a bowl, cover with hot tap water, and let stand for about 5 minutes.

Leavenings The choice of leavening used in baked goods often depends on the other ingredients. **Baking soda** is an alkali and when combined with acidic ingredients such as cocoa, molasses, or buttermilk creates carbon dioxide. The gases are trapped in the dough or batter and make it rise. **Baking powder** can be used with any combination of ingredients, acidic or not. A mixture of alkaline baking soda and acidic cream of tartar, baking powder is often called "double-acting" because it gives off some of its leavening power when moistened, and more when heated in the oven. Obviously, baking soda and baking powder are not interchangeable, but substituting them for each other is a common mistake made by beginning bakers. Store both in airtight containers in a cool, dry place. Both leavenings should be used by the date marked on the container.

Yeast Understanding yeast is very important, for it is the ingredient that leavens bread. As the yeast comes into contact with sugar (either naturally occurring in the flour or added by the baker), it gives off carbon dioxide. This gas is trapped in the "invisible" gluten web in the dough, making the bread rise.

There are two kinds of yeast used in this book—compressed (also called fresh or cake) and dry. In both cases, pay attention to the "use-by" date on the package, as yeast quickly loses its strength after that date. Proofing is a way to check the freshness of the yeast. The yeast is dissolved in warm water with a pinch of sugar, and if the mixture bubbles, it indicates that the yeast is alive and eating the sugar.

I use compressed yeast because of the wonderful, complex flavor it brings to breads and pastries. It also has a stronger rising power than the dried variety and, in my opinion, better flavor. Home bakers are most likely to find compressed yeast during the holiday baking seasons. It is most commonly sold in 2-ounce cakes. Some stores also carry a smaller .6-ounce cube, which is equal to 1 envelope (2¼ teaspoons) of active dry yeast. Look for compressed yeast in the refrigerated section of the supermarket.

Professional bakeries use 1-pound blocks of compressed yeast, which home bakers can often find at restaurant and bakery suppliers and some wholesale clubs. This professional grade is excellent, but it must be purchased in a larger quantity than most home bakers can use up in a reasonable amount of time, before the yeast dies. Buy a pound, and consider sharing the excess with a friend. Compressed yeast must be refrigerated and stored airtight, so wrap any leftover portions well in plastic wrap and store in the refrigerator for no longer than ten days. Freezing does not increase the life of compressed yeast, and in fact can give it a slimy texture, so don't freeze it.

The best way to measure compressed yeast is by weight on a digital scale, because measuring its volume in a spoon isn't nearly as accurate. However, if you must use a measuring spoon, 1 ounce of compressed yeast equals approximately 2 packed tablespoons. (See the chart on the opposite page for other measurements, as well as comparisons of compressed and active dry yeast by volume and weight.) Crumble the yeast into the mixing bowl to help it dissolve.

Unlike dehydrated yeast, compressed yeast does not need to be dissolved in warm water before using. The most efficient way of preparing compressed yeast is the "sugar melt" method, where finely crumbled compressed yeast is mixed with sugar as the first step in the bread-making process. The yeast devours the sugar, and a reaction creates water as a by-product, turning the mixture into a moist paste. Because the yeast is not actually diluted with water, it retains all of its strength. After the yeast liquefies, whisk it well to be sure that it is completely dissolved to avoid bits of yeast in the dough. Compressed yeast can also be dissolved in warm liquid, but the "sugar melt" method is my favorite.

Active dry yeast has a longer shelf life than compressed yeast and can be stored in a cool, dry place, so

Yeast Conversions

COMPRESSED YEAST (WEIGHT/OUNCE)	COMPRESSED YEAST (PACKED TEASPOONS/TABLESPOONS)	ACTIVE DRY YEAST (WEIGHT/OUNCE)	ACTIVE DRY YEAST (LEVEL TEASPOONS)
.5 ounce	1 tablespoon		1¾ teaspoons
.6-ounce cube	1 tablespoon plus 1 teaspoon	(One) ¼-ounce envelope	2¼ teaspoons
.75 ounce	1 tablespoon plus 1½ teaspoons		2¾ teaspoons
.8 ounce	1 tablespoon plus 2 teaspoons		3 teaspoons
1 ounce	2 tablespoons		3½ teaspoons
2-ounce cake	4 tablespoons	(Three) ¼-ounce envelopes	6¾ teaspoons

some home bakers prefer its convenience. Active dry yeast comes in a strip of three ¼-ounce envelopes or in 4-ounce jars.

Active dry yeast must be dissolved in water before using. Although cold water can be used, most manufacturers recommend a water temperature of 105° to 115°F, a temperature range that effectively dissolves the coating around the yeast granules. One of the most common mistakes in bread baking happens when the yeast is killed by hot water. Always use a thermometer to check the water's temperature (with practice, you can tell the temperature by feel). Sprinkle the yeast into the water and let stand for 5 minutes to soften. The mixture may or may not foam, depending on the brand. Stir well with a fork to completely dissolve the softened yeast. Dry yeast softened in milk doesn't dissolve as readily as when the liquid is plain water, so a mini-whisk comes in handy to help break up the granules.

I prefer compressed yeast, but know that it is not easy to find, so I always give instructions for both compressed and active dry yeast in these recipes.

In addition to active dry yeast, you can also buy rapid-rise yeast (also known as bread-machine or instant yeast). This yeast does not need to be dissolved in water, and decreases the rising time of the dough. If you want to try it, go ahead, but I am sticking to compressed yeast.

Nuts Almonds, hazelnuts, pecans, and walnuts all make appearances in my baking. Nuts contain oils that can turn rancid, so it is best to store them in airtight containers in the refrigerator or freezer.

Toasting brings out the flavor in nuts. Spread the nuts on a half-sheet pan and bake in a preheated 350°F oven, stirring occasionally, until they are toasted and fragrant, anywhere from 8 to 12 minutes, depending on the thickness of the nut.

For hazelnuts, bake until the skins are cracked and the nuts underneath look toasted, about 10 minutes. Wrap the nuts in a clean kitchen towel and cool for a few minutes. Using the towel, rub off the skins. Don't be concerned if you can't get every bit of skin off—this adds color and character to baked goods. If you wish, rub the stubborn skin against a wire sieve to scrape it off.

Nuts can be very finely ground into flours. This can be done in an electric revolving blade (not burr) coffee or spice grinder or in a food processor with the blade attachment. (Before using a coffee grinder for grinding nuts, it may be necessary to remove residual coffee or spice flavors: Clean the grinder by processing raw rice until powdery. Toss out the ground rice and brush the interior of the grinder clean.) Add toasted, cooled nuts to the grinder with some of the flour from the recipe as directed and pulse until the nuts are finely ground but not oily.

Salt Sea salt, kosher salt, table, or iodized salt—they may all be sodium chloride, but each one has a distinct flavor and texture. For baking, I use fine sea salt because it dissolves readily in a batter or dough and has a clean flavor and neutral color.

Sugar and Other Sweeteners **Granulated sugar** is a very important baking ingredient, but unfortunately, it can be an unreliable product. Always buy pure cane sugar. If the label doesn't indicate this, you can assume the sugar in the bag is made from sugar beets and, in my opinion, has a rougher texture and doesn't melt easily into caramel.

Superfine sugar is very finely ground granulated sugar, and at the bakery, it is all we use. However, it isn't easy for a home baker to buy in bulk. I use it in recipes where it is extremely important that the sugar dissolves thoroughly. I also like it in recipes where butter and sugar are creamed because it makes an especially tender, fine crumb. You'll find superfine sugar at supermarkets, where it may be labeled baker's sugar or bar sugar. In a pinch, you can grind granulated sugar in a blender or food processor until the crystals are half their original size, a process that takes a minute or two.

Brown sugar used to be a by-product of making granulated sugar, but it is now usually granulated sugar that has been sprayed with molasses to give it a moist consistency. The color of the brown sugar (light or dark) is indicative of the amount and strength of molasses flavor. I usually prefer light brown sugar. To measure brown sugar, pack it firmly into the measuring cup, and level it at the edge of the cup.

Confectioners' sugar is very finely ground sugar that has many uses for the baker in cookies, glazes, or as a garnish. It is sometimes called powdered or 10X sugar. The number means that the sugar has been ground ten times. There are also 6X and 4X sugars, but 10X is a common consumer product.

Honey gives its flavor to some baked goods and provides moisture, too. Use a mild-flavored variety, such as clover or orange blossom. Chestnut and other dark, heavy honeys may be good drizzled on ice cream, but they can be overpowering in baked goods.

Corn syrup is used to give a neutral sweet flavor to moist fillings and a shine to some sauces. Light corn syrup is clear; dark corn syrup has been colored with caramel. Both are used in this book.

Chocolate All chocolate begins with cacao beans that have been harvested, fermented, and ground. The resulting paste is called cacao liquor. How the cacao liquor is processed determines the end product.

I like the subtleties of flavor in **bittersweet and semisweet chocolate.** Both have varying amounts of sugar added, and there is no official standard (the USDA includes them in the same "dark chocolate" category, which is any chocolate with a minimum of 35 percent and a maximum of 88 percent cacao). The sweetness fluctuates by the brand. Some chocolate manufacturers state the percentage of cacao on the product label. Obviously, higher cacao content means a chocolate that is less sweet with a stronger flavor. However, that doesn't mean that the chocolate is better, only that it is more bitter. Unsweetened chocolate is 100 percent cacao liquor without anything added. Also, chocolate with a high percentage of cacao may act differently in a recipe than a moderate-cacao chocolate, especially in a ganache (chocolate melted with heavy cream). A safe cacao content range in chocolate for using in desserts is 52 to 62 percent. **White chocolate** is essentially cocoa butter (the material left after removing the cacao solids from the bean), sugar, and vanilla. Look at the label to be sure the white chocolate is made from cocoa butter, and not a cheaper fat such as palm oil.

When the cacao liquor is dried and pulverized, it becomes **cocoa powder.** However, cocoa powder is a very acidic product, and this property makes it somewhat challenging for bakers. In the 1830s, a Dutch scientist developed a method of treating cocoa with alkali salt to reduce the acidity. The treatment also gave the cocoa a reddish color that turned baked goods a darker, richer brown. I find that Dutch-processed cocoa—also called alkalized cocoa—has a deeper flavor than natural cocoa, and I use it in all of my baking.

Chocolate has two enemies: heat and liquid. It must be melted carefully with gentle heat. Overheated chocolate tastes scorched and has a lumpy texture. For some methods, like tempering (see Chocolate Marmalade Cookies, pages 211 and 212), you cannot splash even a drop of liquid into it, or your chocolate will tighten up or "seize." For other recipes, you have to add at least 2 tablespoons of liquid for every 1 ounce of melted chocolate to provide enough liquid for the chocolate to smooth out.

To melt chocolate, using a serrated knife, coarsely chop the chocolate into uniform pieces. (Some manufacturers make chocolate *pistoles*, small ovals of chocolate that do not need chopping. They are very convenient, and worth searching out.) Place the chocolate in a heatproof bowl that is wider than the saucepan you will be using. Bring 1 inch of water to a simmer in the saucepan. Place the bowl with the chocolate over the hot water and let stand, stirring occasionally, until it is smooth and melted. Do not let the bottom of the bowl touch the water. Remove from the heat. The wide bowl exposes the most chocolate to the heat, and the melting goes quickly, especially with large amounts of chocolate.

Vanilla Some good cooks make the serious error of taking vanilla for granted. By using vanilla beans instead of vanilla extract, your baking will be elevated to another level of sophistication.

The orchid that bears the vanilla bean grows only in the tropics. The flower must be painstakingly pollinated by hand during a very short window of opportunity, and then the harvested bean takes months to develop flavor. The beans are costlier than extract, but worth it.

Vanilla is usually identified by the location of its harvest. I love the rich flavor and full aroma of beans from the islands of Madagascar and Bourbon (now known as Réunion). Mexican beans can be a bargain; however, buy carefully, as the country grows more than one type. Tahitian vanilla has a lovely floral fragrance, and its flavor is more delicate than Madagascar-Bourbon beans.

The flavor compound in vanilla beans is vanillin, which can be commercially extracted from the bean and turned into a liquid flavoring. Vanillin can also be artificially replicated, so there are plenty of imitation vanilla products available. I do not use artificial ingredients in my baking.

In some recipes, particularly creamy fillings or custards, I want the flavor of vanilla seeds, but not their grittiness. To achieve this creamy texture, vanilla beans are plumped in rum (you must use an alcoholic liquor, as it acts as a preservative) for a couple of weeks to soften the interior seeds into a semi-liquid consistency. I give detailed instructions for Plumped Vanilla Beans on page 295. If you haven't thought ahead to plump the vanilla bean, and you want to use an unsoaked bean, split it in half length-wise and scrape out the tiny seeds with the tip of a small sharp knife. When the vanilla is used in a hot liquid (such as crème anglaise), add the emptied bean, split lengthwise, along with the seeds so the bean releases its flavor into the mixture. The bean can be lifted or strained out.

While I (almost) always prefer vanilla beans, I know that there will be times when you may choose to use vanilla extract. Buy only pure vanilla extract made from Madagascar-Bourbon beans.

Almond Paste Finely ground almonds bound with sweeteners, almond paste is used in pastries for its intense flavor. It is available, either packed in a foil tube or canned, in the baking aisle in most supermarkets. Both are acceptable. Almond paste can be quite hard, and should be finely chopped before using, or it may not incorporate well with the other ingredients. If it is very hard, grate it on a box grater. Do not confuse it with marzipan, a similar but much sweeter product. After opening, refrigerate leftover almond paste in an airtight container, where it should keep for a few months, or freeze it for longer storage.

EQUIPMENT AND TOOLS

Here are the utensils and appliances that I can't do without. My choices are very personal, as we have a particular way of doing things at Sarabeth's. (See Sources on page 297 for purveyors.)

Heavy-duty Stand Mixer There is no substitute for the power of a heavy-duty stand mixer. Its wide, deep bowl does a great job of creaming butter and sugar, kneading bread dough, and making buttercream. The 5-quart model is the most versatile size.

The only downside to a heavy-duty stand mixer is that the metal paddle attachment doesn't come into full contact with the bottom and sides of the mixer bowl, and you have to stop and scrape the bowl often to ensure proper mixing. BeaterBlade, a flexible plastic beater that better fits the contours of the bowl, reduces (but does not eliminate) the need for constant scraping.

Handheld Electric Mixer As much as I love my stand mixer, there are times when a smaller, handheld mixer is more efficient. Small amounts of ingredients (say, less than a cup of cream or only a couple of egg whites) will not beat properly in the large bowl of a stand mixer, but a handheld mixer and a small bowl work perfectly. Look for a handheld mixer with a strong motor and large beaters.

Half-sheet Pan This versatile pan has many uses in the bakery. Measuring about 18 by 13 inches with 1-inch-high sides, it is used for everything from baking cookies and other pastries to sheets of génoise. Why is it called a half-sheet pan? A full-sheet pan measures 26 by 18 inches and is used by large commercial kitchens to bake very large amounts of food; a half-sheet pan is half that size. A quarter-sheet pan is 13 by 9 inches, a very convenient size that I use for baking brownies and small sheet cakes. I do not recommend any other kind of baking sheet (inexpensive ones are too small, and buckle and discolor easily), so I always call for a half-sheet pan in the recipes in this book.

Metal Cake and Entremet Rings Professional tools give professional-looking results. This is never more evident than in the case of stainless steel or aluminum rings, which allow the home baker to mold perfectly round desserts with smooth sides. They are available in a huge range of sizes at professional kitchenware shops and online, but I use only three sizes in this book.

For larger desserts, such as layer cakes and cheesecake, I use an 8-inch-diameter by 3-inch-tall metal cake ring. Metal entremet rings are smaller (although some vendors call them cake rings), and are reserved for individual-size baked goods. These rings measure 3 inches in diameter by 1½ inches tall (or 2⅜ inches tall for my bread puddings). Because these rings are made in countries that use the metric measuring system, which doesn't translate exactly to our American system, you may find rings listed as 1⅓ or 1⅝ inches tall rather than 1½ inches. An eighth of an inch either way won't make any difference. Some recipes use ten rings; so if you are buying a large quantity, look for dealers that offer discounts.

These metal rings are hard wearing, so once you make the investment, they will last a long time if you handle them with reasonable care. The stainless rings are more expensive than the aluminum ones, but they are stronger and won't rust or lose their shape with use. As a precaution against rusting, wash the metal rings by hand and dry immediately.

For baking large desserts, place the cake or entremet ring(s) on a half-sheet pan lined with parchment paper. To assemble already-baked desserts, place the cake ring on a clean parchment-lined pan and insert a white cardboard round snugly in the bottom of the ring. This creates a solid supporting surface for the dessert. I much prefer the neutral white cardboard to the dimpled metal bottom of the common springform pan. For smaller desserts, entremet rings are placed directly on the lined pan without the cardboard rounds. Once filled, the rings on the pan go directly to the oven for baking.

Parchment Paper or Silicone Baking Mats Parchment paper usually comes rolled in a box similar to the kind that holds waxed paper. (Waxed paper smokes at temperatures higher than 400°F and is not a substitute for parchment paper.) The problem with rolled parchment paper is that it holds its curl and is difficult to flatten. If you have to use this kind of parchment paper, lightly butter the half-sheet pan first to adhere the paper to the pan. Flat parchment paper is available from some kitchen suppliers.

I also use parchment paper to help transfer dry ingredients into a mixer: Combine the ingredients on the paper, then pick up the parchment on the two long ends and tilt to slide the ingredients into the bowl as the batter mixes. It is also handy when wrapping dough for chilling because some dough will "sweat" when wrapped in plastic wrap.

Silicone nonstick baking mats are somewhat new additions to the nonstick scene. Made from flexible fiber coated with silicone, they are usually imported from France. The typical size is about 18 by 13 inches (again, to fit half-sheet pans), but some brands can be trimmed with scissors to fit smaller pans. They last for about two thousand bakings. They aren't perfect for every single recipe, as they can insulate cookie bottoms and discourage browning.

Whisks You should own a selection of whisks. A large thin-wired balloon whisk is the choice for whipping egg whites or cream, and is also a surprisingly good tool for folding flour into beaten eggs when making génoise cake batter. A medium-size whisk with sturdier wires can get into the corners of a saucepan when cooking pastry cream. Have a mini-whisk to combine ingredients in a small bowl.

Kitchen Scale Nothing discourages a cook from using the European weight method of measuring more than a cheap, rickety, spring-dial kitchen scale. Look for digital scales with easy-to-read numerical readouts and a full range of increments from ¼ ounce to 11 pounds or so. There are many uses for your scale beyond weighing ingredients. For loaves of bread or dinner rolls of the same size, weigh the entire batch of dough, then divide by the appropriate number and weigh each piece as required.

Baking Dishes and Pans All of my favorite baking pans (including loaf pans, fluted tube pans, and cookie sheets) are made from heavy-gauge aluminum. Heavy pans promote even browning because they absorb oven heat more efficiently than thin pans. I am not a fan of nonstick surfaces on baking pans because their dark surfaces absorb the oven heat and can cause overbrowning.

Brioche Tins While these decorative, fluted tins range in size from about 2⅜ to 8 inches in diameter, I prefer to make 3½-inch-wide individual brioche. They are usually made from tin and can rust, so dry them immediately after washing.

Fluted Cake Pans I love the attractive shape of cakes baked in fluted tube pans. Many American bakers are familiar with Bundt pans, but kitchenware shops now carry many other pans with other beautiful

patterns. I prefer a kugelhopf (sometimes called *gugelhupf*) pan, the granddaddy of all tube pans, which resembles a pleated turban. Buy a heavy, cast-metal 10- to 12-cup-capacity pan and avoid dark-colored pans, even if they have a nonstick interior. The dark pans absorb the heat in the oven and make the outside of the cake too brown. A properly buttered-and-floured pan works just as well as a nonstick one. If you must use a nonstick pan, preheat the oven to the recipe's temperature, but reduce the temperature by 25°F after the cake is in the oven, and watch carefully for doneness.

Jelly-roll Pan Measuring 15 by 10 by 1 inch, this pan is the perfect size for baking a sheet cake to be rolled with filling for a roulade. In a pinch, it can be used as a baking sheet.

Loaf Pans The two sizes of loaf pans that I use are 8 by 4 by 2½ inches and 9 by 5 by 3 inches. While they may look very similar, there is a 2-cup volume difference between them. I also use a 14 by 4 by 4-inch covered Pullman loaf pan for my *Pain de Mie* (page 101).

Muffin Pans A good muffin pan feels heavy. While there are now a variety of mini- and maxi-muffin sizes, the old standard, with cups that are each 2¾ inches across and 1½ inches deep with a capacity of about 7 tablespoons, yields muffins of a reasonable size. However, there is quite a variance in size with each manufacturer's "standard" muffin cup. Before starting to bake, determine the capacity of your muffin cup by filling it to the brim with water, then measuring the amount.

Pie Pan Also called a pie plate, this is the familiar dish used to bake pies. The best ones are made from either Pyrex or tin. Both have advantages. Transparent Pyrex lets the baker check the browning of the bottom crust, and metal is a great heat conductor and makes beautifully browned crusts. I use a 9 by 1-inch pan to yield eight servings.

Ramekins These round ceramic dishes are slow to absorb heat, so they are perfect for baking delicate custards. The 6-ounce (¾-cup) ramekin with a 3-inch diameter is a good size.

Tart and Tartlet Pans Made from tinned steel, these pans with removable bottoms come in a range of sizes. The tart pan size used in this book is 9 inches in diameter with 1¼-inch-tall sides. For tartlets, use 3¾-inch-diameter pans with ¾-inch-high sides.

Cookie and Biscuit Cutters Buy a set of cutters with graduated diameters and round fluted edges for cutting out cookies and biscuits. The most familiar cookie cutters are made from stainless steel or tin. Unless tin cutters are washed and dried immediately, they can rust. I highly recommend professional-quality pastry cutters made from white composite plastic. These cutters are expensive, but like so many culinary tools, the investment will last a lifetime if the tools are well cared for.

Wire Cooling Racks Baked goods will cool more quickly if transferred to wire cooling racks. While they are available in a variety of sizes, the large rack (about 18 by 13 inches), designed to fit a half-sheet pan, is very useful for cooling a sheet cake.

Rolling Pins There are a lot of rolling pins out there, truly something for everyone. Some bakers prefer a French-style rolling pin that resembles a thick dowel, or the standard American model with a cylinder on ball bearings. Pins with tapered ends are essential for rolling out the "cloverleaf" flaps for layered dough; the flaps are too narrow for wider pins. Silicone-coated rolling pins are especially useful for sticky, delicate dough with high sugar content. Of all the tools in my bakery, I have a special attachment to my European-made Matfer nylon rolling pin.

It is very helpful to have rolling pins for different uses. Laminated yeast doughs (such as croissant, puff pastry, or Danish) absolutely require a large, heavy pin to weight and stretch the densely layered dough. The one I use is about 18 inches long and weighs 4 pounds, and does a great job. A smaller pin that is easier to maneuver is better for rolling out tart or pie dough.

Whichever you choose, never wash your wooden rolling pin with soap and water or it could warp. Just scrape off any clinging dough with a plastic bowl scraper, and wipe the pin clean with a towel.

Cardboard Cake Rounds A sturdy corrugated cardboard round, produced specifically for bakers, provides a solid surface for transporting large baked goods. An 8-inch-diameter round fits perfectly in an 8-inch cake ring, or you can trim larger rounds as needed. The white side of the round always faces up.

Bench Scraper A professional baker would be lost without this squat, wide, spatula-like tool, which is also called a bench knife or dough scraper. My bench scraper is by my side all day long. With a couple of swipes, it scrapes the work surface clean of dough scraps (to avoid scratching, be careful if using it on stone surfaces), and nothing cuts up dough more efficiently. Once you start using one, you'll be hooked.

Hand Blender Cooks often use this handy tool to puree soups and other mixtures right in the pot. Bakers will find it particularly useful for blending eggs for a wash to glaze pastries before baking. It takes a lot of violent hand whisking to correctly combine the yolk and white, and the chalazae (the opaque white cords attached to the yolk) will never dissolve, making for a lumpy glaze. A hand blender does the job in a couple of seconds.

Plastic Bowl Scraper This plastic tool is curved (some look like a kidney) to fit the interior of a mixing bowl, and lets the baker clean every last drop of clinging batter.

Portion Scoops Ever hassle with dropping sticky dough into a muffin pan or scooping up balls of cookie dough? Solve the problem with a small ice-cream scoop, sometimes called a portion scoop. The three scoops I use most often have 1½-inch (for small cookies), 2-inch (for moderately sized cookies), and 2½-inch (for filling muffin cups) diameters.

Pizza Wheel/Cutter This tool is indispensable for cutting dough and pastry. Make sure to use one with a 4-inch diameter. My favorite is the sturdy one with a replaceable blade, from Dexter.

Pastry Bags and Tips A few pastry tips, specified in each recipe, can create a variety of decorations. Choose a pastry bag that is at least 14 inches long so you don't have to refill it often.

Ruler/Yardstick At the bakery, we always have a ruler and a yardstick handy for measuring pastry to get uniform results. The ruler is also used for measuring the thickness of pie, tart, and cookie doughs; a yardstick will help determine the dimensions of croissant, puff pastry, and Danish doughs, which are rolled into fairly large sheets. Use it as a guide with a pizza wheel to cleanly cut the dough.

Brushes For glazing the tops of pastries, use a natural bristle brush, which gives an even coating. To glaze individual pastries, a 1- to 1½-inch diameter works well. A wider brush (3 to 4 inches wide) does a quick job of brushing the flour off pastry during rolling. A cylinder-shaped brush is excellent for buttering the insides of baking pans (especially fluted tube and muffin pans), as it gets into the crevices better than a flat brush.

Spatula, Silicone Sturdier, heat-resistant up to 600°F, and less odor-absorbent than a rubber spatula, this tool can be used to stir cooking mixtures in a saucepan, as well as to perform its traditional role for folding ingredients together.

Spatula, Offset Metal Also called an icing spatula, this tool has a thin, flexible metal blade that is offset from the handle. It is perfect for spreading batter into the corners of a rectangular baking pan and applying icing onto cakes at awkward angles. You should have both sizes, large (9½-inch blade) and small (4½-inch blade).

Thermometers Do not underestimate the importance of an oven thermometer. Very few ovens are spot-on accurate, and without a thermometer, the baker is at a big disadvantage. For the most accurate reading, place an oven thermometer on the center of the rack, not too close to the hot metal sides of the oven. A digital instant-read thermometer is necessary for checking the temperature of delicate items like crème anglaise and for tempering chocolate.

Zester When removing the flavorful, fragrant zest from citrus fruit, it is important to collect only the colored peel and not the bitter white pith. A Microplane zester, which looks like a rasp with very fine teeth, grates the surface of the fruit and can also be used for grating nutmeg.

Chapter One

Morning Pastries

Croissants, cheese danish, fruit turnovers . . . these quintessential examples of the baker's art can be enjoyed at any time of day, although they are favored for breakfast. Morning pastries are some of the most beloved in the baker's repertoire.

The French have a name for this family of sweet breads—*Viennoiserie*, or "Viennese specialties," which refers to the city where this kind of sophisticated baking originated and was perfected. The refined flavor and texture of these delicacies come from prodigious amounts of butter. Croissant and Danish dough and puff pastry are called layered or laminated doughs, as the butter is carefully manipulated to form thin sheets that give the pastries their unique flakiness. An impressive amount of butter is beaten into brioche dough, contributing to its golden color.

When I knew that I had mastered the intricacies of *Viennoiserie*, I was truly proud. I want to teach you how to make these incomparable treats so you can share this joyful feeling of accomplishment.

A LESSON ON MORNING PASTRIES

Layered Dough When making dough or batter, the handling of the butter is a major factor in the final baked texture of the pastry. To give pastry dough a flaky texture, the butter is rolled into the dough to create thin sheets. The technique of folding the dough and butter together is called a turn. The butter melts during baking, and gives off steam that separates the dough into very thin, flaky layers. Dough that uses this technique is called layered dough.

Puff pastry is the most basic layered dough, made from thin layers of unyeasted dough and butter. Croissant dough is similar, but the dough contains yeast and sugar. Danish dough is closely related to croissant, but the dough is enriched with eggs and more butter. Bakers new to layered dough may want to start with puff pastry, as it shares elemental techniques with the other two. Brioche is not a layered dough, but its buttery richness makes it a member of the morning pastry family.

Classic French pastry nomenclature is used by bakers in many nations to describe the various parts of making dough. The basic flour-and-liquid component of layered dough is called the *détrempe*. The butter factor is called the *beurrage*. The two are carefully rolled and folded in no less than four sequences. The final dough may look cohesive, but it is composed of many distinct layers. If the butter gets too warm, it will soften and absorb into the dough, and the steam that makes the dough flaky during baking won't form. Therefore, temperature plays a big part in successfully making layered dough. The dough is refrigerated at regular intervals to firm the butter to a consistency and temperature that facilitate rolling into the necessary thin layers. These resting periods also relax the gluten in the dough so it is less elastic and easier to roll.

Beyond their incomparable flavor and flakiness, there is another reason why bakers love layered dough: There is little actual labor involved in making them, and that action repeats the "turning" of the dough. Most of the time is spent waiting for the dough to relax in the refrigerator between the turns. Once you become familiar with the technique, you can whip up one of these doughs very easily.

In order to make laminated dough properly, you must have sufficient ingredients to perform the techniques of layering the butter and flour components. Therefore, you will end up with about two pounds of dough. To give the home baker flexibility and the chance to make a variety of pastries from the same batch of dough, I have divided the finished dough in half to give two pieces of about one pound each. Now you can make a dozen croissants on one day, and another dozen (or something else) later.

Starting Out To make the *détrempe*, flour, salt, and liquids are mixed together in a heavy-duty stand mixer with the paddle attachment just until the dough comes together and cleans the sides of the bowl. The dough will be very moist and sticky, which will not be a problem because it will absorb plenty of flour during the subsequent rolling and folding. With yeasted croissant and Danish doughs, the gluten will be activated with all of the handling involved, so kneading is not necessary.

Once the dough is mixed, turn it out onto a floured work surface and shape into a ball. Place the ball of dough on a lightly floured half-sheet pan. Cut a 1-inch-deep X in the top of the dough to mark it into quadrants. Do not cut all the way through the dough. In the next step, each of these quadrants will be rolled into thin flaps to surround the *beurrage* and start the layering. Sprinkle the top of the dough with flour to discourage a skin from forming, and refrigerate for 20 minutes to relax the activated gluten.

To make the *beurrage*, the butter must be beaten to give it a malleable texture and should be at a cool temperature that can withstand rolling into a thin sheet without breaking up into pieces. Clean excess dough from the bowl and paddle. Add chilled cubed butter to the bowl and beat with the paddle attachment on medium-high speed until almost smooth, about 30 seconds. Scrape down the bowl and remove any butter clinging to the beater. Add flour and continue beating until the mixture has melded into a smooth mass, about 30 seconds more. Scrape down the sides of the bowl. Transfer the butter to a floured work surface, and shape into a 4-inch square. The butter should feel cool. Place on the half-sheet pan next to the ball of dough and refrigerate for the remainder of the dough's resting time, about 15 minutes.

Incorporating the Butter To simplify the rolling of the resilient dough, you should use two different rolling pins. A tapered pin helps create the thin flaps of dough that enclose the *beurrage*, and a large, heavy pin is necessary in the folding process. After the first resting period, the *détrempe* and the *beurrage* will feel cool but still be malleable enough for rolling out. Place the dough on a floured work surface with the ends of the X at approximately 2, 4, 7, and 10 o'clock positions. There will be four quadrants of dough between the crosses of the X at the north, south, east, and west positions. Dust the top of the dough with flour. Using the heel of your hand, flatten and stretch each quadrant out about 2½ inches to make a cloverleaf shape with an area in the center that is thicker than the "leaves." Use a tapered rolling pin to roll each "cloverleaf" into a flap about 6 inches long and 5 inches wide, leaving a raised square in the center. Using the side of the rolling pin, press the sides of the raised area to demark the square.

Place the butter square in the thicker center area of the cloverleaf. Gently stretch and pull the north flap of dough down to cover the top and the south side of the butter square, brushing away any excess flour. If the dough tears, just repair the tear as best as you can by pinching. Now stretch and pull the south-facing flap of dough up to cover the top and north side of the butter square. Turn the dough so the open ends of the square face north and south. Repeat folding and stretching the north- and south-facing flaps (originally the east and west flaps) of dough to completely cover the butter square, making a butter-filled packet of dough about 6 inches square.

Flour the work surface again. Turn the dough over so the four folded flaps face down. Be sure that the open seam faces you. Dust the top of the dough with flour. Switch to a large, heavy rolling pin. Holding it at a slight angle, lightly pound the top of the dough to widen it to 9 inches. This gentle pounding also begins to distribute the butter inside the dough.

The First Turn Layered doughs are fairly resilient, and are rolled into relatively large rectangles. Rolling will be facilitated by using a heavy rolling pin at least 16 inches long. (If the pin is shorter, be careful that the ends of the pin do not dig into the dough.) Use plenty of flour when rolling out the dough to prevent it from sticking to the work surface. Brush off the excess flour before folding the dough.

Next, roll the dough into a 17 by 9-inch rectangle. Fold the dough into thirds, like a business letter, brushing away excess flour. This is a called a single turn. Roll the rectangle lightly to barely compress the layers. Return the dough to the pan and refrigerate for about 20 minutes. Do not chill the dough for more than 20 minutes, or the butter could be too hard to roll in the next step. While the dough is resting, use a bench scraper to clean the work surface.

The Second Turn You now have a rectangle of dough with three layers. The next turn folds the dough into quarters, quadrupling the layers to twelve. This fold is called a double or book turn.

Dust the work surface again with flour. Place the dough on the surface with the open seam of dough facing you. This is another important detail, as it always keeps the butter and flour layers in the same direction as before, and encourages even rising. Dust the dough with flour. Roll out the dough again into a 17 by 9-inch rectangle. Fold the right side of the dough over 2 inches to the left. Fold the left side of the dough over to meet the right side. Fold the dough in half vertically from left to right, which should be about 2 inches to the left of the point where the two ends of dough meet. By folding the dough off-center in this manner, you avoid a center crease that can widen during rolling and disrupt the layering. Roll the rectangle lightly to barely compress the layers. Return to the half-sheet pan and refrigerate for 20 minutes.

The Final Turns For puff pastry, roll out the dough again into a double turn, then refrigerate for 20 minutes, and finish with a single turn. Croissant and Danish doughs need only a final single turn. In all cases, be sure that you always start rolling with the long open seam facing you, and use plenty of flour.

An entire batch of dough is called a *paton*. Again, with the long seam facing you, cut the dough in half vertically. Wrap each half well in plastic wrap.

Freezing the Dough The dough now is frozen for at least 24 hours, which firms the layers and makes them more distinct than just refrigerating them. In the case of the croissant and Danish doughs, which have lots of sugar for the yeast to feed on and create carbon dioxide, the cold temperature keeps them from rising too quickly. This is known as retarding the dough, and each recipe gives the maximum freezing time. Before using, defrost the dough overnight in the refrigerator. Defrosted dough should be used within a few hours or the dough will get sticky and hard to handle. Each recipe has recommendations for the maximum time that the defrosted dough can wait before using.

Shaping, Baking, and Serving All of these pastries are best served the day of baking. If you want freshly baked pastries, shape them about three hours before serving to allow time for proofing, baking, and cooling. Unless you are a very early riser (remember, bakers work in the middle of the night), it is probably most practical to serve your home-baked morning pastries for brunch.

The instructions for cutting and shaping each of the pastries are included in the individual recipes. When cutting the dough, it is important to use a sharp pizza wheel. Even sharp knives can drag and compress the pastry layers and inhibit rising. For the best control over the pizza wheel, move it from top to bottom, as it is trickier to guide the wheel if you go from bottom to top. A yardstick will be very useful to measure the dimensions of the dough.

After shaping yeasted layered doughs, the pastries must rise before baking (this procedure is called proofing). Usually, the pastries are covered with plastic wrap or kitchen towels to discourage the dough from drying on the surface. However, my doughs are very delicate and would stick to their coverings. At the bakery, they are proofed in warm, humid cabinets called proofing boxes. I have created a simple setup to simulate a proofing box with a tall "kitchen-sized" plastic bag (see page 85).

Puff Pastry

Makes about 2 pounds, 3 ounces dough

....

With countless amazingly thin, buttery layers that shatter when bitten into, puff pastry is the classic layered dough. Most bakers make their dough with water. I use heavy cream, and the added butterfat gives the pastry another dimension of flavor and crispness. Colleagues tell me that this defies logic, but they want the recipe nonetheless.

BAKER'S NOTE: Puff pastry is used to make Apple Turnovers (page 31). It is also the main component of Mille-Feuille with Summer Berries and Palmiers (pages 167 and 219). • To achieve its multiple layers, puff pastry has four turns: single, double, double, and single. • Use two rolling pins: a tapered pin for creating the thin flaps to cover the *beurrage*, and a large, heavy pin for the rolling steps. • Make, freeze, and defrost puff pastry at least 2 days before baking. This firms the butter and flour layers, and encourages them to bake into an extra-flaky texture. It also relaxes the dough better than refrigeration alone. • Puff pastry can be frozen for up to 3 weeks. After that time, the flour discolors, and the layering won't be as distinct. • Defrost the dough in the refrigerator for 8 to 12 hours. Do not refrigerate the defrosted dough for longer than 12 hours, or the dough could get wet from the thawed ice crystals and make it difficult to roll out and handle.

Détrempe

2 cups unbleached all-purpose flour, plus more for rolling out the dough	½ teaspoon fine sea salt
	About 1⅓ cups heavy cream, as needed

Beurrage

¾ pound (3 sticks) unsalted butter, chilled and cut into tablespoons • 3 tablespoons unbleached all-purpose flour

1 Make the dough at least 2 days before using. To make the *détrempe*, combine the flour and salt together in the bowl of a heavy-duty stand mixer. Attach the bowl to the mixer and fit with the paddle attachment. On low speed, gradually add enough of the cream to make a stiff but sticky dough. Do not overmix, as the dough will be worked and will absorb more flour during the rolling and folding processes. Transfer the dough to a floured work surface, knead a few times to smooth the surface, and shape into a ball.

2   Dust a half-sheet pan with flour. Place the dough on the flour and cut an X about 1 inch deep in the top of the ball to mark it into quadrants. Sprinkle with flour on top and refrigerate.

3   Immediately make the *beurrage*. Clean the work bowl and paddle attachment. Add the butter to the bowl and beat on medium speed until the butter is almost smooth, about 30 seconds. Add the flour and continue beating until the mixture is smooth, cool, and malleable, about 30 seconds more. Transfer to a lightly floured work surface and press any remaining lumps of butter out with the heel of your hand, and shape into a 4-inch square. Place the *beurrage* on the pan with the *détrempe* and refrigerate together for about 15 minutes (figure 1). The *détrempe* and the *beurrage* should be about the same consistency and temperature after this slight chilling.

4   Flour the work surface again. Place the dough on the work surface with the ends of the X at approximately 2, 4, 7, and 10 o'clock positions. You will notice four quadrants of dough between the crosses of the X at the north, south, east, and west positions. Dust the top of the dough with flour. Using the heel of your hand, flatten and stretch each quadrant out about 2½ inches to make a cloverleaf shape with an area in the center that is thicker than the "leaves" (figure 2). Use a tapered rolling pin to roll each "cloverleaf" into a flap about 6 inches long and 5 inches wide, leaving a raised square in the center (figure 3). Using the side of the rolling pin, press the sides of the raised area to demark the square.

5   Place the butter square in the center of the cloverleaf. Gently stretch and pull the north-facing flap of dough down to cover the top and sides of the butter square, brushing away any excess flour (figure 4). (This dough is on the stiff side, so just cover the butter square as best as you can without tearing the dough.) Now stretch and pull the south-facing flap of dough up to cover the top and sides of the butter square (figure 5). Turn the dough so the open ends of the square face north and south. Repeat folding and stretching the north- and south-facing flaps of dough (originally the east and west flaps) to completely cover the butter square, making a butter-filled packet of dough about 6 inches square (figure 6).

6   Dust the work surface with flour. Turn the dough over so the four folded flaps face down. Be sure that the open seam faces you. Dust the top of the dough with flour. Using a large, heavy rolling pin held at a slight angle, lightly pound the top of the dough to widen it slightly and help distribute the butter inside the dough (figure 7). Roll the dough into a 17 by 9-inch rectangle (figure 8). Fold the dough into thirds, like a business letter, brushing away excess flour. This is called a single turn (figure 9). Roll the rectangle lightly to barely compress the layers. Transfer to the pan and refrigerate for about 20 minutes.

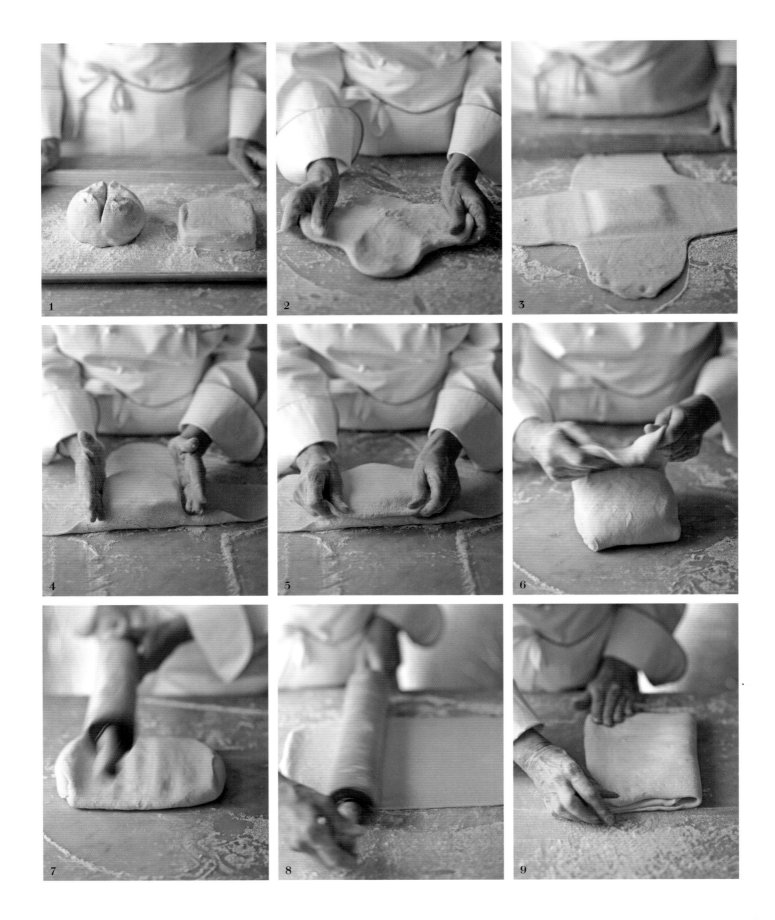

7 Dust the work surface with flour. Place the dough on the surface with the long open seam of dough facing you. Dust the dough with flour. Roll out the dough into a 17 by 9-inch rectangle. Fold the right side of the dough over 2 inches to the left. Fold the left side of the dough over to meet the right side (figure 10). Fold the dough in half vertically from left to right, which should be about 2 inches to the left of the point where the two ends of dough meet. This is a double turn (also known as a book turn). Roll the rectangle lightly to barely compress the layers (figure 11). Return to the half-sheet pan and refrigerate for another 20 minutes.

8 Repeat rolling and folding the dough into a second double turn (figures 10 and 11). Refrigerate for another 20 minutes.

9 Repeat rolling and folding the dough into a final single turn (figure 9). With the long seam facing you, cut the dough in half vertically (figure 12). Wrap each piece of dough tightly in plastic wrap, then wrap again. Freeze for at least 24 hours or up to 3 weeks.

10 The night before using the dough, transfer the frozen dough to the refrigerator and let thaw overnight, about 8 but no longer than 12 hours.

Croissant Dough

Makes about 2 pounds, 6 ounces dough

....

O f course, croissant dough is used to bake the classic crescent-shaped breakfast icons, but it also makes other treats. Without butter and egg yolks mixed into the *détrempe*, croissant dough is "leaner" than Danish, but it is no less delicious. To give the flour the right amount of gluten for strength and flakiness, bread and pastry flours are combined.

BAKER'S NOTE: Croissants, Almond Croissants, *Pains au Chocolat*, *Pains de Matin*, and *Pains aux Raisins* (pages 33, 36, 38, 40, and 43) all use this dough. Croissant dough has three turns: single, double, and single. • Use two rolling pins: a tapered pin for creating the thin flaps to cover the *beurrage*, and a large, heavy pin for the rolling steps. • For dry yeast, refer to the adjusted liquid measurements in the directions. • Make, freeze, and defrost croissant dough at least 2 days before baking. This firms the butter and flour layers, and encourages them to bake into an extra-light texture. It also relaxes the dough better than refrigeration alone. • Croissant dough can only be frozen for up to 4 days. After that time, the flour discolors and the yeast loses strength.

Détrempe

.75 ounce (1 packed tablespoon plus 1½ packed teaspoons) compressed yeast or 2¾ teaspoons active dry yeast

¼ cup granulated sugar

1¼ cups whole milk

1¾ cups bread flour, plus more for rolling out the dough

1¼ cups pastry or unbleached cake flour, sifted

1 teaspoon fine sea salt

Beurrage

½ pound (2 sticks) unsalted butter, chilled and cut into tablespoons • 2 tablespoons bread flour

1   Make the dough at least 2 days before using. To make the *détrempe*, finely crumble the yeast into the bowl of a heavy-duty stand mixer. Add the sugar and let stand until the yeast gives off some moisture, about 3 minutes. Whisk well to dissolve the yeast. Stir in the milk. (If using dry yeast, sprinkle the yeast over ¼ cup warm, 105°to 115°F, milk in a small bowl. Let stand until the yeast softens, about 5 minutes. Whisk well to dissolve. Pour into the mixer bowl, then add the sugar. Add the remaining 1 cup cold milk.)

2   Mix the bread and pastry flours together. Add 2 cups of the flour mixture and the salt to the bowl. Attach the bowl to the mixer and fit with the paddle attachment. Mix on low speed, adding enough of the remaining flour mixture to make a soft, sticky dough. Do not overmix, as the dough will be worked and absorb more flour during the rolling and folding processes. Transfer the dough to a floured work surface, knead a few times to smooth the surface, and shape into a ball. The ball will hold its shape but spread slightly during standing.

3   Dust a half-sheet pan with flour. Place the dough on the flour and cut an X about 1 inch deep in the top of the ball to mark it into quadrants. Sprinkle with flour on top and refrigerate.

4   Immediately make the *beurrage*. Clean the mixer bowl and paddle attachment. Add the butter to the bowl and beat with the paddle attachment on medium speed until the butter is almost smooth, about 30 seconds. Add the flour and continue beating until the mixture is smooth, cool, and malleable, about 30 seconds more. Transfer to a lightly floured work surface and press any remaining lumps of butter out with the heel of your hand, and shape the butter into a 4-inch square. Place the *beurrage* on the half-sheet pan with the *détrempe* and refrigerate together for about 15 minutes (see page 22, figure 1). The *détrempe* and the *beurrage* should be the same consistency and temperature after this slight chilling.

5   Flour the work surface again. Place the dough on the work surface with the ends of the X at approximately 2, 4, 7, and 10 o'clock positions. You will notice four quadrants of dough between the crosses of the X at the north, south, east, and west positions. Dust the top of the dough with flour. Using the heel of your hand, flatten and stretch each quadrant out about 2½ inches to make a cloverleaf shape with an area in the center that is thicker than the "leaves" (see page 22, figure 2). Use a tapered rolling pin to roll each "cloverleaf" into a flap about 6 inches long and 5 inches wide, leaving a raised square in the center (see page 22, figure 3). Using the side of the rolling pin, press the sides of the raised area to demark the square.

6   Place the butter square in the center of the cloverleaf. Gently stretch and pull the north-facing flap of dough down to cover the top and sides of the butter square, brushing away any excess flour (see page 22, figure 4). (This dough is very extendable and will stretch easily, but don't tear it.) Now stretch and pull the south-facing flap of dough up to cover the top and sides of the butter square (see page 22, figure 5). Turn the dough so the open ends of the square face north and south. Repeat folding and stretching the north- and south-facing flaps of dough (originally the east and west flaps) to completely cover the butter square, making a butter-filled packet of dough about 6 inches square (see page 22, figure 6).

7 Dust the work surface with flour. Turn the dough over so the four folded flaps face down with the open seam facing you. Dust the top of the dough with flour. Using a large, heavy rolling pin held at a slight angle, lightly pound the top of the dough to widen it slightly and help distribute the butter inside the dough (see page 22, figure 7). Roll the dough into a 17 by 9-inch rectangle (see page 22, figure 8). Fold the dough into thirds, like a business letter, brushing away excess flour. This is called a single turn (see page 22, figure 9). Roll the rectangle lightly to barely compress the layers. Transfer to a half-sheet pan and refrigerate for about 20 minutes.

8 Lightly flour the work surface. Place the dough on the work surface with the long open seam of dough facing you. Dust the dough with flour. Roll out the dough into a 17 by 9-inch rectangle. Fold the right side of the dough over 2 inches to the left. Fold the left side of the dough over to meet the right side (see page 23, figure 10). Fold the dough in half vertically from left to right. This is a double turn (also known as a book turn). Roll the rectangle lightly to barely compress the layers (see page 23, figure 11). Return to the half-sheet pan and refrigerate for another 20 minutes.

9 Repeat rolling and folding the dough into a final single turn (see page 22, figure 9). With the long seam facing you, cut the dough in half vertically (see page 23, figure 12). Wrap each piece of dough tightly in plastic wrap, then wrap again. Freeze for at least 24 hours or up to 4 days.

10 The night before using the dough, transfer the frozen dough to the refrigerator and let thaw overnight, about 8 hours. Once defrosted it will begin to rise, so make sure to roll it out immediately.

Danish Dough

Makes about 2 pounds, 4 ounces dough

....

I f the French call this kind of pastry *Viennoiserie*, and it hails from Vienna, why do Americans call it Danish? In the mid-nineteenth century, there was a bakers' strike in Copenhagen, and the strikers were replaced with Viennese workers, who baked their own national recipes. When the strike was over, the customers had developed a taste for the Viennese style of baking. Danish immigrants brought the layered dough recipe with them to America, and the bakeries that they opened featured this new, irresistible pastry.

Enriched with eggs, butter, and sugar, this golden dough is responsible for many of the most beloved morning pastries, particularly with my New York clientele who have deep nostalgia for fruit Danish and cream cheese Danish. The butter layers give the pastries a deliciously light texture.

BAKER'S NOTE: Use this dough for Cheese and Raisin Danish, Fruit Danish, and Chocolate Babka (pages 44, 49, and 51). • Danish dough has three turns: single, double, and single. • Use two rolling pins: a tapered pin for creating the thin flaps to cover the *beurrage*, and a large, heavy pin for the rolling steps. • For dry yeast, refer to the adjusted liquid measurements in the directions. • Make, freeze, and defrost Danish dough at least 2 days before baking. This firms the butter and flour layers, and encourages them to bake into an extra-flaky texture. It also relaxes the dough better than refrigeration alone. • Danish dough can be frozen for up to 4 days. After that time, the flour discolors and the yeast loses strength.

Détrempe

.75 ounce (1 packed tablespoon plus 1½ packed teaspoons) compressed yeast or 2¼ teaspoons active dry yeast

2 tablespoons granulated sugar

⅔ cup whole milk

1 large egg plus 4 large egg yolks

Seeds from 1 Plumped Vanilla Bean (page 295)

2⅔ cups unbleached all-purpose flour, plus more for rolling out the dough

¼ teaspoon fine sea salt

4 tablespoons (½ stick) unsalted butter, cut into tablespoons, well softened

Beurrage

½ pound (2 sticks) unsalted butter, chilled and cut into tablespoons • 2 tablespoons unbleached all-purpose flour

1   Make the dough at least 2 days before using. To make the *détrempe*, finely crumble the yeast into the bowl of a heavy-duty stand mixer. Add the sugar and let stand until the yeast gives off some moisture, about 3 minutes. Whisk well to dissolve. Stir in the milk. (If using dry yeast, sprinkle the yeast over ⅓ cup warm, 105° to 115°F, milk in a small bowl. Let stand until the yeast softens, about 5 minutes. Whisk well to dissolve. Pour into the mixer bowl, then add the sugar. Add the remaining ⅓ cup cold milk.)

2   Add the egg, yolks, and vanilla seeds and whisk to combine. Attach the bowl to the mixer and fit with the paddle attachment. Mix on low speed, and add 2 cups of the flour and the salt to the bowl. Add the butter, 1 tablespoon at a time. Add enough of the remaining flour to make a soft, sticky dough that almost cleans the sides of the bowl. Do not overmix, as the dough will be worked and absorb more flour during the rolling and folding processes. Transfer the dough to a floured work surface, knead a few times to smooth the surface, and shape into a ball. The ball should hold its shape, but it will widen slightly upon standing.

3   Dust a half-sheet pan with flour. Place the dough on the flour and cut an X about 1 inch deep in the top of the ball to mark it into quadrants. Sprinkle with flour on top and refrigerate.

4   Immediately make the *beurrage*. Clean the mixer bowl and paddle attachment. Add the butter to the bowl and beat with the paddle attachment on medium speed until the butter is almost smooth, about 30 seconds. Add the flour and continue beating until the mixture is smooth, cool, and malleable, about 30 seconds. Transfer to a lightly floured work surface and press any remaining lumps of butter out with the heel of your hand, and shape the butter into a 4-inch square. Place the *beurrage* on the half-sheet pan with the *détrempe* and refrigerate together for about 15 minutes (see page 22, figure 1). The *détrempe* and the *beurrage* should be the same consistency and temperature after this slight chilling.

5   Flour the work surface again. Place the dough on the work surface with the ends of the X at approximately 2, 4, 7, and 10 o'clock positions. You will notice four quadrants of dough between the crosses of the X at the north, south, east, and west positions. Dust the top of the dough with flour. Using the heel of your hand, flatten and stretch each quadrant out about 2½ inches to make a cloverleaf shape with an area in the center that is thicker than the "leaves" (see page 22, figure 2). Use a tapered rolling pin to roll each "cloverleaf" into a flap about 6 inches long and 5 inches wide, leaving a raised square in the center (see page 22, figure 3). Using the side of the rolling pin, press the sides of the raised area to demark the square.

6   Place the butter square in the center of the cloverleaf. Gently stretch and pull the north-facing flap of dough down to cover the top and the sides of the butter square, brushing away any excess flour (see page 22, figure 4). (This dough is very extendable and stretches easily; be careful not to tear it.) Now stretch and pull the south-facing flap of dough up to cover the top and sides of the butter square (see page 22, figure 5). Turn the dough so the open ends of the square face north and south. Repeat folding and stretching the north- and south-facing flaps of dough (originally the east and west flaps) to completely cover the butter square, making a butter-filled packet of dough about 6 inches square (see page 22, figure 6).

7   Dust the work surface with flour. Turn the dough over so the four folded flaps face down, with the open seam facing you. Dust the top of the dough with flour. Using a large, heavy rolling pin held at a slight angle, lightly pound the top of the dough to widen it slightly and help distribute the butter inside the dough (see page 22, figure 7). Roll the dough into a 17 by 9-inch rectangle (see page 22, figure 8). Fold the dough into thirds, like a business letter, brushing away excess flour. This is called a single turn (see page 22, figure 9). Roll the rectangle lightly to barely compress the layers. Transfer to a half-sheet pan and refrigerate for about 20 minutes.

8   Dust the work surface with flour. Place the dough on the work surface with the long open seam of dough facing you. Dust the dough with flour. Roll out the dough into a 17 by 9-inch rectangle. Fold the right side of the dough over 2 inches to the left. Fold the left side of the dough over to meet the right side (see page 23, figure 10). Fold the dough in half vertically from left to right. This is a double turn (also known as a book turn). Roll the rectangle lightly to barely compress the layers (see page 23, figure 11). Return to the half-sheet pan and refrigerate for another 20 minutes.

9   Repeat rolling and folding the dough into a final single turn (see page 22, figure 9). With the long seam facing you, cut the dough in half vertically (see page 23, figure 12). Wrap each piece of dough tightly in plastic wrap, then wrap again. Freeze for at least 24 hours or up to 4 days.

10   The night before using the dough, transfer the frozen dough to the refrigerator and let thaw overnight, about 8 hours. Once the dough defrosts it will begin to rise, so be sure to roll it out immediately or it could develop a yeasty taste.

Apple Turnovers

Makes 9 turnovers

....

With only puff pastry and some apple preserves, you can have these delectable turnovers ready for serving in no time. While you can use other preserves that suit your fancy, I think that apple is the best. No matter what you choose, be sure to resist temptation and let them cool before serving—the filling will be extremely hot when the turnovers are fresh from the oven.

½ recipe Puff Pastry (page 20)

Unbleached all-purpose flour, for rolling out the dough

¾ cup Chunky Apple Preserves (page 275)

Granulated sugar, for sprinkling

Confectioners' sugar, for serving

1   Place the puff pastry on a lightly floured work surface. Lightly dust the top of the pastry with flour. Using a large, heavy rolling pin, roll out the pastry into a 13 by 13-inch square. Fold into thirds, place on a half-sheet pan, and refrigerate for 15 minutes.

2   Position a rack in the center of the oven and preheat to 400°F. Line a half-sheet pan with parchment paper. Unfold the pastry onto the work surface. Using a yardstick and pizza wheel, trim the pastry into a 12 by 12-inch square. Cut the pastry vertically into three 4-inch strips, then horizontally into three 4-inch strips to make 9 squares.

3   For each turnover, spoon a tablespoon of apple preserves slightly off-center in the pastry square. Lightly brush two adjoining sides of the square with water. Starting with the point opposite the moistened sides, fold the turnover in half diagonally. Press the open seams closed with the sides of your thumbs. Place the turnovers 1 inch apart on the half-sheet pan and refrigerate until chilled, about 15 minutes. Using the tines of a fork, press the seams in a few places to seal again. Pierce the top of each turnover with the fork.

4   Lightly brush the tops of the turnovers with water and sprinkle with granulated sugar. Bake for 15 minutes. Reduce the oven temperature to 375°F and continue baking until the turnovers are golden brown, about 15 minutes more.

5   Let the turnovers cool on the pan for 15 minutes. Transfer to a wire cooling rack and let cool completely. Just before serving, sift confectioners' sugar over the tops.

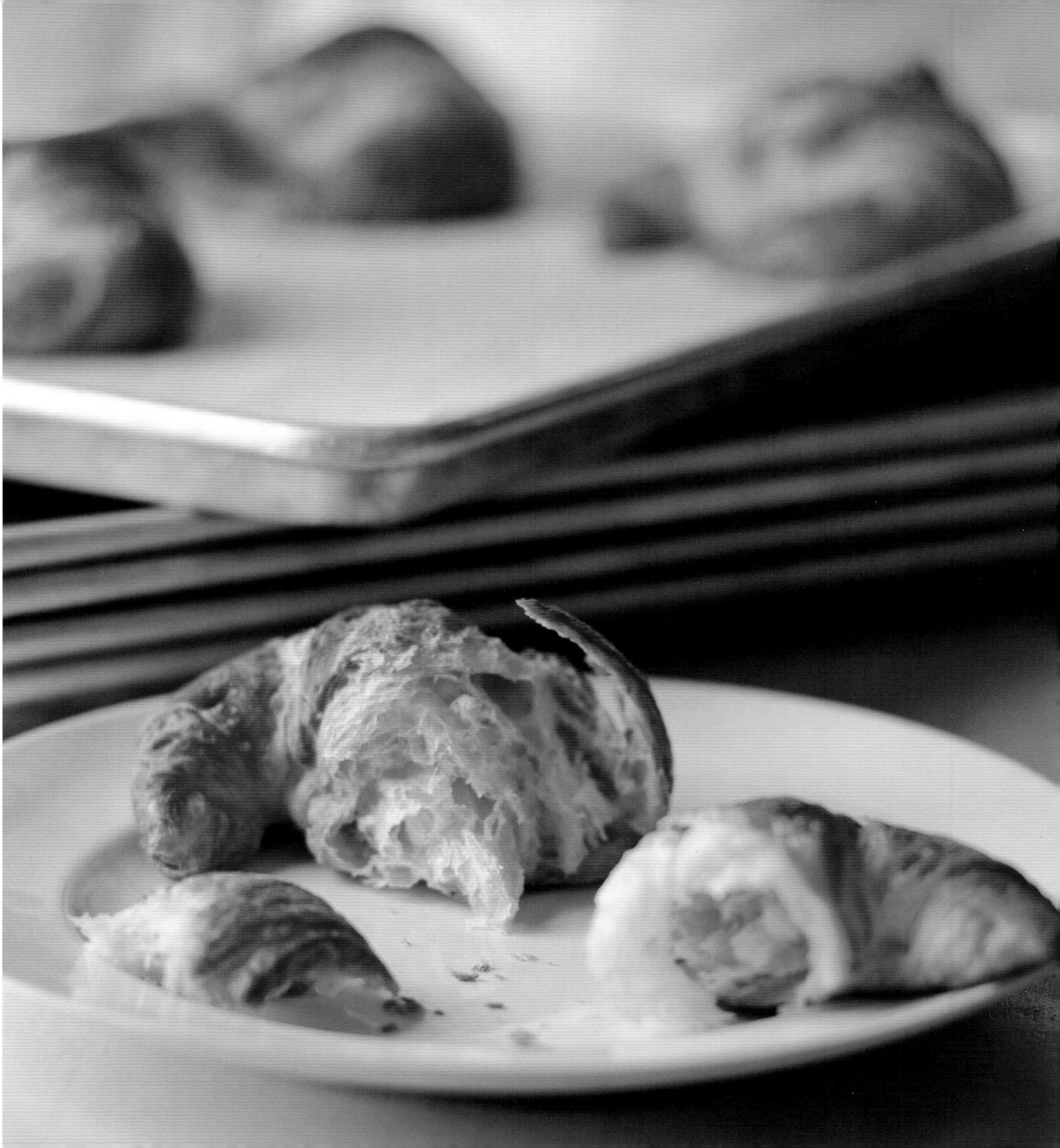

Croissants

Makes 14 croissants

....

What a pleasure it is to present a basket of home-baked croissants to guests. And what a sense of satisfaction it will be for the home baker to create these masterpieces of the baker's art. You'll know that you've mastered the rolling technique if you tug at the end of a baked croissant and the dough unfurls in a single, long spiral. These wonderful pastries are surprisingly easy to make.

BAKER'S NOTE: Have a yardstick and a pizza wheel at your side to help keep the cuts straight. Always cut from top to bottom. You will have better control over the wheel than if you cut from the bottom up. • At the bakery, we combine the half-triangle scraps of dough with trimmings from the Danish dough to make *Pains de Matin* (page 40), sweet breakfast rolls. However, it is unlikely that a home baker will collect enough scraps to make baking these rolls practical. I don't want to waste the croissant trimmings, so I give instructions for piecing the half-triangles together to make full-size croissants. They will not be perfect, but it is possible that no one will notice.

Unbleached all-purpose flour, for rolling the dough   *1 large egg, well beaten with a hand blender*

½ recipe Croissant Dough (page 24)

1   Line two half-sheet pans with parchment paper. Dust the work surface well with flour. Place the dough on the work surface with the open seam of dough facing you. Dust the top of the dough with flour. Using a large, heavy rolling pin, roll out the dough into a 16 by 12-inch rectangle. Don't press the dough too hard; let the weight of the pin do much of the work. If you changed the position of the dough while rolling, it is important to keep track of which side contains the seam.

2   Turn the dough with the seam facing you. (If you've lost track, look carefully at the sides of the dough, and you should be able to discern it, even though it is faint.) Using a pizza wheel and a yardstick, neatly trim the rough edges. Cut the dough in half lengthwise to make two 16 by 6-inch rectangles. Fold each rectangle into thirds, place on a half-sheet pan, and refrigerate uncovered for about 15 minutes.

3   Remove the dough strips from the refrigerator. Work with one dough strip at a time. Using a pizza wheel, starting at the top left corner of one strip, cut down to make a half-triangle with a 2-inch base; set aside. Measure 3½ inches from the top left corner of the strip and mark a notch with the wheel at this point. Cut down diagonally from the notch to meet the bottom left edge of the dough strip to make another triangle with a 3½-inch base. Continue cutting, alternating diagonal cuts, to cut out 6 triangles (figure 1). The last cut will also yield a half-triangle with a 2-inch-wide base. Repeat with the second strip of dough to make 6 more large triangles and 2 half-triangles. You should have a total of 12 large triangles and 4 half-triangles.

4   Place a single "complete" triangle on the work surface with the base of the triangle facing you. Stretch the bottom slightly so it is about 5 inches wide. Pick up the triangle. With one hand, hold the dough triangle at the bottom and stretch it with your other hand until it is about 7 inches long (figure 2). Return the triangle to the work surface. Starting at the bottom, roll up the triangle, and finish with the tip underneath the croissant (figures 3, 4, 5, and 6). Place on the pan. Curve the croissant by bringing the two ends together and then cross one end over the other, and press together. Repeat rolling the remaining dough triangles, placing them 1½ inches apart on the pan. Overlap 2 of the half-triangles at their long sides, and press the seam together. Roll up as described for the large triangles and add to the pan. Repeat with the remaining half-triangles.

5 Choose a warm place in the kitchen for proofing. Slip each pan into a tall "kitchen-sized" plastic bag. Place a tall glass of very hot water near the center of each pan. Wave the opening of each bag to trap air and inflate it like a balloon to create "head room," being sure that the plastic does not touch the delicate dough. Twist each bag closed. Let stand until the croissants look puffy but not doubled, 1½ to 2 hours.

6 Meanwhile, position racks in the center and top third of the oven and preheat to 375°F. Remove the glasses from the bags, then the pans. Lightly brush the croissants with the beaten egg. Bake for 10 minutes. Reduce the heat to 350°F and continue baking until the croissants are crisp and golden brown, about 15 minutes longer. Serve warm or cool to room temperature.

Almond Croissants

Makes 14 croissants

....

Even though they aren't curved into the traditional crescent shape, these glorious *pains aux amandes* are still considered croissants. Each one is filled with almond cream, then glazed and topped with more almonds after baking.

BAKER'S NOTE: Have a yardstick and a pizza wheel at your side to help keep the cuts straight. Always cut from top to bottom. You will have better control over the wheel than if you cut from the bottom up. • At the bakery, we combine the half-triangle scraps of dough with trimmings from the Danish dough to make *Pains de Matin* (page 40), sweet breakfast rolls. However, it is unlikely that a home baker will collect enough scraps to make baking these rolls practical. I don't want to waste the croissant trimmings, so I give instructions for piecing the half-triangles together to make full-size croissants. They will not be perfect, but it is possible that no one will notice.

Unbleached all-purpose flour, for rolling the dough

½ recipe Croissant Dough (page 24)

Almond Cream (page 51)

1 large egg, well beaten with a hand blender

Confectioners' Glaze

½ cup confectioners' sugar, sifted • 5 teaspoons water, as needed

3 tablespoons sliced almonds, toasted (page 5)

1   Line two half-sheet pans with parchment paper. Dust the work surface well with flour. Place the dough on the work surface with the open seam of dough facing you. Dust the top of the dough with flour. Using a large, heavy rolling pin, roll out the dough into a 16 by 12-inch rectangle. Don't press the dough too hard; let the weight of the pin do much of the work. If you changed the position of the dough while rolling, it is important to keep track of which side contains the seam.

2   Turn the dough with the seam facing you. (If you've lost track, look carefully at the sides of the dough, and you should be able to discern it, even though it is faint.) Using a pizza wheel and a yardstick, neatly trim the rough edges. Cut the dough in half lengthwise to make two 16 by 6-inch rectangles. Fold each rectangle into thirds, place on a half-sheet pan, and refrigerate uncovered for about 15 minutes.

3 Remove the dough strips from the refrigerator. Work with one dough strip at a time. Using a pizza wheel, starting at the top left corner of one strip, cut down to make a half-triangle with a 2-inch base; set aside. Measure 3½ inches from the top left corner of the strip and mark a notch with the wheel at this point. Cut down diagonally from the notch to meet the bottom left edge of the dough strip to make another triangle with a 3½-inch base. Continue cutting, alternating diagonal cuts, to cut out 6 triangles (see page 34, figure 1). The last cut will also yield a half-triangle with a 2-inch-wide base. Repeat with the second strip of dough to make 6 more large triangles and 2 half-triangles. You should have a total of 12 large triangles and 4 half-triangles.

4 Fit a pastry bag with a ⅜-inch-diameter plain tip, such as Ateco #804, and fill with the almond cream. Place a single "complete" triangle on the work surface with the base of the triangle facing you. Stretch the bottom slightly so it is about 5 inches wide. Pick up the triangle. With one hand, hold the dough triangle at the bottom and stretch it with your other hand until it is about 7 inches long (see page 34, figure 2). Return the triangle to the work surface. About ¼ inch up from the bottom of the triangle, pipe a 2-inch-long strip of almond cream. Fold the base of the triangle up to cover the almond cream. Starting at the bottom, roll up the triangle and finish with the tip under the croissant (see pages 34 and 35, figures 3, 4, 5, and 6). Place on the pan, keeping the croissant straight (this croissant is not curved). Repeat filling and rolling the remaining triangles, placing them 1½ inches apart. Overlap 2 of the half-triangles at their long sides, and press the seam together. Fill and roll up as described for the large triangles and add to the pan. Repeat with the remaining half-triangles.

5 Choose a warm place in the kitchen for proofing. Slip each pan into a tall "kitchen-sized" plastic bag. Place a tall glass of very hot water near the center of each pan. Wave the opening of each bag to trap air and inflate it like a balloon to create "head room," being sure that the plastic does not touch the delicate dough. Twist each bag closed. Let stand until the croissants look puffy but not doubled, 1½ to 2 hours.

6 Meanwhile, position racks in the center and top third of the oven and preheat to 375°F. Remove the glasses from the bags, then the pans. Lightly brush the croissants with the beaten egg. Bake for 10 minutes. Reduce the heat to 350°F and continue baking until the croissants are crisp and golden brown, about 15 minutes longer.

7 To make the confectioners' glaze, whisk the confectioners' sugar and enough of the water to make a glaze about the consistency of half-and-half. Brush the glaze over the warm croissants and sprinkle with the toasted almonds. Let cool until the glaze sets. Serve warm or at room temperature.

Pains au Chocolat

Makes 12 pastries

....

Another use for croissant dough, these have almost more "French" cachet than their crescent-shaped ancestor. Use your favorite eating chocolate for the filling, from sweet to the darkest bittersweet.

BAKER'S NOTE: Have a yardstick and a pizza wheel at your side to help keep the cuts straight. Always cut from top to bottom. You will have better control over the wheel than if you cut from the bottom up. • While you can buy chocolate strips (*bâtons*) specifically for *pains au chocolat* at bakery suppliers or on-line, it is more convenient for the home baker to make his or her own from a standard 3½-ounce chocolate bar. If the chocolate bar is too cold, it will snap into shards instead of cutting into strips. Let the bar stand in a warm spot in the kitchen for about 30 minutes to soften slightly. Or, if you have a large pocket in your apron, put the chocolate bar in there and let it warm from your body heat. Even if the bar does shatter, it can still be used—just keep track of the pieces and use an equal amount for each *pain*.

Unbleached all-purpose flour, for rolling the dough

½ recipe Croissant Dough (page 24)

One 3½-ounce semisweet or bittersweet chocolate bar, cut crosswise into 12 strips

1 large egg, well beaten with a hand blender

1   Line a half-sheet pan with parchment paper. Dust the work surface well with flour. Place the dough on the work surface with the open seam of dough facing you. Dust the top of the dough with flour. Using a large, heavy rolling pin, roll out the dough into a 16 by 12-inch rectangle. Don't press the dough too hard; let the weight of the pin do much of the work. If you changed the position of the dough while rolling, it is important to keep track of which side contains the seam. Using a yardstick and a pizza wheel, neatly trim the rough edges of the rectangle. Fold the dough into thirds, place on the half-sheet pan, and refrigerate uncovered for 15 minutes.

2   Unfold the dough onto the work surface. Cut the dough horizontally into thirds and vertically into quarters to make 12 squares. Place a chocolate strip about ¼ inch up from the bottom of a dough square. Roll from the bottom up and place, seam side down, on the pan. Repeat with the remaining dough and chocolate, placing the *pains* 1½ inches apart. Using a very sharp thin knife, make a 1-inch slit in the center of the *pains*, cutting just down to the chocolate. Make two more 1-inch slits, ¾ inch on either side of the center slit.

3   Choose a warm place in the kitchen for proofing. Slip the pan into a tall "kitchen-sized" plastic bag. Place a tall glass of very hot water near the center of the pan. Wave the opening of the bag to trap air and inflate it like a balloon to create "head room," being sure that the plastic does not touch the delicate dough. Twist the bag closed. Let stand until the *pains au chocolat* look puffy but not doubled, 1½ to 2 hours.

4   Meanwhile, position a rack in the center of the oven and preheat to 375°F. Remove the glass from the bag, then the pan. Lightly brush the *pains* with the beaten egg. Bake for 10 minutes. Reduce the heat to 350°F and continue baking until the *pains* are crisp and golden brown, about 15 minutes longer. Serve warm or at room temperature.

Pains de Matin

Makes 12 pastries

....

At the bakery, we make these light and buttery "morning breads" by collecting the trimmings from our croissant and Danish doughs. It is unlikely that a home baker will gather enough trimmings, so this recipe uses one pound of each dough. Once the doughs are made (and remember that the majority of time used to make them happens during the resting periods), these will come together in no time. Make them for a very special brunch.

Unbleached all-purpose flour, for rolling out the dough

½ recipe Croissant Dough (page 24)

½ recipe Danish Dough (page 27)

6 tablespoons superfine sugar

½ teaspoon ground cinnamon

Softened unsalted butter, for the muffin pan

Confectioners' sugar, for garnish

1   Lightly dust a work surface with flour. Place the croissant dough on the surface and dust the top with flour. Using a large, heavy rolling pin, roll out the dough ¼ inch thick. Using a pizza wheel, cut the dough into ½-inch pieces. Lightly dust them with flour so they do not stick together. Transfer to a large bowl. Repeat with the Danish dough. Add the sugar and cinnamon to the bowl and toss the dough pieces with your hands to coat well.

2   Brush the inside of 12 muffin cups well with softened butter, then brush the top of the pan. Divide the dough pieces evenly among the muffin cups. Using your fingertips, firmly press the tops to compress and level them.

3   Choose a warm place in the kitchen for proofing. Slip the pan into a tall "kitchen-sized" plastic bag. Place two tall glasses of very hot water on the counter next to two opposing corners of the pan. Wave the opening of the bag to trap air and inflate it like a balloon to create "head room," being sure that the plastic does not touch the delicate dough. Twist the bag closed. Let stand until the *pains* look puffy but not doubled, 1½ to 2 hours.

4   Meanwhile, position a rack in the center of the oven and preheat to 350°F. Remove the glasses from the bag, then the pan. Bake until golden brown, about 25 minutes. Cool slightly, then remove the *pains* from the pan. Serve warm or at room temperature, with confectioners' sugar sifted on top.

Pains aux Raisins

Makes 12 pastries

....

These may look like the prosaic snail pastries that you find in bakeries across America, but with their buttery croissant dough, they are as French as the Eiffel Tower. A layer of pastry cream provides extra flavor and moisture.

Unbleached all-purpose flour, for rolling the dough

½ recipe Croissant Dough (page 24)

½ cup Pastry Cream (page 286)

½ cup seedless raisins

1 large egg, well beaten with a hand blender

Apricot Glaze (page 293), hot

Confectioners' Glaze (page 36)

1 Line a half-sheet pan with parchment paper. Dust the work surface well with flour. Place the dough with the open seam facing you, and dust with flour. Using a large, heavy rolling pin, roll the dough into a 16 by 12-inch rectangle; let the weight of the pin do much of the work. Keep track of which side contains the seam. Using a yardstick and a pizza wheel, neatly trim the rough edges of the rectangle. Fold into thirds, place on the half-sheet pan, and refrigerate uncovered for 15 minutes.

2 Unfold the dough onto the work surface. Spread with pastry cream, leaving a ½-inch border, then sprinkle with raisins. Starting from the top, roll down the dough. Do not pinch the long seam closed. Cut crosswise into 1-inch pieces. Tuck the loose end of each pastry underneath the roll, and place, tucked side down, on the pan, 1½ inches apart. Cover with parchment paper and a half-sheet pan. Gently press on pan to slightly widen the pastries. Remove the top pan and the parchment paper.

3 Choose a warm place in the kitchen for proofing. Slip the pan into a tall "kitchen-sized" plastic bag. Place a tall glass of hot water near the center of the pan. Wave the opening of the bag to trap air and inflate it like a balloon to create "head room," being sure the plastic does not touch the delicate dough. Twist the bag closed. Let stand until the *pains* look puffy but not doubled, 1½ to 2 hours.

4 Meanwhile, position a rack in the center of the oven and preheat to 375°F. Remove the glass from the bag, then the pan. Lightly brush the *pains* with the beaten egg. Bake for 10 minutes. Reduce the heat to 350°F and continue baking until the *pains* are crisp and golden brown, about 15 minutes longer. Brush the hot apricot glaze over the hot *pains*, followed by the confectioners' glaze. Let cool until the glazes set. Serve warm or cool to room temperature.

Cheese and Raisin Danish

Makes 12 pastries

....

At most bakeries, all Danish have the same round shape, and you can tell one kind from another only by the topping. At Sarabeth's, each version has a distinct shape. These flavorful pastry pockets are filled with cream cheese and raisins.

Cream Cheese and Raisin Filling

3 tablespoons seedless raisins	*1 tablespoon superfine sugar*
1 cup hot water	*½ teaspoon pure vanilla extract*
6 ounces cream cheese, softened	

Unbleached all-purpose flour, for rolling the dough	*Apricot Glaze (page 293), hot*
½ recipe Danish Dough (page 27)	*Confectioners' sugar, for garnish*
1 large egg, well beaten with a hand blender	

1   To make the filling, soak the raisins in the hot water for 1 hour. Drain well. Pat the raisins dry with a paper towel. Mash the cream cheese, sugar, and vanilla with a silicone spatula in a small bowl until smooth. Stir in the soaked raisins. Using a 1½-inch-diameter scoop, portion 12 balls of the mixture onto a plate. Refrigerate until ready to use.

2   Dust the work surface well with flour. Place the dough on the work surface with the open seam of dough facing you. Dust the top of the dough with flour. Using a large, heavy rolling pin, roll out the dough into a 16 by 12-inch rectangle. Don't press the dough too hard; let the weight of the pin do much of the work. If you changed the position of the dough while rolling, it is important to keep track of which side contains the seam. Using a yardstick and a pizza wheel, neatly trim the rough edges of the rectangle. Fold the dough into thirds, place on a half-sheet pan, and refrigerate uncovered for 15 minutes.

3   Line a half-sheet pan with parchment paper. Unfold the dough onto the work surface. Cut the dough horizontally into thirds and vertically into quarters to make 12 squares. Set a cream-cheese ball in the center of each square (figure 1).

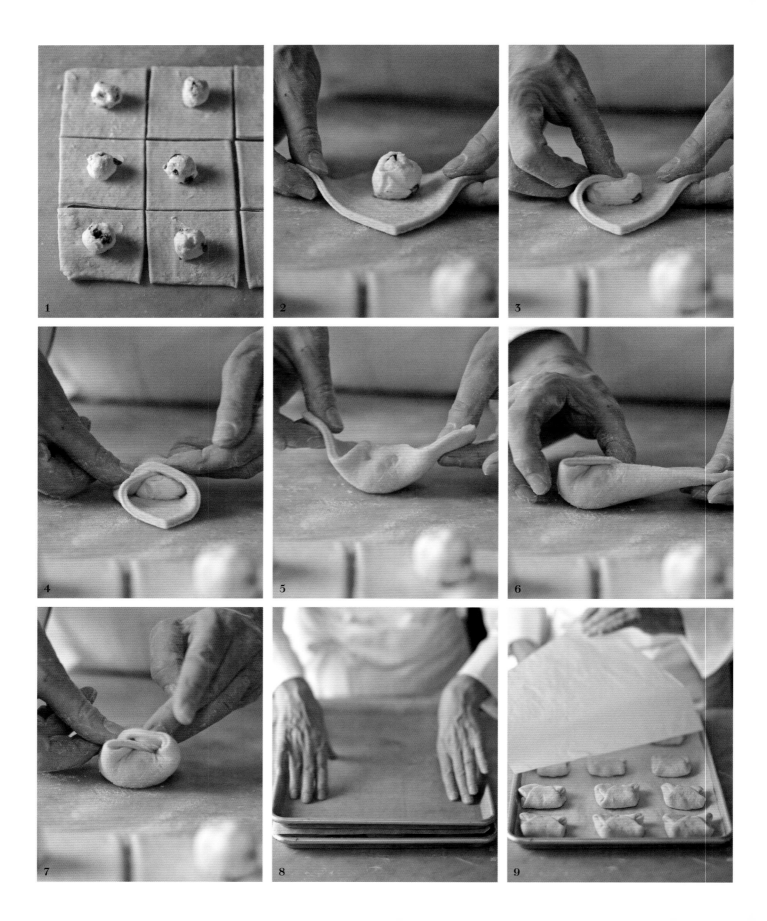

4 Place a dough square in front of you, with a point at the top (figure 2). Take the right point of the square and push it into the center of the cheese ball with your thumb (figure 3). Pull and stretch the left point to the right of the cheese ball, and press it into the side of the pastry with your thumb to secure it (figure 4). Turn the pastry so the unfolded points run horizontally (figure 5). Pull and stretch the right point to the left side of the cheese, and tuck it into the pastry with your thumb (figure 6). Repeat with the left point, pulling, stretching, and pushing with your thumb until the right side of the pastry completely encloses the cheese (figure 7). Repeat with the remaining dough and cheese balls. Place the packets on the pan, spacing them 1½ inches apart. Cover the packets with parchment paper and a half-sheet pan. Gently press the top pan to slightly widen the packets (figure 8). Remove the top pan and paper (figure 9).

5 Choose a warm place in the kitchen for proofing. Slip the pan into a tall "kitchen-sized" plastic bag. Place a tall glass of very hot water near the center of the pan. Wave the opening of the bag to trap air and inflate it like a balloon to create "head room," being sure that the plastic does not touch the delicate dough. Twist the bag closed. Let stand until the packets look puffy but not doubled, 1½ to 2 hours.

6 Meanwhile, position a rack in the center of the oven and preheat to 350°F. Remove the glass from the bag, then the pan. Lightly brush the packets with the beaten egg. Bake until the Danish are golden brown, about 25 minutes. Gently brush the hot apricot glaze over the hot Danish. Let cool slightly. Sift confectioners' sugar over the tops and serve warm or at room temperature.

Fruit Danish

Makes 12 Danish

....

Fruit Danish is another pastry that, in the wrong hands, can become predictable. Our fruit Danish are not just baked; they are handcrafted to become as beautiful as they are delicious. Use your favorite jam or preserves, from raspberry to apricot, as the fruit component. This tender dough absolutely melts in your mouth.

Unbleached all-purpose flour, for rolling the dough

½ recipe Danish Dough (page 27)

1 tablespoon superfine sugar

⅛ teaspoon ground cinnamon

*¼ cup Raspberry Jam (page 276),
or use your favorite, as needed*

1 large egg, well beaten with a hand blender

Apricot Glaze (page 293), hot

1   Dust the work surface well with flour. Place the dough on the work surface with the open seam of dough facing you. Dust the top of the dough with flour. Using a large, heavy rolling pin, roll out the dough into a 12 by 16-inch rectangle. Don't press the dough too hard; let the weight of the pin do much of the work. If you changed the position of the dough while rolling, it is important to keep track of which side contains the seam. Fold the dough into thirds, place on a half-sheet pan, and refrigerate uncovered for 15 minutes.

2   Line a half-sheet pan with parchment paper. Return the dough to the work surface. Position the dough with the short side (with the seam) facing you. Mix the sugar and cinnamon together, and sprinkle over the dough. Fold the dough in half horizontally. Gently roll the pin over the folded dough to lightly compress the layers. Using a yardstick and a pizza wheel, neatly trim the side edges of the rectangle. Cut the dough vertically into twelve 1-inch-wide strips.

3   Working with one strip at a time, hold the closed end with one hand and roll the open end underneath your palm to twist the strip into a 12-inch-long spiral (figure 1). Hold the folded end of the strip in place with one hand. With the other hand, wrap the strip in a counterclockwise motion into a snail shape (figure 2). Tuck the loose end underneath the pastry to secure it (figure 3). Place the pastries on the pan, tucked side down, spacing them 1½ inches apart.

4   Choose a warm place in the kitchen for proofing. Slip the pan into a tall "kitchen-sized" plastic bag. Place a tall glass of very hot water near the center of the pan. Wave the opening of the bag to trap air and inflate it like a balloon to create "head room," being sure that the plastic does not touch the delicate dough. Twist the bag closed. Let stand until the pastries look puffy but not doubled, 1½ to 2 hours.

5   Meanwhile, position a rack in the center of the oven and preheat to 350°F. Remove the glass from the bag, then the pan. Lightly moisten your index fingers with tepid water and gently depress the center of each pastry. Be careful not to deflate the surrounding proofed dough. Place a rounded ½ teaspoon of preserves in each center.

6   Lightly brush the pastries with the beaten egg. Do not egg wash the jam. Bake until the Danish are golden brown, about 25 minutes. Gently brush the hot Danish with the hot apricot glaze. Let cool slightly and serve warm or at room temperature.

Chocolate Babka

Makes one large 9 by 5-inch loaf

....

This streusel-topped loaf of Danish dough, swirled with an almond cream, chocolate, raisins, and cinnamon, is a classic Eastern European holiday bread. But don't just reserve it for special holidays, as it is a welcome addition to a brunch menu. If the trick of twisting the filled dough into its distinctive three-humped loaf shape seems unfamiliar, it will become clear after some practice.

Soaked Raisins

½ cup seedless raisins • ½ cup hot water • 1 tablespoon dark rum

Streusel

⅔ cup unbleached all-purpose flour

2 tablespoons superfine sugar

2 tablespoons light brown sugar

¼ teaspoon ground cinnamon

4 tablespoons (½ stick) unsalted butter, melted

Almond Cream

4 tablespoons (½ stick) unsalted butter, at room temperature

2 tablespoons superfine sugar

1 large egg yolk

1 tablespoon plus 1 teaspoon almond paste, finely chopped

⅓ cup (1¼ ounces) sliced almonds, toasted (page 5) and finely chopped

½ teaspoon dark rum

½ teaspoon pure vanilla extract

Softened unsalted butter, for the pan

1 tablespoon superfine sugar

¼ teaspoon ground cinnamon

Unbleached all-purpose flour, for rolling out the dough

½ recipe Danish Dough (page 27)

6 ounces semisweet or bittersweet chocolate, finely chopped

1 large egg, well beaten with a hand blender

2 ounces semisweet or bittersweet chocolate, melted (page 7), for decorating

Confectioners' sugar, for garnish

1
2
3

1 At least 2 hours before baking the babka, prepare the soaked raisins. Combine the raisins, hot water, and rum in a small bowl. Let stand until the raisins are plump, about 1 hour. Drain well and pat dry with paper towels.

2 To make the streusel, combine the flour, sugars, and cinnamon in a bowl. Gradually stir in the butter and mix, squeeze, and break up the mixture with your hands until it resembles coarse crumbs.

3 To make the almond cream, beat the butter and sugar together in a small bowl with a handheld electric mixer until the mixture is light in color and texture, about 2 minutes. Beat in the yolk. Add the almond paste and beat well until the mixture is smooth (the almond paste will take some time to break down), about 1 minute. Add the almonds, rum, and vanilla and mix until combined.

4 Generously butter a 9 by 5-inch metal loaf pan. Sprinkle about half of the streusel inside the pan and tilt to coat the pan. Tap the excess streusel back into the bowl of remaining streusel. Set the pan and the bowl of streusel aside.

5 Mix the sugar and cinnamon together; set aside. On a lightly floured work surface, roll out the Danish dough into a 14 by 8-inch rectangle. Spread the dough with the almond cream, leaving a 1-inch border at the bottom. Sprinkle the cream with the drained raisins, then the chopped chocolate and cinnamon sugar. Starting at the top, roll down the dough. Brush the empty border of dough with the beaten egg, and pinch the long seam closed. Roll the dough underneath your hands to stretch to 18 inches. Fold the dough in half into a curve, with the front length 3 inches longer than the back

length. Using the side of your hand, dent the dough at its bend (figure 1). Fold the longer length of dough over the back length twice to make two humps (figure 2). Twist the dough to create a third hump, and tuck the two open ends under the loaf (figure 3). You should have a loaf about 9 inches long with three humps.

6   Transfer to the prepared pan, being sure that the open ends are well secured under the loaf. Brush the top with the beaten egg and sprinkle with the reserved streusel. Don't worry if some of the streusel falls into the corners of the pan. Place the babka, in the loaf pan, on a half-sheet pan.

7   Choose a warm place in the kitchen for proofing. Slip the babka on the pan into a tall "kitchen-sized" plastic bag. Place a tall glass of very hot water near the loaf pan. Wave the opening of the bag to trap air and inflate it like a balloon to create "head room," being sure that the plastic does not touch the delicate dough. Twist the bag closed. Let stand until the dough has risen about 1 inch over the top of the pan, about 1½ hours.

8   Position a rack in the center of the oven and preheat to 325°F.

9   Remove the glass from the bag, then the loaf pan on the half-sheet pan. Bake until the babka is deep golden brown, the dough in the crevices looks fully baked, and an instant-read thermometer inserted into the center of the babka reads at least 195°F, 45 to 50 minutes. If the loaf threatens to burn, cover the top loosely with aluminum foil.

10 Cool in the pan on a wire rack for 10 minutes. Carefully unmold the babka from the loaf pan onto the rack, and let cool completely. Drizzle the melted chocolate from a silicone spatula over the top of the babka, and let cool until set. Sift confectioners' sugar over the top. When serving, slice the babka with a serrated knife.

Brioche

Makes twelve 3 ½-inch brioche

....

I s there a more perfect breakfast than brioche, fresh from the oven, served with fruit preserves? Glorious, golden brown brioche gets its glow from lots of egg yolks and a healthy amount of butter. To give the dough its light-as-a-feather texture, avoid adding too much flour during mixing (it should be just cohesive enough to barely hold its shape when it is removed from the mixing bowl) and handle it gently during shaping. This is my favorite morning pastry. I think it may become yours as well.

BAKER'S NOTE: The butter must be very soft (but not melted) so it can incorporate into the dough. Cut it into tablespoon-size pieces, and let stand at room temperature for at least 1 hour before using. • For dry yeast, refer to the adjusted liquid measurements in the directions. • Leftover baked brioche can be frozen for up to 2 weeks. They are great toasted.

1 ounce (2 packed tablespoons) compressed yeast or
3 ½ teaspoons active dry yeast

2 tablespoons superfine sugar

⅓ cup plus 1 tablespoon whole milk

8 large egg yolks

2 ¼ cups unbleached all-purpose flour, as needed

¼ teaspoon fine sea salt

8 tablespoons (1 stick) unsalted butter,
cut into tablespoons, well softened, plus more
for the bowl and brioche tins

1 large egg, well beaten with a hand blender

1   Crumble the compressed yeast finely into the bowl of a heavy-duty stand mixer. Add the sugar and let stand until the yeast gives off some moisture, about 3 minutes. Whisk well to dissolve. Add the cold milk and yolks and whisk to combine. (If using dry yeast, sprinkle the yeast over ⅓ cup warm, 105° to 115°F, milk in a small bowl. Let stand until softened, about 5 minutes, then stir to dissolve. Add to the mixer bowl with 1 tablespoon cold milk, the sugar, and yolks, and whisk.)

2   Attach the bowl to the mixer and fit with the paddle attachment. With the machine on low speed, add 2 cups of the flour and the salt. Mix until the mixture forms a sticky, batter-like dough that clings to the sides of the bowl. Increase the speed to medium. One tablespoon at a time, beat in the softened butter, letting each addition become absorbed before adding another. Remove the paddle attachment.

3 Using a spatula, scrape the dough into the center of the bowl. Attach the dough hook to the mixer. Knead the dough on medium-high speed until it is gathers into a ball around the hook. Return to medium speed and knead, adding tablespoons of the remaining flour, until the dough is smooth but feels tacky and sticks to the bottom of the bowl, about 3 minutes.

4 Generously butter a medium bowl. Turn the dough out onto a lightly floured work surface. Gently shape the dough into a ball. Turn the ball, smooth side down, in the bowl, and turn right side up to lightly coat the ball in butter. Cover the bowl with plastic wrap and let stand in a warm place until doubled, 1½ to 2 hours (figure 1).

5 Butter twelve 3½-inch-wide brioche tins. Turn the dough out onto a lightly floured work surface, but do not punch down the dough—its texture should remind you of a feather-filled pillow. Cut the dough into 12 equal portions. (If you have a kitchen scale, each portion will weigh 2 ounces.)

6 One at a time, shape each portion of dough into a ball on the work surface, taking care not to break the exterior of the dough (figure 2). To do this, cup both hands around the dough. Carefully turn the dough in your cupped hands to gently shape into a ball—overhandling will melt the butter in the dough. Place the dough on its side, with the rough underside of the dough to one side (either right or left, depending on your dominant hand). Lightly dust the side of your hand with flour. Place the side of your hand about 1 inch from the smooth end of the dough. Using the upper part of your hand, including the last finger, move your hand back and forth to cut into the dough, forming a small ball that is attached to the larger portion by a thin piece of dough (figures 3 and 4).

7 Transfer the shaped dough to a brioche tin, holding the larger portion in one hand and the small ball in the other, taking care not to break the connection. Place the larger portion of dough in the bottom of the tin (figure 5). Using your thumb and first two fingers, still holding the small ball of dough, force a hole into the center of the larger portion of dough, reaching all the way down to the bottom of the tin, and stick the smaller ball in the hole (figure 6). This keeps it from popping off during baking. Repeat with the remaining balls of dough. Place the tins on a half-sheet pan. Lightly brush the tops of the brioche with some of the beaten egg, reserving the rest.

8 Choose a warm spot in the kitchen for proofing. Slip the half-sheet pan into a tall "kitchen-sized" plastic bag. Place two tall glasses of very hot water near the center of the pan. Wave the opening of the bag to trap air and inflate the bag like a balloon to create "head room," being sure that the plastic does not touch the sticky dough. Twist the bag closed. Let stand in a warm place until the brioche looks puffy, about 1 hour.

9 Position a rack in the center of the oven and preheat to 350°F. Remove the glasses from the bag, and then the pan. Lightly brush the tops of the brioche again with the reserved egg. Bake until the brioche are golden brown, about 20 minutes. Let cool in their tins for 5 minutes. Remove the brioche from their tins, and serve warm or at room temperature.

Chapter Two
Muffins and More

MUFFINS AREN'T FANCY, BUT THEY SURE ARE DELICIOUS. WHETHER YOU ENJOY ONE WITH YOUR MORNING COFFEE, OR SAVE THE CALORIES FOR later in the day as an afternoon snack, they always seem to hit the spot. But like the other pastries at the bakery, I think that ours are a step above the typical muffin.

Many muffin recipes simply stir the wet and dry ingredients together, which can make a good muffin, but not always. (Exceptions include the Blueberry Crumb Muffins and Maple Muffins on pages 65 and 69.) For the lightest texture and most delicate crumb, the butter and sugar are creamed, eggs beaten in, then the flour added—just like cake batter. With the hundreds of thousands of muffins Sarabeth's has made over the years, there must be plenty of people who agree with me. In fact, the Pumpkin Muffin (page 71) was once our bakery logo.

Muffins may also be popular because of their size, each one representing a single little cake that is yours and yours alone. And they come in a large range of flavors, from bran and corn to banana and pumpkin. Personally speaking, it would be hard to choose a favorite. Biscuits and scones, simply prepared but utterly delicious little pastries, are included in this chapter; you'll find two of my favorites here.

A LESSON ON MUFFINS

Keep It Cool A perfectly made muffin doesn't just taste delicious, it must have the classic domed shape. If the batter is too soft, the muffins will be flat. The trick is to use chilled butter, cut into tablespoons, and a heavy-duty stand mixer, which is strong enough to soften the butter for creaming. A handheld electric mixer will do if the butter is allowed to stand about 15 minutes—the butter should feel quite cool, but be malleable. Beat the butter for a minute or two until it becomes smooth, then gradually add the sugar, and cream together until the mixture is very light in color and texture. Be sure to stop the machine and scrape down the batter a few times during the creaming process. For a couple of recipes, the batter should be beaten an extra 15 seconds after it comes together. You will recognize the proper stage of beating by a sheen on the batter. This helps strengthen the batter so it rises evenly. When the relatively cool batter is scooped into the muffin cups, it will hold its shape and bake into a dome.

Making Muffins I am not a fan of muffin (cupcake) liners. Yes, they help when you clean the muffin pan, but I don't like peeling off paper or foil from my muffin. In the process of the peeling, you usually end up with a crumby mess. I much prefer to butter the muffin cups, which imparts a wonderful rich flavor to the outside crust as a bonus. Don't use nonstick muffin pans, as the dark coating absorbs heat from the oven and tends to overbake the muffin at the sides.

To butter a muffin tin, use well-softened butter and a cylinder-shaped brush with natural white bristles—flat brushes don't work as well. In a pinch, use a folded paper towel. Butter the cup thoroughly and evenly without any gaps or lumps. To be sure the muffin tops don't stick to the pan, brush the top (the flat area between the cups) of the muffin tin, too.

A picture-perfect muffin has a gorgeous domed top. The best way to achieve this shape is to portion out the batter with an ice-cream scoop. The advantages of scooping the batter over spooning it into the cups are many—not only does the muffin rise better into the desired rounded shape, but it is less messy and you get excellent uniformity from one muffin to another. The right-size scoop has a 2½-inch diameter with about 6 tablespoons capacity.

While a simple scooping of the batter works, to get a more rounded ball of batter that ensures a domed top, I often use a two-handed technique. Scoop the batter with one hand, filling the scoop to overflowing. Your instinct may be to level the batter, but instead, use your other hand to quickly mold and shape the exposed batter into a gently rising mound in the scoop. You will have a roughly shaped sphere in the scoop. Release the batter into the prepared muffin cup.

To test for doneness, a wire cake tester is the best tool. It is thin enough that it doesn't leave a hole in the muffin. Or, lightly press the muffin with your fingertips—if the muffin is done, it will spring back.

Unlike cakes, muffins cool quickly, and a cooling rack is unnecessary. Let the muffins sit in the pan for 10 minutes (no longer, or moisture will collect on their bottoms) to set up and cool slightly, then remove them from the pan. Let them cool on a half-sheet pan covered with parchment paper or on a rack, if you prefer. The muffins are best served the day they are baked.

Banana Streusel Muffins

Makes 12 muffins

....

Streusel crumbs give a jaunty finish to these extremely tender muffins. For the best flavor, use well-ripened bananas, but not ones that are blackened, with an alcohol aroma. The sour cream makes this muffin nice and moist.

BAKER'S NOTE: Be sure to let the muffins cool and firm up for at least 10 minutes before removing them from the pan. If removed too soon, they can collapse.

Muffin Streusel

6 tablespoons unbleached all-purpose flour	*⅛ teaspoon ground cinnamon*
1 tablespoon superfine sugar	*2½ tablespoons unsalted butter, melted*
1 tablespoon light brown sugar	*¼ teaspoon pure vanilla extract*

Softened unsalted butter, for the pan	*Grated zest of ½ lemon*
3 cups unbleached all-purpose flour	*Seeds from ½ Plumped Vanilla Bean (page 295) or ½ teaspoon pure vanilla extract*
1 tablespoon baking powder	
½ teaspoon fine sea salt	*2 large eggs, at room temperature, beaten*
8 tablespoons (1 stick) unsalted butter, chilled and cut into ½-inch cubes	*½ cup whole milk*
	1 cup sour cream
1 cup superfine sugar	*4 small ripe bananas, peeled and cut into ¼-inch-thick slices*

1 Position a rack in the center of the oven and preheat to 400°F. Brush the insides of 12 muffin cups with softened butter, then brush the top of the pan.

2 To make the streusel, mix the flour, superfine sugar, brown sugar, cinnamon, butter, and vanilla with your fingers in a small bowl until combined and crumbly. Set aside.

3 Sift the flour, baking powder, and salt together into a medium bowl. Beat the butter in the bowl of a heavy-duty stand mixer fitted with the paddle attachment on high speed until smooth, about 1 minute. Gradually add the sugar and continue beating, scraping the sides of the bowl often with

a silicone spatula, until the mixture is very light in color and texture, about 5 minutes. Beat in the lemon zest and vanilla. Gradually beat in the eggs, then the milk. Reduce the mixer speed to low. In thirds, add the flour, alternating with two additions of the sour cream, scraping the sides of the bowl and beating briefly after each addition. Do not overbeat. Fold in the bananas.

4   Using a 2½-inch-diameter ice-cream scoop, portion the batter, rounded side up, into the prepared muffin cups. Generously sprinkle the tops with the streusel.

5   Bake for 10 minutes. Reduce the oven temperature to 375°F and bake until the muffin tops are golden brown and a wire cake tester inserted into the center of a muffin comes out clean, about 15 minutes more.

6   Cool in the pan for 10 minutes. Remove the muffins from the pan and cool completely.

Blueberry Crumb Muffins

Makes 10 muffins

....

Although my usual muffin batter technique calls for creaming the butter and sugar, here is an excellent recipe that uses the more standard "stir it all together" technique. Orange juice and zest give these a hint of citrus that beautifully complements the blueberries. I wouldn't be surprised if this becomes your "go-to" muffin recipe.

Softened unsalted butter, for the pan

1 large seedless orange

⅔ cup corn oil

½ cup plus 1 tablespoon whole milk

2 large eggs, at room temperature

2¼ cups bread flour

1 cup packed light brown sugar, rubbed through a medium-mesh sieve to remove any lumps

1 tablespoon baking powder

¼ teaspoon fine sea salt

1 cup fresh or frozen blueberries

Muffin Streusel (page 62)

1   Position a rack in the center of the oven and preheat to 400°F. Brush the insides of 10 muffin cups with softened butter, then brush the top of the pan.

2   Grate the zest from the orange; set aside. Juice the orange and measure; you should have ⅓ cup. Whisk the oil, milk, orange juice, orange zest, and eggs together in a medium bowl. Whisk the flour, brown sugar, baking powder, and salt together in another bowl. Add to the liquids and stir with a spoon just until combined; do not overmix. Fold in the blueberries.

3   Using a 2½-inch-diameter ice-cream scoop, portion the batter, rounded side up, into the prepared muffin cups. Generously sprinkle the tops with the streusel.

4   Bake for 10 minutes. Reduce the oven temperature to 375°F and continue baking until the tops of the muffins are golden brown and a wire cake tester inserted into the center of a muffin comes out clean, about 15 minutes more. If using frozen berries, allow a few extra minutes.

5   Cool in the pan for 10 minutes. Remove the muffins from the pan and cool completely.

Raspberry Crumb Muffins: Substitute fresh or frozen raspberries for the blueberries.

Bran Muffins

Makes 10 muffins

....

These muffins are everything a bran muffin should be. They're packed with wheat flavor and fiber, but aren't heavy. They're lightly sweetened, but fragrant with honey and studded with plenty of raisins. I love to cut them lengthwise into two chunks, then heat in a toaster oven until crisp around the edges.

Softened unsalted butter, for the pan

1⅔ cups wheat bran (not bran breakfast cereal)

1⅔ cups unbleached all-purpose flour

1 tablespoon baking powder

¼ teaspoon fine sea salt

10 tablespoons (1¼ sticks) unsalted butter, chilled and cut into ½-inch cubes

¼ cup superfine sugar

⅓ cup plus 1 tablespoon mild honey, such as clover or blended blossom

2 large eggs, at room temperature, beaten

1 cup whole milk

1 cup seedless raisins

1 Position a rack in the center of the oven and preheat to 400°F. Brush the insides of 10 muffin cups with softened butter, then brush the top of the pan.

2 Whisk the bran, flour, baking powder, and salt together in a medium bowl. Beat the butter in the bowl of a heavy-duty stand mixer fitted with the paddle attachment on high speed until smooth, about 1 minute. Gradually add the sugar. Beat, scraping the sides of the bowl often with a silicone spatula, until the mixture is very light in color and texture, about 5 minutes. Add the honey and beat for 1 minute. Gradually beat in the eggs, beating well after each addition. Reduce the mixer speed to low. In thirds, beat in the bran mixture, alternating with two equal additions of the milk, scraping down the sides of the bowl often, and mix until smooth. Stir in the raisins.

3 Using a 2½-inch-diameter ice-cream scoop, portion the batter, rounded side up, into the cups.

4 Bake for 10 minutes. Reduce the oven temperature to 375°F and continue baking until the tops of the muffins are browned, and a wire cake tester inserted into the center of a muffin comes out clean, about 15 minutes more.

5 Cool in the pan for 10 minutes. Remove the muffins from the pan and cool completely.

Double Corn Muffins

Makes 10 muffins

T his muffin is bursting with corn flavor. When corn is in season, you can substitute ¾ cup cooked fresh kernels for canned. I prefer canned to frozen when fresh isn't available. The little kernels make this muffin special.

Softened unsalted butter, for the pan

1¼ cups unbleached all-purpose flour

¼ cup stone-ground yellow cornmeal

1 tablespoon baking powder

¼ teaspoon fine sea salt

8 tablespoons (1 stick) unsalted butter, chilled and cut into ½-inch cubes

½ cup superfine sugar

2 large eggs, at room temperature, beaten

¾ cup whole milk

One 7-ounce can vacuum-packed corn, well drained

1 Position a rack in the center of the oven and preheat to 400°F. Brush the insides of 10 muffin cups with softened butter, then brush the top of the pan.

2 Whisk the flour, cornmeal, baking powder, and salt together in a medium bowl. Beat the butter and sugar in the bowl of a heavy-duty stand mixer fitted with the paddle attachment on high speed, scraping the sides of the bowl often with a silicone spatula, until the mixture is very light in color and texture, about 5 minutes. Gradually beat in the eggs, beating well after each addition. Reduce the mixer speed to low. In thirds, beat in the flour mixture, alternating with two equal additions of the milk, scraping down the sides of the bowl often, and mix until smooth. Stir in the corn.

3 Using a 2½-inch-diameter ice-cream scoop, portion the batter, rounded side up, into the cups.

4 Bake for 10 minutes. Reduce the oven temperature to 375°F and continue baking until the tops of the muffins are golden brown and a wire cake tester inserted into the center of a muffin comes out clean, about 15 minutes more.

5 Cool in the pan for 10 minutes. Remove the muffins from the pan and cool completely.

Maple Muffins

Makes 12 muffins

....

This recipe was literally forced upon me by a customer who said her family had made these muffins for more than a hundred years. She promised they would be fantastic, and she was right! Their rich, bold maple flavor and crunchy tops are simply irresistible.

BAKER'S NOTE: Grade B maple syrup refers to its color and flavor, which are darker and stronger than Grade A. It does not mean that it is inferior. See page 263 for more on maple syrup.

Softened unsalted butter, for the pan	*1½ cups pure maple syrup, preferably Grade B*
2¼ cups unbleached all-purpose flour	*12 tablespoons (1½ sticks) unsalted butter, melted*
¼ cup whole wheat flour	*½ cup whole milk*
1 tablespoon baking powder	*1 large egg plus 1 large egg yolk, at room temperature*
½ teaspoon fine sea salt	*1 cup coarsely chopped walnuts, toasted (page 5)*

1   Position a rack in the center of the oven and preheat to 400°F. Brush the insides of 12 muffin cups with softened butter, then brush the top of the pan.

2   Whisk the unbleached flour, whole wheat flour, baking powder, and salt together in a medium bowl. Whisk the maple syrup, melted butter, and milk together in another bowl, then whisk in the egg and yolk. Add the dry ingredients to the wet ingredients and stir just until smooth. Stir in the walnuts. Let the batter stand so the dry ingredients can absorb the liquids, about 5 minutes.

3   Using a 2½-inch-diameter ice-cream scoop, portion the batter, rounded side up, into the prepared muffin cups.

4   Bake for 10 minutes. Reduce the oven temperature to 375°F and bake until the tops of the muffins are golden brown and a wire cake tester inserted into the center of a muffin comes out clean, about 15 minutes more.

5   Cool in the pan for 10 minutes. Remove the muffins from the pan and cool completely.

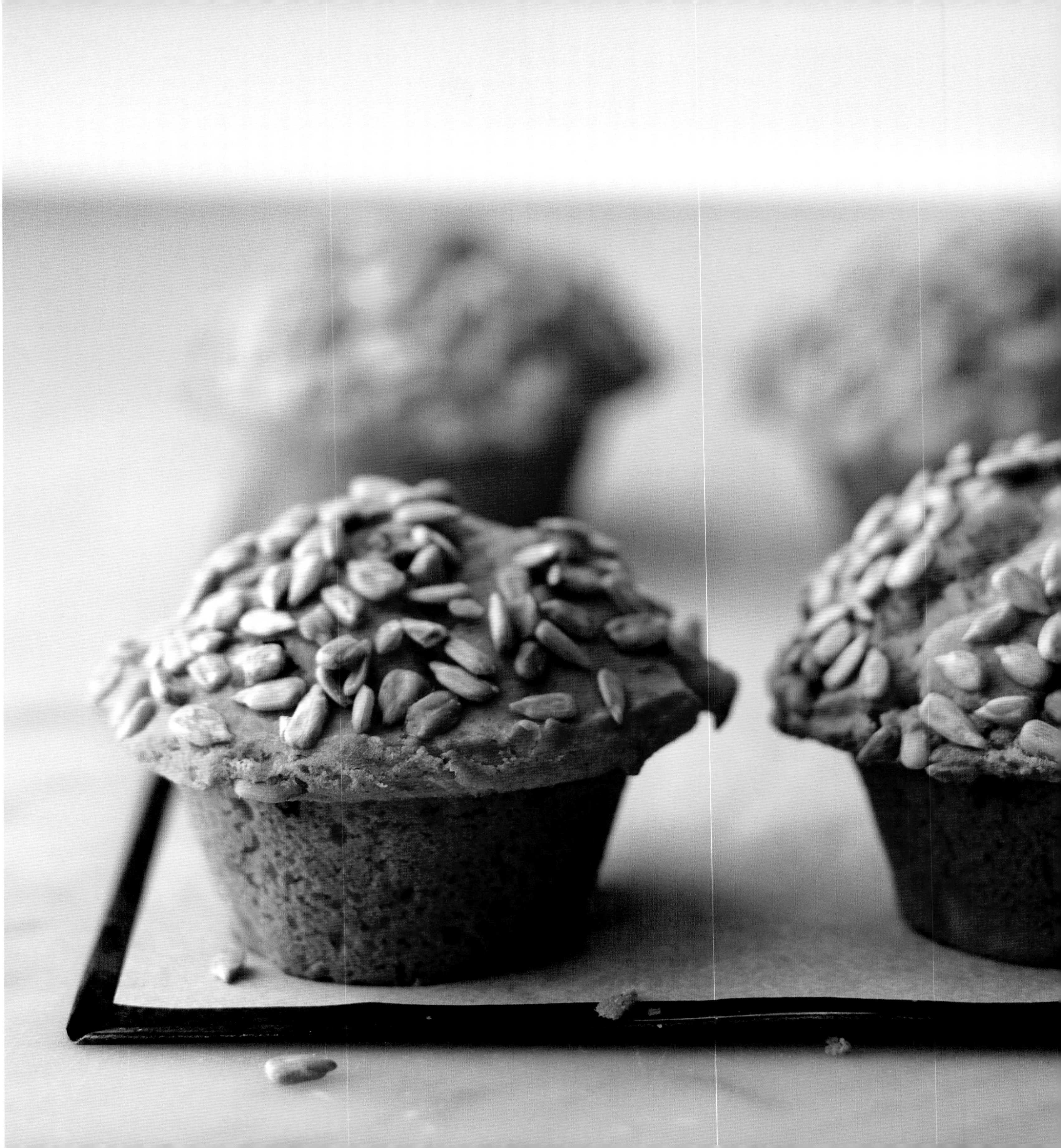

Pumpkin Muffins

Makes 12 to 14 muffins

....

I t seems naïve to talk about building a business on a single muffin, but in the case of this pumpkin muffin, it's the truth. Instead of the heavy, dark-brown pumpkin muffins people expected, we offered them a light-textured, attractive, pastel orange mini-cake, sprinkled with sunflower seeds. Word about my baking spread, thanks to the success of those muffins. Thank you, Peggy Cullen, for sharing these beauties.

BAKER'S NOTE: If you use generous scoops of batter, the yield will be 12 muffins. For smaller muffins, use 7 muffin cups in each of 2 muffin pans. Distribute the batter in a random pattern (not in rows) in each pan so the muffins bake evenly. Butter only the cups that you are going to use, or the butter in the empty cups will burn.

Softened unsalted butter, for the pan	8 tablespoons (1 stick) unsalted butter, chilled and cut into ½-inch cubes
3⅔ cups pastry flour, sifted	
1 tablespoon plus 1 teaspoon baking powder	1⅓ cups superfine sugar
1 teaspoon ground cinnamon	4 large eggs, at room temperature, beaten
¼ teaspoon ground ginger	One 15-ounce can solid-pack pumpkin
¼ teaspoon freshly grated nutmeg	1 cup seedless golden or dark raisins
¼ teaspoon fine sea salt	¼ cup hulled unsalted sunflower seeds

1   Position a rack in the center of the oven and preheat to 400°F. Brush the insides of 12 to 14 muffin cups with softened butter, then brush the top of the pan.

2   Sift the flour, baking powder, cinnamon, ginger, nutmeg, and salt together into a medium bowl. Beat the butter in the bowl of a heavy-duty stand mixer fitted with the paddle attachment on high speed until creamy, about 1 minute. Gradually beat in the sugar, and continue beating, scraping the sides of the bowl often with a silicone spatula, until the mixture is very light in color and texture, about 5 minutes. Gradually beat in the eggs. Reduce the mixer speed to low. Beat in the pumpkin; the mixture may look curdled. In thirds, beat in the flour mixture, scraping down the sides of the bowl often, and mix until smooth. Add the raisins. Increase the speed to high and beat until the batter has a slight sheen, about 15 seconds, no longer.

3 Using a 2½-inch-diameter ice-cream scoop, portion the batter, rounded side up, into the prepared cups. Sprinkle the tops with the sunflower seeds.

4 Bake for 10 minutes. Reduce the oven temperature to 375°F and continue baking until the tops of the muffins are golden brown and a wire cake tester inserted into the center of a muffin comes out clean, about 15 minutes more.

5 Cool in the pan for 10 minutes. Remove the muffins from the pan and cool completely.

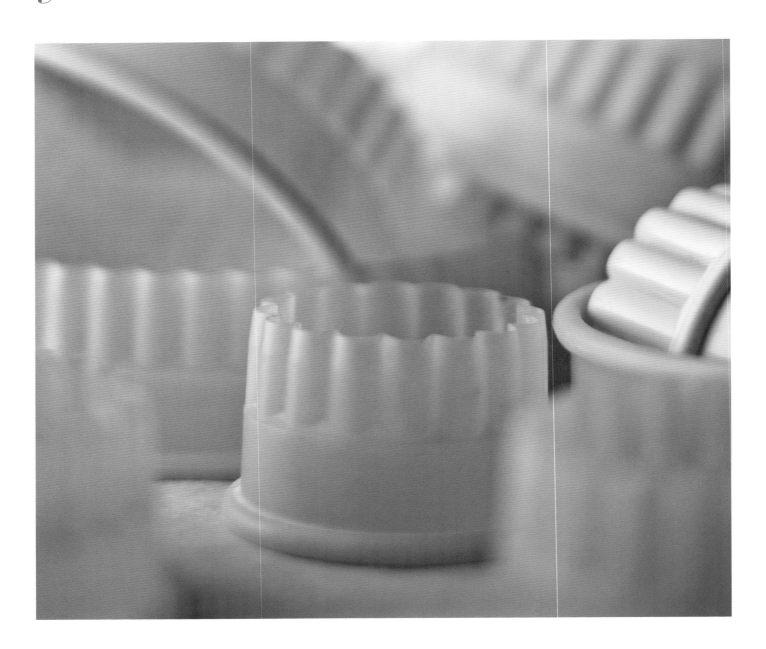

Currant Scones

Makes 12 scones

....

I n Britain, these are teatime favorites, but in the States, we like them for breakfast, too. Just follow the advice in the Baker's Note for Buttermilk Biscuits on page 77, and you'll get tall, flaky, buttery scones that are excellent partners with your finest jams.

¾ cup whole milk	*¼ teaspoon fine sea salt*
2 large eggs, chilled	*A few gratings of fresh nutmeg*
3 cups unbleached all-purpose flour, plus more as needed	*10 tablespoons (1¼ sticks) unsalted butter, chilled and cut into ½-inch cubes*
1 tablespoon plus 1 teaspoon baking powder	*½ cup dried currants*
2 tablespoons superfine sugar	*1 large egg, well beaten with a hand blender, for glazing*

1 Position a rack in the center of the oven and preheat to 425°F. Line a half-sheet pan with parchment paper.

2 TO MAKE THE DOUGH BY HAND: Whisk the milk and 2 eggs together in a small bowl; set aside. Sift the flour, baking powder, sugar, salt, and nutmeg into a medium bowl. Add the butter and mix quickly to coat the butter with the flour mixture. Using a pastry blender, cut the butter into the flour, scraping the butter off the blender as needed, until the mixture resembles coarse bread crumbs with some pea-size pieces of butter (figures 1 and 2). Mix in the currants. Using a wooden spoon, stir in the milk mixture and mix just until the dough clumps together (figure 3).
TO USE A MIXER: Whisk the milk and 2 eggs together in a small bowl; set aside. Sift the dry ingredients together into the bowl of a heavy-duty stand mixer. Add the butter. Attach the bowl to the mixer and fit with the paddle attachment. Mix on medium-low speed until the mixture looks mealy with some pea-size bits of butter. Mix in the currants. Reduce the mixer speed to low. Add the milk mixture, mixing just until the dough barely comes together.

3 Turn the dough out onto a well-floured work surface and sprinkle about 2 tablespoons of flour on top. Knead the dough a few times, just until it doesn't stick to the work surface. Do not overwork the dough. The surface will be floured, but the inside of the dough should remain on the wet side (figure 4). Gently roll out the dough into a ¾-inch-thick round (figure 5).

4 Using a 2½-inch fluted biscuit cutter, dipping it into flour between cuts, cut out the scones (cut straight down and do not twist the cutter) and place 1½ inches apart on the prepared half-sheet pan. To get the most biscuits out of the dough, cut out the scones close together in concentric circles (figure 6). Gather up the dough scraps, knead very lightly, and repeat to cut out more scones. You should get two scones from the second batch of scraps. Brush the tops of the scones lightly with the beaten egg, being sure not to let the egg drip down the sides (which would inhibit a good rise).

5 Place the scones in the oven and immediately reduce the heat to 400°F. Bake until golden brown, about 20 minutes. Cool on the pan for a few minutes, then serve warm or cool completely.

Buttermilk Biscuits

Makes 16 biscuits

....

I n some lucky parts of the country (mainly south of the Mason-Dixon line), fresh-baked biscuits are still everyday fare. They are so easy to make, they should be baked at home often. So make these for breakfast, lunch, or dinner.

BAKER'S NOTE: The key to tender biscuits is to avoid overhandling, which activates the gluten in the flour and makes tough biscuits. You can gather up the scraps for a second cutting, but don't do a third. Also, be sure your cutters are good and sharp—dull edges compress the sides of the biscuit and discourage a good rise.

3¼ cups unbleached all-purpose flour	*⅛ teaspoon fine sea salt*
2 tablespoons superfine sugar	*12 tablespoons (1½ sticks) unsalted butter, chilled, cut into ½-inch cubes*
1 tablespoon plus 2 teaspoons baking powder	*1½ cups buttermilk*

1 Position a rack in the center of the oven and preheat to 400°F. Line a half-sheet pan with parchment paper.

2 Sift the flour, sugar, baking powder, and salt together into the bowl of a heavy-duty stand mixer. Attach the bowl to the mixer and fit with the paddle attachment. Add the butter. Mix on low speed until the mixture resembles coarse meal with some pea-size pieces of butter. Add the buttermilk, mixing just until the dough barely comes together.

3 Scrape the dough onto a lightly floured surface and knead a few times until the dough is smooth. Sprinkle the top of the dough with flour and roll out a little more than ¾ inch thick. Using a 2¼-inch fluted biscuit cutter, dipping the cutter into flour between cuts, cut out the biscuits and place 1 inch apart on the pan. Gently press the scraps together (do not overhandle the dough). Repeat rolling and cutting (see page 74, figures 4, 5, and 6).

4 Bake until the biscuits are well risen and golden brown, 18 to 20 minutes. Serve hot or warm. To reheat the biscuits, wrap them in aluminum foil and bake in a preheated 350°F oven for about 10 minutes.

English Muffins

Makes 12 muffins

....

These aren't classic English muffins, which are usually baked on a griddle like pancakes. I wanted to make a better-looking, oven-baked version, and this is what I came up with. Leavened with yeast, these golden muffins are one of my most unusual and popular creations.

BAKER'S NOTE: This is really more like a thick batter than a dough. You will need a 2½-inch-diameter ice-cream scoop to portion it into the entremet rings for baking. • For dry yeast, refer to the adjusted liquid measurements in the directions. • These are baked in 12 metal entremet rings, 3 inches wide by 1½ inches tall, to shape the batter into their attractive mushroom shape. Do not confuse them with the standard English muffin rings, which are smaller and shallower. • The batter should be chilled no longer than 8 hours for the best results and flavor. Make the batter in the morning and bake the muffins later in the day after chilling. Day-old muffins are wonderful toasted and buttered—with my jam, of course.

1 cup whole milk	1 ounce (2 tablespoons) compressed yeast, or 3½ teaspoons active dry yeast
1 cup water	
2½ tablespoons unsalted butter, cut into small pieces	1 large egg, beaten
2 tablespoons granulated sugar	4 cups unbleached all-purpose flour
1 teaspoon fine sea salt	Softened unsalted butter, for the rings
	½ cup instant polenta, for the rings

1   At least 4 hours before making the muffins, bring the milk, water (for dry yeast, use ¾ cup water), butter, sugar, and salt to a simmer in a medium saucepan over medium heat, stirring often to dissolve the butter. Transfer to the bowl of a heavy-duty stand mixer and cool to room temperature.

2   Crumble the compressed yeast into the mixer bowl, let stand for 5 minutes, then stir to dissolve. (If using dry yeast, sprinkle the yeast over ¼ cup warm, 105° to 115°F, water in a small bowl. Let stand for 5 minutes. Whisk well to dissolve. Add to the mixer bowl.) Add the egg. Attach the bowl to the mixer and fit with the paddle attachment. With the mixer on low speed, gradually beat in the flour to make a sticky batter. When the batter forms, increase the speed to high and beat for 30 seconds. Remove the bowl and attachment from the mixer and scrape down the sides of the bowl with a silicone spatula. Cover the bowl tightly with plastic wrap and refrigerate for at least 4 and up to 8 hours.

3   Butter the insides of 12 metal entremet rings (3 inches in diameter and 1½ inches tall). Place the polenta in a small bowl, and coat the rings with it. Reserve the remaining polenta. Line a half-sheet pan with parchment paper. Arrange the rings on the parchment, spacing them about 1½ inches apart. Sprinkle a light, even coating of polenta into each of the rings (approximately ¼ teaspoon per ring).

4   Stir down the chilled batter—it will be very sticky. Using a 2½-inch-diameter ice-cream scoop dipped in cold water, scoop level portions of the batter into the rings. Lightly sprinkle the muffin tops with the remaining polenta.

5   Choose a warm spot in the kitchen for proofing the muffins. Slip the half-sheet pan with the rings into a tall "kitchen-sized" plastic bag. Place two tall glasses of very hot water near the center of the pan. Wave the opening of the bag to trap air and inflate the bag to create "head room," being sure that the plastic does not touch the batter. Twist the bag closed. Let stand until the batter just begins to dome over the tops of the rings, about 1½ hours.

6   Position a rack in the bottom third of the oven and preheat to 350°F. Carefully remove the glasses from the bag, then the pan with the rings. Bake the muffins until the tops are golden brown, about 25 minutes. Let stand for 5 minutes, then remove the muffins from the rings (if left in the rings too long, the muffins will steam and get a "cinched waist" look), protecting your hands with a kitchen towel. Cool slightly and serve warm or at room temperature.

Chapter Three

Beautiful Breads

BAKING HOMEMADE BREAD IS NOT ONLY FULFILLING AND SATISFYING, IT IS JUST PLAIN FUN. IT REQUIRES PATIENCE AND, AS THE SAYING GOES, PATIENCE has its rewards. Because the dough is actually alive with yeast, you must keep an eye on it, or it will overproof and the yeast will lose its ability to rise.

Bread baking is a very personal art, and every baker has favorite techniques and tips. At Sarabeth's Bakery, we have become known for our old-fashioned, home-style loaves. I have purposely concentrated on perfecting breads that may be just like your grandmother or mother would have made. I enjoy and make crusty, artisan breads, but I also know that they are very complicated, sometimes requiring special sourdough starters that can take weeks to make. I would rather share recipes that I know give great results in a reasonable amount of time. These are tender, fluffy breads for slicing and slathering with jam and butter, or turning into a mouthwatering sandwich.

A LESSON ON BREAD

Mixing It Up The amount of bread we bake at the bakery requires a huge mixing machine. Even at home, the simplicity of making bread with a mixer makes it my preference over the bowl-and-spoon method. A heavy-duty stand mixer (be sure it has a 5-quart or higher capacity) makes bread baking a much less physical procedure, which is not necessarily a bad thing. That doesn't mean that you won't be touching the dough! Bread dough loves to be handled, and good bakers are happy to oblige. The dough may be mixed and initially kneaded in the mixer, but it gets a final kneading and shaping by hand before baking. I give general instructions below for hand mixing and kneading, too.

In general, when using a heavy-duty mixer, first the liquid ingredients are combined in the mixer bowl, then the flour is added gradually to make the dough. I use cold water when making yeast dough because warm water speeds up the rising process. Long rising gives the bread a much better flavor, so I don't want to hurry this step.

All of these recipes make two loaves of bread. It takes no more time to mix a double batch of dough than a single one. If you suspect that your mixer can't handle the large batch (although I have made these in a variety of mixers without any problems), divide the mixed dough in half, cover one half with plastic wrap, and knead the dough in the mixer one half at a time. Knead the two portions together by hand for the first rising.

Start by crumbling compressed yeast into the bowl and adding the sugar. Let it stand for a few minutes until the yeast melts into a moist paste, then whisk until smooth. If you are using active dry yeast, the liquid in the recipe (which could be water or milk) is reduced by either ¼ or ⅓ cup to compensate for the warm liquid used to dissolve the yeast. Sprinkle the dry yeast over the warm, 105° to 115°F, liquid in a small bowl. Let stand for a few minutes to soften, then stir well to dissolve the yeast. (Dry yeast doesn't dissolve easily in milk, so if that is your liquid, you may want to use a mini-whisk to help dissolve the yeast granules.) Add the dissolved yeast to the bowl with the remaining liquid ingredients.

If you are making a recipe that calls for the sponge method, combine either type of yeast and liquid in the mixer bowl, let stand to soften, then stir to dissolve the yeast. Add the flour and stir well (at least 50 strokes) to make a smooth, sticky, batter-like dough. Cover the bowl tightly with plastic wrap and let stand until the mixture has lots of tiny bubbles (resembling the surface of a sponge), about 20 minutes.

Attach the bowl to the mixer and fit with the paddle attachment. (Some bakers use a dough hook to mix the dough at this point, but the paddle attachment is much more efficient in a home mixer.) Gradually beat in half of the flour, then add the salt. Salt is a very important addition to bread dough. Without it, bread tastes dull, and equally important, the salt controls the potency of the yeast so it grows at a controlled rate. Salt should never come into direct contact with yeast or it could weaken the yeast's strength too much. Always be sure that there is plenty of flour already in the dough to act as a buffer before adding the salt.

Now mix in enough of the remaining flour to make a soft, rough-looking dough that cleans the sides of the bowl. The flour measurement in the recipe's ingredient list is an estimate, and the exact amount needed will be variable. Atmospheric moisture affects the dryness of the flour and the amount of liquid it will absorb on a given day. You may have to use more or less flour than estimated in the recipe. Aim for the texture of the dough, not a precise measurement of flour.

Replace the paddle attachment with the dough hook. Knead the dough at medium-low speed until it is smooth and elastic (if you pull the dough apart about an inch, it snaps back into shape), about 6 minutes. If the dough is soft, it may climb up the hook—simply stop the machine, push the dough down, and continue kneading. To check if the dough has been kneaded enough, remove the dough and shape it into a ball—it should hold its shape.

After the dough is smooth, transfer it to an unfloured work surface and knead by hand a bit to check its consistency. Rich dough containing eggs, butter, or sugar will feel slightly sticky, but it shouldn't stick to the work surface. If necessary, knead in a bit more flour by hand.

If you prefer, the dough can be made by hand. It's simply a matter of mixing all of the liquids and the dissolved yeast in the bowl. Stir in half of the flour and the salt, then enough of the remaining flour to make a rough dough that is too stiff to stir. Turn out the dough onto a well-floured work surface.

To knead by hand, fold the top quarter of the dough mass into the center. Place the heel of one hand in the center of the dough and press and push the dough away from you. Turn the dough a quarter of a turn, and fold and push out the dough again. Repeat kneading and turning the dough a quarter after each push, and adding the remaining flour a tablespoon at a time, until the dough doesn't stick to the work surface. (Keep in mind that some doughs are supposed to have a tacky texture, so follow my instructions in the recipes.) Continue kneading until it is smooth and supple, about 6 minutes more.

The First Proofing Proofing the yeast means testing it for freshness, but proofing the dough means letting it rise. The first proofing allows the yeast in the kneaded dough to grow and give off gases to flavor the dough. Gather the dough into a ball and place in a lightly buttered or oiled bowl. Turn to lightly coat the dough with butter, which will prevent the exposed top from drying out, and cover tightly with plastic wrap. For most dough, the buttering step is unnecessary, because the plastic keeps out the air. I do it anyway as a precautionary step. If you wish, let the dough rise in an ungreased, tightly sealed plastic container—tall 3- to 4-quart storage containers are ideal.

Dough requires a relatively warm, draft-free place to rise. A temperature of 75°F is optimum (no warmer) because the longer the rise, the better the flavor. If the environment is too cold, the dough takes too long to rise. But if the rising area is too warm, the dough can overferment, giving the loaf a poor shape and an aggressively yeasty flavor. This is why cold, not warm, liquids should be used to make dough, as the cool liquids keep the yeast from rising too fast.

The dough should rise to about double the original volume. If you use a covered plastic container or a glass bowl, it's easy to gauge the dough's progress by sight. You can even mark the side of the container or bowl with a marker at the height of the unproofed dough so you can tell at a glance how much it has risen. Otherwise, to check if the dough has risen enough, press a finger about ½ inch into the dough—if it leaves an impression, the dough is ready to shape. If the impression fills in quickly, it needs more time. The typical rising time is about 1½ hours.

Shaping the Loaves After the first proofing, the dough is deflated, shaped into loaves, and allowed to rise a second time before baking.

To deflate the dough, turn it out onto the work surface and knead it gently to push out some of the air. This also reinvigorates the dough for another burst of carbon dioxide and a strong final proofing. Just give it a few kneads. In some cases where extra-light bread is desired, you may be directed to handle the dough very carefully to retain the air.

The dough is almost ready for shaping. Deflating reactivates the gluten in the dough, so some dough will be too elastic and retractable to shape at this point, and will need a short rest period to relax the gluten. Cut the dough in half and shape on the counter into two large, taut balls. Cover with plastic wrap or a moistened towel and let stand for 15 minutes.

Bread can be baked in pans or shaped and baked directly on a baking stone. For loaf-shaped breads, use heavy-gauge aluminum pans with a dull finish. In this chapter, I use a standard pan size, 8 by 4 by 2½ inches. It's just the right size for a perfectly proportioned loaf.

To shape the bread into the standard American "sandwich" loaf to be baked in a pan, place half of the dough in front of you on an unfloured work surface. Pat, press, and stretch the dough into a rectangle approximately an inch longer than the pan (that is, about 9 by 8 inches for an 8 by 4-inch pan). Fold the short sides in about ½ inch. Starting at the top edge, roll the dough into a thick cylinder, pressing the seal closed after each turn. Pinch the final long seam closed with your fingers. Transfer the loaf, seam side down, to the bread pan. Press the dough so the top is level and fills the corners of the pan.

The Second Proofing Most cookbooks recommend covering the rising loaves with plastic wrap. That works for most doughs, but moist ones will stick to the plastic and tear when it is removed.

In professional bakeries, shaped dough rises in a proof box, a tall temperature- and humidity-controlled cabinet that keeps the dough warm and moist and protects it against drafts that would make it fall. (Actually, our proof box is the size of a walk-in closet.) In a home kitchen, there is a clever way to make a homemade proof box from a large plastic bag.

The idea is to provide a warm, moist atmosphere that encourages yeast growth and keeps the dough surface from drying out. First, place a tall "kitchen-sized" garbage bag on the work surface. Slip the dough (either in loaf pans or shaped on a parchment paper–covered half-sheet pan) into the bag. Place a tall glass or two of very hot, steaming tap water in the bag to give off a small amount of steam and to lift the plastic away from the dough. Give the open end of the bag a wave to inflate the bag a bit, then twist the bag closed to trap the air—the bag should look like a partially inflated balloon. (In some cases, with very sticky dough, inflate the bag more thoroughly to be sure that it doesn't touch the dough.)

Baking Your Bread A baking stone, which provides a flat, hot surface for baking, is a good tool for bakers wanting crusty artisan breads. But a stone can create a thick bottom crust in breads baked in pans, so I don't use one in this book. The loaf pans can be placed on a half-sheet pan for easy transfer to and from the oven.

Position a rack in the center of the oven. Heat rises, and if the bread is baked too high in the oven, the crust could brown before the bread is done. In some ovens, the heat source is on the bottom of the oven, so if the rack is too low, the bottoms will burn. Allow at least 20 minutes for the oven to preheat.

All of the senses come into play to determine when the bread is done. You will be able to see the lovely golden brown color of the crust, which will often give off a caramelized scent from the sugars in the dough. But your senses of touch and hearing are also invaluable indicators. The bread will feel and sound hollow when tapped on the bottom. Breads that were baked in pans need to be removed from the pans for testing—be sure to protect your hands with clean, dry kitchen towels or potholders when unmolding the hot loaves. Even if the top crust looks nicely browned, the area of crust protected by the pan could remain pale. If that happens, just slip the bread back into the pan and bake for a few more minutes, protecting the top with a piece of aluminum foil to prevent darkening.

Transfer the loaves to wire racks for cooling. For breads in pans, let them cool on the rack for 5 minutes, then remove from the pans and let cool further on the racks. If the loaves remain in the pans too long, steam will build up and soften the loaves. As tempting as it is to slice the hot, fragrant bread, let it cool for at least 1 hour before slicing, or the bread will lose its beautiful structure.

Without the preservatives found in mass-produced bread, your loaves will probably be soft for only a couple of days. No matter: Stale bread lives on as toast, bread pudding, French toast, and the like, which I love almost as much as fresh bread.

You may want to serve one loaf for immediate consumption and store the second for another time. Freeze the extra, cooled loaf in a freezer bag for up to 1 month. Remove the loaf from the freezer bag; it will defrost in a couple of hours at room temperature.

Apple Cinnamon Loaf

Makes 2 loaves

....

There are so many possibilities for serving this puffy bread packed with apples that I hardly know where to start. As a breakfast toast topped with sweet butter, it is sublime. Turn it into French toast, and you'll have them lining up outside your kitchen (just as we have at the restaurants). No matter how you slice it, it's wonderful. The procedure for forming the loaf is probably unlike any other bread you've ever made, but just follow the instructions and you'll be fine.

BAKER'S NOTE: I use Granny Smith apples because they are tasty and available throughout the year. You can experiment with other apples, as long as you know that they will hold their shape during baking. • For dry yeast, refer to the adjusted liquid measurements in the directions.

.8 ounce (1 packed tablespoon plus 2 packed teaspoons) compressed yeast or 3 teaspoons active dry yeast

3 tablespoons granulated sugar

¼ cup cold whole milk

⅔ cup cold water

1 large egg yolk

1 teaspoon pure vanilla extract

4 cups unbleached all-purpose flour, as needed

1¼ teaspoons fine sea salt

4 tablespoons (½ stick) unsalted butter, at room temperature, plus additional for the bowl and pans

Apple Filling

2 large Granny Smith apples (about 1½ pounds), peeled, cored, and cut into ½-inch cubes

1 large egg yolk

2 tablespoons granulated sugar

¼ teaspoon ground cinnamon

1. To make the dough, crumble the compressed yeast finely into the bowl of a heavy-duty stand mixer. Add the sugar and let stand until the yeast gives off some moisture, about 3 minutes. Whisk well to dissolve the yeast. Add the milk, water, egg yolk, and vanilla and whisk to combine. (If using dry yeast, sprinkle the yeast over ⅓ cup warm, 105° to 115°F, water in a small bowl. Let stand until the yeast softens, about 5 minutes, then stir to dissolve. Pour into the mixer bowl. Add the milk, ⅓ cup cold water, the sugar, egg yolk, and vanilla and whisk to combine.)

2   Attach the bowl to the mixer and fit with the paddle attachment. On low speed, gradually add half of the flour, then the salt. One tablespoon at a time, add the butter. Gradually mix in enough of the remaining flour to form a rough dough. Replace the paddle attachment with the dough hook. Knead on medium-low speed, adding more flour if needed, until the dough cleans the bowl. Continue kneading until the dough is soft, smooth, and elastic, about 6 minutes.

3   Transfer the dough to a lightly floured work surface and knead briefly to check the dough's texture—it should be slightly sticky. Form into a ball. Lightly butter a large bowl. Place the dough in the bowl, smooth side down. Turn to coat with butter, ending with the smooth side up. Cover the bowl tightly with plastic wrap. Let stand in a warm place until doubled in volume, about 1½ hours.

4   When the dough has risen, prepare the apple filling. Mix the cut apples, egg yolk, sugar, and cinnamon in a medium bowl.

5   Butter two 8 by 4 by 2½-inch metal loaf pans. Line the bottoms of the pans with parchment paper. Dust the insides of the pans with flour (no need to butter the paper) and tap out the excess flour.

6   Place the dough on a lightly floured work surface. Stretch or roll the dough into a 16 by 12-inch rectangle. Spread the filling over the dough. Starting at the top of the dough, roll it down. Using a bench scraper or a large knife, cut the dough into 1-inch-thick slices. Now cut through the slices to make 1- to 1½-inch pieces. It will look like quite a mess, but you're doing the right thing. Using the bench scraper, scoop up the dough-apple mixture and divide equally among the prepared loaf pans (a kitchen scale comes in handy here), distributing it as evenly as possible.

7   Choose a warm spot in the kitchen for proofing. Place the pans on a half-sheet pan. Slip the pan with the loaf pans into a large "kitchen-sized" plastic bag. Place a tall glass of very hot water on the pan between the loaves to keep the plastic from touching the dough. Tightly close the bag, trapping air in the bag to partially inflate it. Let stand until the dough has just risen to the top of the pans (the dough will look lumpy), about 1 hour.

8   Position a rack in the center of the oven and preheat to 350°F. Remove the glass from the pan, then the pan with the loaf pans from the bag. Bake the loaves on the half-sheet pan for 35 minutes. Cover the loaves loosely with aluminum foil and continue baking until the tops are golden brown and an instant-read thermometer inserted into the center of the loaves reads 210°F, about 25 minutes.

9   Transfer the loaf pans to a wire cooling rack and let stand for 5 minutes. Unmold the loaves onto the rack. Remove the parchment paper. Turn the loaves right sides up and let cool completely.

Challah

Makes two 12-inch loaves

....

Golden with eggs and braided into a fat, fluffy twist, challah is traditionally eaten at the Sabbath meal. Even my non-Jewish clientele appreciates this bread for its luxurious texture. Save a loaf to have on hand for French toast.

BAKER'S NOTE: For an evenly shaped challah, braid from the center of the trio of dough "ropes," then turn the group over and braid from the center to the other end. • For dry yeast, refer to the adjusted liquid measurements in the directions.

1 ounce (2 packed tablespoons) compressed yeast or 3½ teaspoons active dry yeast

¼ cup mild honey, such as orange blossom

1 cup cold water

2 large eggs plus 2 large egg yolks

¼ cup corn oil, preferably cold-pressed, or other vegetable oil, plus additional for the bowl

4½ cups unbleached all-purpose flour, as needed

1½ teaspoons fine sea salt

1 large egg, beaten with a hand blender, for the glaze

1 Crumble the compressed yeast finely into the bowl of a heavy-duty stand mixer. Add the honey and let stand until the yeast gives off some moisture, about 3 minutes. Whisk well to dissolve the yeast. Add the water, the 2 eggs, the yolks, and oil and whisk again. (If using dry yeast, sprinkle the yeast over ¼ cup warm, 105° to 115°F, water in a small bowl. Let stand for 5 minutes to soften the yeast, then stir to dissolve. Pour into the mixer bowl. Add ¾ cup cold water, the honey, the 2 eggs, the yolks, and oil, and whisk to combine.)

2 Attach the bowl to the mixer and fit with the paddle attachment. On low speed, gradually add half of the flour, and then the salt. Gradually mix enough of the remaining flour to form a soft, rough dough that cleans the bowl. Replace the paddle attachment with the dough hook. Knead on medium-low speed until the dough is smooth, soft, and elastic, about 6 minutes.

3 Transfer the dough to a lightly floured work surface. Knead briefly to check the dough's texture. It should feel slightly sticky, but you can knead in a little more flour if necessary. Lightly oil a large bowl. Shape the dough into a ball and place, smooth side down, in the bowl. Turn to coat the ball with the oil, ending with the smooth side up. Cover the bowl tightly with plastic wrap. Let stand in a warm place until doubled in volume, about 1½ hours.

4   Working carefully to preserve the dough's light and puffy texture, turn the dough out onto a clean, unfloured work surface. Do not knead the dough. Gently shape the dough into a thick rectangle and cut the dough into 6 equal pieces. For the best results, weigh each piece on a scale.

5   In order to roll the dough into ropes for braiding, there must be some traction between the dough and the work surface. The tiniest bit of flour will make the surface too slick. To remedy this, scrape your work surface completely clean. Using a damp kitchen towel, wipe a very thin film of water on the work surface. Working with one piece of dough at a time, shape into a thick cylinder. Starting at the center and working outward, roll the dough back and forth on the work surface, pressing down on the dough at the same time, slowly moving your hands apart as you roll until the dough is stretched into a 13-inch-long rope, with the center of the rope plumper than the two ends. Repeat with the other 5 ropes. As the ropes are formed, cover them loosely with plastic wrap.

6   Line two half-sheet pans with parchment paper. Vertically line up 3 ropes next to each other. Begin the braid from the center to one bottom end, dropping the ropes loosely into place without stretching them. When you have finished half of the braid, pinch the ends together. Flip the dough over with the unbraided ropes facing you. Braid from the center to the other end, and pinch the ends together. Turn the dough over again, and transfer to a prepared pan. Be sure that the ends of the loaf are pinched and the points are tucked under. Repeat with the other 3 ropes of dough and transfer to a second prepared pan.

7   Choose a warm spot in the kitchen for the proofing. Slip each pan into a tall "kitchen-sized" plastic bag, place a tall glass of very hot water on each pan to keep the plastic from touching the dough. Tightly close each bag, trapping air in the bag to partially inflate it. Let stand until the braids look quite puffy and seem a bit more than doubled in volume, 45 to 60 minutes. Meanwhile, position racks in the center and top third of the oven and preheat to 375°F. Remove the glass from each pan, then the pans. Brush the top of each braid lightly but thoroughly with the beaten egg.

8   Bake for 15 minutes. Switch the position of the breads from top to bottom and front to back. Reduce the oven temperature to 350°F and continue baking until the loaves are golden brown and the bottoms sound hollow when tapped with your knuckles, about 30 minutes. If the loaves seem to be browning too deeply, cover them loosely with aluminum foil. Transfer the loaves to a wire rack and cool completely.

Raisin Challah: After the dough has come together in the mixer (after about 2 minutes of kneading), add 1 cup seedless raisins.

Cinnamon Raisin Loaf

Makes 2 loaves

....

Toast slices of this loaf for breakfast, and your kitchen will be perfumed for hours with the spicy aroma of cinnamon. Use it to make one of my favorite treats—cinnamon toast. Spread a slice with soft butter and sprinkle with sugar and more cinnamon, or my Lemony Pear-Pineapple Preserves (page 277).

BAKER'S NOTE: For dry yeast, refer to the adjusted liquid measurements in the directions.

.8 ounce (1 packed tablespoon plus 2 packed teaspoons) compressed yeast or 3 teaspoons active dry yeast

3 tablespoons granulated sugar

1 cup cold water

¼ cup whole milk

3 cups unbleached all-purpose flour, plus more as needed

2 cups whole wheat flour

2 teaspoons ground cinnamon

1½ teaspoons fine sea salt

3 tablespoons unsalted butter, at room temperature, plus more for the bowl and pans

1 cup seedless raisins

1 large egg, beaten with a hand blender, for the glaze

1   Crumble the yeast finely into the bowl of a heavy-duty stand mixer. Add the sugar and let stand until the yeast gives off some moisture, about 3 minutes. Whisk well to dissolve the yeast. Add the water and milk and whisk to combine. (If using dry yeast, sprinkle the yeast over ¼ cup warm, 105° to 115°F, water in a small bowl. Let stand until softened, about 5 minutes, then stir to dissolve. Pour into the mixer bowl. Add ¾ cup cold water with the milk and sugar and whisk to combine.)

2   Attach the bowl to the mixer and fit with the paddle attachment. Mix the unbleached and whole wheat flours in a large bowl. On low speed, gradually add half of the flour, then the cinnamon and salt. One tablespoon at a time, mix in the butter. Gradually mix in enough of the remaining flour to form a rough dough that cleans the bowl. Replace the paddle attachment with the dough hook. Knead on medium-low speed until the dough is soft, smooth, and elastic, about 6 minutes. During the last minute or so, add the raisins.

3   Transfer the dough to a lightly floured work surface and knead briefly to check the dough's texture—it will be slightly sticky but will hold its shape. Form into a ball. Lightly butter a large bowl.

Place the dough in the bowl, smooth side down. Turn to coat with butter, ending with the smooth side up. Cover the bowl tightly with plastic wrap. Let stand in a warm place until doubled in volume, about 1½ hours.

4 Turn out the dough onto a lightly floured work surface and cut in half. Shape into two balls, cover with plastic wrap, and let stand for 15 minutes.

5 Lightly butter two 8 by 4 by 2½-inch metal loaf pans. Working with one ball at a time, gently pressing to deflate the dough, shape into a 9 by 5-inch rectangle (see page 100, figure 1). To shape into a loaf, fold in the right and left sides of the dough about ½ inch, and pinch the seams closed. Starting from a long side, roll the dough into a plump loaf and press the seam closed (see page 100, figure 2). Fit the loaf into the pan, seam side down, and press it gently to fill the corners of the pan (see page 100, figure 3). Repeat with the second ball and place the loaf pans on a half-sheet pan.

6 Choose a warm spot in the kitchen for the proofing. Slip the pan with the loaf pans into a tall "kitchen-sized" plastic bag, place a tall glass of very hot water on the pan between the loaves to keep the plastic from touching the dough. Tightly close the bag, trapping air in the bag to partially inflate it. Let stand until the dough domes about 1 inch over the pans, about 45 minutes.

7 Position a rack in the center of the oven and preheat to 350°F. Remove the glass from the bag, then the pan with the loaf pans. Brush the tops of the loaves lightly but thoroughly with the beaten egg. Bake until the loaves are nicely browned and the bottoms sound hollow when tapped, about 35 minutes. Cool on a wire rack for 5 minutes. Remove the loaves from the pans and cool completely on the rack.

Dinner Rolls

Makes 18 rolls

....

Present these light and buttery rolls in a linen-lined basket at your next dinner party and your guests are bound to sing your praises. This is the perfect recipe for a beginning baker, as the rolls do not require special ingredients like buttermilk or mashed potatoes, and it still gives excellent, old-fashioned results.

BAKER'S NOTE: Sometimes, instead of baking these in two pans, I love to make them in petite loaf pans (about 3½ by 2½ inches) to create individual rolls that look like tiny loaves of bread. Lightly butter 18 petite loaf pans. Cut the dough into 18 equal pieces, and shape each into a small loaf. Using a dough scraper or knife, cut each loaf vertically into four equal pieces. Holding the pieces together, fit each loaf into a pan. Bake as directed. • For dry yeast, refer to the adjusted liquid measurements in the directions.

1 ounce (2 packed tablespoons) compressed yeast or 3 ½ teaspoons active dry yeast

2 tablespoons granulated sugar

1 cup whole milk

1 large egg plus 1 large egg yolk

3 ¾ cups all-purpose flour, as needed

1 teaspoon fine sea salt

12 tablespoons (1½ sticks) unsalted butter, cut into tablespoons, well softened

1   Crumble the yeast finely into the bowl of a heavy-duty stand mixer. Add the sugar and let stand until the yeast gives off some moisture, about 3 minutes. Whisk to dissolve the yeast. Add the milk, egg, and yolk. (If using active dry yeast, sprinkle the yeast over ¼ cup warm, 105° to 115°F, milk in a small bowl. Let stand until the yeast softens, about 5 minutes, then stir well to dissolve. Pour into the mixing bowl. Add ¾ cup cold milk, the sugar, egg, and yolk, and whisk to combine.)

2   Attach the bowl to the mixer and fit with the paddle attachment. Mix on low speed, adding 2 cups of the flour and the salt. One tablespoon at a time, beat in the butter, letting each addition become absorbed before adding another. Add another cup of the flour to make a soft dough that cleans the sides of the bowl.

3   Using a silicone spatula, scrape the dough into the center of the bowl. Replace the paddle attachment with the dough hook. Knead on medium-low speed until the dough is supple, about 4 minutes. One tablespoon at a time, add as much of the remaining flour as needed for the dough to become smooth.

4   Generously butter a medium bowl. Turn the dough out onto a lightly floured work surface. Shape the dough into a ball. Place the ball, smooth side down, in the bowl, and turn right side up to lightly coat the ball in butter. Cover the bowl with plastic wrap and let stand in a warm place until doubled, about 1½ hours.

5   Lightly butter two 9-inch round cake pans. Cut the dough into 18 equal portions. (If you have a kitchen scale, each portion will weigh 2 ounces.) To shape into balls, one portion at a time, place the dough on an unfloured work surface. Cup one hand over the dough and move your hand in a tight circular motion, letting your palm gently touch the top of the dough. For each pan, arrange 7 balls inside the perimeter of the pan, with 2 balls in the center, spacing the balls equally apart. There will be space between the balls until they proof.

6   Choose a warm spot in the kitchen for the proofing. Slip the pans into a tall "kitchen-sized" plastic bag, place a tall glass of very hot water between the pans to keep the plastic from touching the dough. Tightly close the bag, trapping air in the bag to partially inflate it. Let stand until the rolls look puffy, about 45 minutes.

7   Position a rack in the center of the oven and preheat to 350°F. Remove the glass from the bag, then the pans. Bake until the rolls are golden brown, about 20 minutes. Let cool in the pans for 5 minutes. Remove from the pans, then separate the rolls from each other and serve hot.

Rosemary Focaccia

Makes 12 servings

Focaccia, the chewy Italian bread, should be redolent with the scent and taste of fine extra-virgin olive oil, so use a high-quality brand with fresh, fruity notes. This flatbread excels as an accompaniment to a Mediterranean-style dinner, but at the bakery, we use it as the bread for our grilled vegetable sandwiches. Just heap whatever vegetables you like (eggplant, zucchini, yellow squash, red bell peppers, and/or tomatoes) with pesto and fresh mozzarella on the bread.

BAKER'S NOTE: The bread should have a generous coating of olive oil on both its top and bottom, so don't be alarmed by the amount. • For a lovely presentation that is perfect for a breadbasket at a formal meal, slice the focaccia vertically into ½-inch-wide strips. • For dry yeast, refer to the adjusted liquid measurements in the directions.

2 cups cold water	*4½ cups unbleached all-purpose flour, as needed*
2 teaspoons finely chopped fresh rosemary	*1¼ teaspoons fine sea salt*
1 ounce (2 packed tablespoons) compressed yeast or 3½ teaspoons active dry yeast	*4 tablespoons high-quality, fruity extra-virgin olive oil, divided, plus additional for the bowl*

1   Place the water and rosemary into the bowl of a heavy-duty stand mixer. Crumble the yeast into the bowl. Let stand 2 minutes, then whisk to dissolve the yeast. (If using active dry yeast, sprinkle the yeast over ¼ cup warm, 105° to 115°F, water in a small bowl. Let stand 5 minutes, then stir to dissolve. Pour into the mixer bowl. Add 1¾ cups cold water and the rosemary and whisk to combine.)

2   Attach the bowl to the mixer and fit with the paddle attachment. With the mixer on low speed, gradually add half of the flour, then the salt. Add enough of the remaining flour to make a soft dough. Replace the paddle attachment with the dough hook. Knead on medium-low speed just until the dough is smooth and it cleans the bowl, about 3 minutes. Do not overknead. Gather up the dough and shape into a ball.

3   Coat the inside of a medium bowl generously with olive oil. Place the ball of dough in the bowl, and turn to coat with oil. Cover the bowl tightly with plastic wrap. Let stand in a warm place until doubled in volume, about 1 hour.

4   Pour 2 tablespoons of the oil in a half-sheet pan, and spread evenly with your fingers. Punch down the dough and transfer to the oiled pan. Using your hands, coax and stretch the dough to fill the pan. If the dough is too elastic, cover the dough in the pan with plastic wrap and let rest for 5 minutes, then try again.

5   Choose a warm place in the kitchen for proofing. Slip the pan into a tall "kitchen-sized" plastic bag and place two tall glasses of very hot water in the bag at opposite ends of the pan to keep the plastic from touching the dough. Tightly close the bag, trapping air in the bag to partially inflate it. Let stand in a warm place until the dough looks puffy, about 45 minutes.

6   Position a rack in the center of the oven and preheat to 450°F. Fill a spray bottle with water. Remove the glasses from the bag, and then the pan. Using your fingers, gently dimple the top of the dough. Drizzle the remaining 2 tablespoons oil over the top of the dough. Using the palms of your hands, taking special care not to deflate the dough, very lightly spread the oil over the focaccia.

7   Place the focaccia in the oven. Aiming for the walls of the oven (and not the top of the focaccia), spray water into the oven. The water will create steam to help crisp the focaccia. Bake until the focaccia is golden brown, about 20 minutes. Cool in the pan for 20 minutes before serving. Cut into rectangles and serve warm or at room temperature.

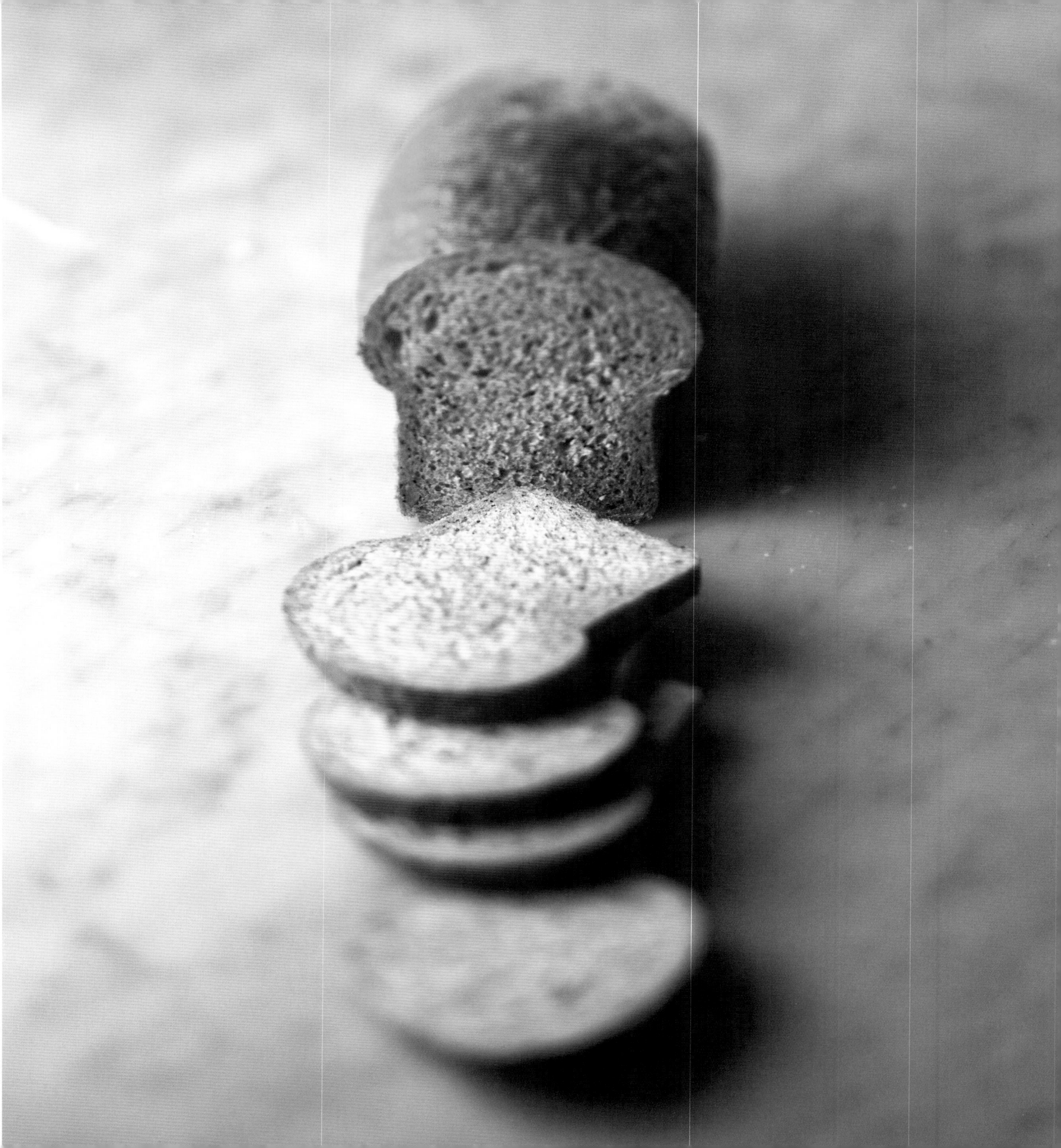

Sarabeth's House Bread

Makes 2 loaves

....

Ever since Sarabeth's Bakery was opened, this bread, with its irresistible nutty-sweet flavor, has graced the display case. While it makes great sandwiches, try it with nothing more than a slather of unsalted butter—now, that's bread.

BAKER'S NOTE: Bread dough made with a high proportion of whole grains has a tacky, almost sticky exterior. If you notice this texture when handling the dough, do not try to adjust it with more flour. As long as the dough isn't sticking to the kneading surface, it is fine. • For dry yeast, refer to the adjusted liquid measurements in the directions.

1 ounce (2 packed tablespoons) compressed yeast
or 3½ teaspoons active dry yeast

¼ cup honey

2¼ cups cold water

2¼ cups whole wheat flour

2¼ cups bread flour, plus more as needed

2 tablespoons stone-ground yellow cornmeal

2 tablespoons poppy seeds

2 tablespoons sesame seeds

1½ teaspoons fine sea salt

2 tablespoons hulled sunflower seeds

Softened unsalted butter, for the bowl and pans

1 large egg, beaten with a hand blender, for the glaze

1 Crumble the yeast finely into the bowl of a heavy-duty stand mixer. Add the honey and let stand until the yeast gives off some moisture, about 3 minutes. Whisk well to dissolve the yeast. Add the water and whisk to combine. (If using active dry yeast, sprinkle the yeast over ¼ cup warm, 105° to 115°F, water in a small bowl. Let stand 5 minutes to soften the yeast, then stir to dissolve. Pour into the mixer bowl. Add 2 cups cold water and the honey and whisk to combine.)

2 Attach the bowl to the mixer and fit with the paddle attachment. Combine the whole wheat flour, 2¼ cups of the bread flour, the cornmeal, poppy seeds, sesame seeds, and salt in a large bowl. With the mixer on low speed, add the flour and seed mixture. Beat until a dough begins to form. Gradually add enough of the remaining bread flour to form a rough dough that cleans the sides of the bowl. Replace the paddle attachment with the dough hook. Knead on medium-low speed until the dough is smooth and slightly sticky, about 5 minutes, again adding a little more flour only if necessary—keep the dough soft. During the last minute or so, add the sunflower seeds.

1 2 3

3 Transfer the dough to a clean work surface. Knead with your hands to check the dough's texture: It should be slightly sticky but not stick to the work surface. Knead in more flour only if needed. Butter a medium bowl. Shape the dough into a taut ball. Place in the bowl, turn to coat with butter, and turn smooth side up. Cover tightly with plastic wrap. Let stand in a warm place until the dough doubles in volume, about 1¼ hours.

4 Cut the dough in half. Shape each piece into a ball. Place on a lightly floured work surface and cover with plastic wrap. Let stand for 15 minutes. Butter two 8 by 4 by 2½-inch loaf pans. Working with one ball of dough at a time, gently press to deflate the dough (figure 1). Pat the dough gently into a thick 8-inch-long rectangle. Starting from the long side, roll and shape into an 8-inch-long loaf and pinch the long seam closed (figure 2). Place, seam side down, in the pan (figure 3). Repeat with the remaining dough. Place the pans on a half-sheet pan.

5 Choose a warm spot in the kitchen for proofing. Slip the pan with the loaf pans into a tall "kitchen-sized" plastic bag. Place a tall glass of hot water on the pan between the loaves to keep the plastic from touching the dough. Tightly close the bag, trapping air in the bag to partially inflate it. Let stand until the loaves gently dome about an inch above the tops of the pans, about 45 minutes.

6 Position a rack in the center of the oven and preheat to 375°F. Remove the glass from the bag, then the pan with the loaf pans. Brush the tops lightly but thoroughly with the beaten egg. Bake until the loaves are browned and the bottoms sound hollow when tapped, about 40 minutes. Cool on a wire rack for 5 minutes. Remove the loaves from the pans and cool completely on the rack.

Pain de Mie

Makes one 14-inch loaf

....

P*ain de mie* ("crumb bread" in French) may be the epitome of sandwich bread. It gets its name from its firm, tight crumb—your sandwich ingredients won't be slipping through any holes in this bread. I prefer to use a large, covered 14-inch Pullman loaf pan to create a large, perfectly rectangular loaf. If you don't want to invest in a Pullman pan, see page 102 for baking two loaves in standard loaf pans.

BAKER'S NOTE: For dry yeast, refer to the adjusted liquid measurements in the directions.

.5 ounce (1 packed tablespoon) compressed yeast or 1¼ teaspoons active dry yeast

2 tablespoons plus 2 teaspoons granulated sugar

1⅓ cups whole milk

3½ cups bread flour, as needed

1 teaspoon fine sea salt

3 tablespoons unsalted butter, well softened, plus more for the bowl and pan

1   Crumble the yeast finely into the bowl of a heavy-duty stand mixer. Add the sugar and let stand until the yeast gives off some moisture, about 3 minutes. Whisk well to dissolve the yeast. Stir in the milk. (If using active dry yeast, sprinkle the yeast over ⅓ cup warm, 105° to 115°F, milk in a small bowl. Let stand 5 minutes, then stir well to dissolve. Pour into the mixer bowl. Add 1 cup cold milk and the sugar and whisk to combine.)

2   Attach the bowl to the mixer and fit with the paddle attachment. On low speed, beat in half of the flour, then the salt. Add the softened butter, 1 tablespoon at a time, and mix until it is absorbed into the dough. Continue adding enough of the flour to make a soft dough that cleans the bowl. Replace the paddle attachment with the dough hook. Knead on medium-low speed until smooth and elastic, about 6 minutes.

3   Butter a medium bowl. Shape the dough into a taut ball. Place in the bowl and turn to coat with butter. Cover tightly with plastic wrap. Let stand in a warm place until the dough doubles in volume, about 1¼ hours.

4   Lightly butter a 14 by 4 by 4-inch covered Pullman loaf pan, including the underside of the lid. Turn out the dough onto a lightly floured work surface. Gently pressing to deflate the dough, shape

it into a 15 by 8-inch rectangle (see page 100, figure 1). To shape into a loaf, fold in the right and left sides of the dough about ½ inch, and pinch the seams closed. Folding over one-third of the dough at a time, roll up into a plump loaf, pressing the seam closed with the heel of your hand at every turn. Using your fingertips, pinch the final seam closed (see page 100, figure 2). Transfer the loaf, seam side down, to the pan, pressing down gently to fit it flat into the pan (see page 100, figure 3). Cover the pan, leaving the lid open about 1 inch. Let stand in a warm place until the dough has risen to ½ inch beneath the edge of the pan, about 1 hour.

5   Position a rack in the center of the oven and preheat to 350°F.

6   Close the lid completely. Bake until the top crust is golden brown, about 35 minutes. Do not under-bake or the loaf will collapse. Let stand for 5 minutes.

7   Remove the loaf from the pan. Transfer to a wire rack and let cool completely.

To Make Two Standard Loaves: Butter two 8 by 4 by 2½-inch loaf pans. Divide the dough in half. Shape each portion of dough into an 8-inch loaf and fit into the pans. Proof in the plastic bag with a glass of hot water until the loaves have risen about 1 inch over the tops of the pans, then remove the pans from the bag. Bake the loaves, uncovered, until golden brown, 35 to 40 minutes. Cool in the pans for 5 minutes, unmold onto racks, and cool completely.

Stollen

Makes 2 loaves

....

I n old New York at Christmastime, bakeries sold stacks of paper-wrapped and be-ribboned stollen, the beloved German holiday bread. When I serve samples of fresh-baked stollen at the bakery, the customers' faces light up with discovery. Once I served it and a customer asked what he was eating. "It's stollen," I said. With a straight face, he replied, "Well, you should give it back!" This recipe, inspired by pastry chef Dieter Schorner, is extraordinarily light and flavored with rum-scented raisins and other fruits and nuts.

BAKER'S NOTE: This bread uses the "sponge" method of bread making. An initial thin dough is made with some of the flour mixed with milk and yeast, which gives the yeast a head start on developing flavor. The rest of the flour is added with the other ingredients to finish the dough. • The bread's folded shape and sugary coating are said to represent the pure white swaddling clothes described in the Nativity story.

Rum Raisins

½ cup seedless raisins • 2 tablespoons dark rum • ¼ teaspoon pure vanilla extract

1 ounce (2 packed tablespoons) compressed yeast or 3½ teaspoons active dry yeast

½ cup warm (105° to 115°F) whole milk

2½ cups bread flour, divided, plus more as needed

10 tablespoons (1¼ sticks) unsalted butter, cut into tablespoons, well softened, plus more for the bowl

½ cup superfine sugar

½ teaspoon fine sea salt

⅛ teaspoon almond extract

Grated zest of ½ lemon

Grated zest of ½ orange

¼ cup (⅓-inch) diced dried apricots

¼ cup dried cherries

¼ cup (⅓-inch) diced dried pears

⅓ cup (1¼ ounces) toasted and coarsely chopped pecans (page 5)

¼ cup (1 ounce) toasted sliced almonds (page 5)

Coating

⅔ cup superfine sugar

Seeds from ½ Plumped Vanilla Bean (page 295)

6 tablespoons (¾ stick) unsalted butter, melted

1 cup confectioners' sugar

1   The day before baking the stollen, prepare the rum raisins. Place the raisins in a heatproof bowl and add enough hot water to cover. Let stand until the raisins are plumped, about 30 minutes. Drain

well and pat dry with paper towels. Return to the bowl. Add the rum and vanilla and toss together. Cover and refrigerate for 8 to 16 hours.

2   To make the stollen, crumble the compressed yeast (or sprinkle the dry yeast) over the warm milk in the bowl of a heavy-duty stand mixer. Let stand 5 minutes, then whisk to dissolve the yeast. Add ¾ cup of the flour and stir well to make a thin, sticky dough. Cover with plastic wrap and let stand in a warm place until bubbly and doubled in volume, about 20 minutes.

3   Add the remaining flour, the butter, sugar, salt, almond extract, lemon zest, and orange zest. Attach the bowl to the mixer and fit with the paddle attachment. Mix on medium-low speed just until the dough comes together. Replace the paddle attachment with the dough hook. Knead on medium-low speed until the dough is smooth, adding more flour if needed, about 3 minutes. Add the rum raisins, apricots, cherries, pears, pecans, and almonds, and mix until they are incorporated into the dough. Gather up the dough and shape into a ball. Transfer the dough to a large bowl. Cover tightly with plastic wrap and let stand in a warm place until the dough has doubled in volume, about 1½ hours.

4   Turn the dough out onto a very lightly floured work surface. Cut the dough in half. Very gently shape each portion into a ball—do not knead the dough, as you want to retain its light texture. Place the balls on the floured work surface and cover each with a clean kitchen towel. Let stand in a warm place until the dough looks puffy but not doubled, about 45 minutes.

5   Line two half-sheet pans with parchment paper or silicone baking mats. Press one ball into a thick round about 7½ inches in diameter. Fold the dough in half from top to bottom. Starting about one-third from the bottom, using your thumbs, firmly press a deep semicircular trough in the dough, reaching almost through the dough. This will keep the stollen layers from separating when baked. Repeat with the second ball. Transfer each to a prepared pan and cover with the towels. Let stand in a warm place until the dough looks puffy but not doubled, about 30 minutes.

6   Position racks in the center and top third of the oven and preheat to 325°F. Uncover the loaves and bake, switching the positions of the pans from top to bottom and front to back, until deep golden brown, almost walnut-colored, about 35 minutes. The stollen may look a shade darker than you might expect, but do not underbake them.

7   To make the coating, combine the superfine sugar and vanilla seeds on a half-sheet pan. Brush the hot stollen twice with warm melted butter. Roll each loaf in vanilla sugar to coat well. Return to the pans and sprinkle with the remaining vanilla sugar. Cool completely. Generously sift confectioners' sugar on top. (Store at room temperature, wrapped in plastic wrap, for up to 3 days.)

Viennese Kugelhopf

Makes 8 to 12 servings

....

Kugelhopf, with its distinctive ribbed "Turk's turban" shape, could very well be the ultimate coffee cake. Finely textured, and not too sweet with a buttery crumb, it impresses with its quiet dignity. Every bakery and cafe in Austria tries to outdo the competition with its version, which can be yeasted, like this one, or leavened with baking powder. I received this recipe many years ago from an anonymous customer who promised that it would produce a very special and authentic kugelhopf, and she told the truth.

BAKER'S NOTE: This is another recipe that uses the sponge method. The bread is meant to be plain, so you can savor the buttery flavor, and it is rarely served with a glaze. You may top it off with a dusting of confectioners' sugar, but that's all that is needed. • A kugelhopf pan is similar to a Bundt pan, but it has more delicate curves. Made from molded metal, it rarely has a nonstick interior. For authenticity's sake, bake your kugelhopf in such a pan, but you can use a Bundt, if you wish.

Soaked Raisins

½ cup seedless raisins • ½ cup hot water • 2 tablespoons dark rum

1 ounce (2 packed tablespoons) compressed yeast or 3½ teaspoons active dry yeast

½ cup warm (105° to 115°F) whole milk

1 cup unbleached all-purpose flour

10 tablespoons (1¼ sticks) unsalted butter, at room temperature, plus more for the pan

⅔ cup confectioners' sugar, sifted

2 large eggs plus 1 large yolk

¼ teaspoon fine sea salt

¼ cup cool whole milk

Grated zest of 1 lemon

Seeds from 1 Plumped Vanilla Bean (page 295) or 1 teaspoon pure vanilla extract

¼ teaspoon freshly grated nutmeg

2¼ cups bread flour, as needed

10 to 12 whole blanched almonds

Confectioners' sugar, for garnish

1   At least 1 hour before making the kugelhopf dough, prepare the soaked raisins. Combine the raisins, water, and rum in a small bowl and let stand until the raisins are plumped, at least 1 and up to 2 hours. Drain well and pat dry with paper towels. Set the raisins aside.

2 To make the kugelhopf, crumble the compressed yeast (or sprinkle the dry yeast) over the warm milk in the bowl of a heavy-duty stand mixer. Let stand until the yeast softens, about 5 minutes. Add the all-purpose flour and stir well with a wooden spoon. Scrape down the sponge from the sides of the bowl with a silicone spatula. Cover with plastic wrap and let stand in a warm place until doubled in volume and bubbly, about 20 minutes.

3 Combine the butter and confectioners' sugar in the bowl of a heavy-duty stand mixer. Attach the bowl to the mixer and fit with the paddle attachment. Beat on medium-high speed until the mixture is light in color and texture, about 3 minutes. In a separate bowl, whisk the eggs, egg yolk, and salt until combined. Gradually beat the egg mixture into the creamed butter, scraping down the sides of the bowl as needed. Add the sponge, cool milk, lemon zest, vanilla, and nutmeg.

4 Reduce the mixer speed to low. Add enough of the bread flour to make a very thick, sticky, batter-like dough that sticks to the sides of the bowl. Do not add too much flour. Replace the paddle attachment with the dough hook. Knead on medium speed for 3 minutes—the dough's texture will not noticeably change. Add the drained raisins and mix just until they are incorporated into the dough.

5 Scrape down the dough from the sides of the bowl with a silicone spatula. (The dough will be loose and very sticky, but it will hold its shape in the bottom of the bowl.) Cover the bowl with plastic wrap and let stand in a warm place until doubled in volume, about 1½ hours.

6 Generously butter the inside of a 10-cup kugelhopf pan. Place the whole almonds, as needed, in the decorative indentation in the crown of the pan. Using buttered hands, transfer the dough to a lightly floured work surface. Shape the dough into a 7-inch-diameter ball. Using your fingers, poke a hole in the center of the ball. Place the ball, smooth side down, in the pan, stretching the hole to fit over the tube in the pan and taking care not to disturb the almonds in the pan. Cover the pan with a clean kitchen towel and let stand until the dough looks puffy, about 40 minutes.

7 Position a rack in the center of the oven and preheat to 325°F. Uncover the pan and bake until the kugelhopf is browned and pulls away slightly from the sides of the pan, about 35 minutes. If the top threatens to burn, loosely cover it with aluminum foil.

8 Let cool in the pan on a wire rack for 10 minutes. Invert and unmold onto the rack and let cool completely. Sift a light coating of confectioners' sugar on top. To serve, slice with a serrated knife.

Chapter Four
Everyday Cakes

I AM OFTEN ASKED ABOUT THE INFLUENCES ON MY BAKING STYLE. COULD IT BE THE CLASSIC BAKERIES OF PARIS? OR THE SIMPLE BUT SATISFYING BAKING of the American heartland kitchen? Most people are surprised to hear that my first real mentor and inspiration was my mother-in-law, Margaret.

Margaret Firestone took an inexperienced cook and instilled a love for cooking that became a passion. She made cooking look easy, and because of her years of experience and skill, it was. Margaret specialized in simple but incredibly delicious desserts, especially cakes. Made in the European style (Margaret was Hungarian), her cakes were so buttery and delectable that they rarely needed frosting. I remember many a family gathering with everyone chatting over endless cups of coffee and servings of her perfect cakes. To this day, her cakes, and those of her friends and relatives, many of whom were also accomplished bakers, are the standard that I strive for at the bakery. We still name cakes at the bakery for their creators: The espresso cake is "Margaret," and the chocolate pound cake is "Mrs. Stein," yet another relative. Were they still alive, they would be thrilled to know how their cakes live on.

All of the cakes in this chapter are created from a straightforward formula, a variation of the beloved pound cake, baked in fluted tube pans, served plain or simply glazed. They're perfect for a sweet breakfast, a lunchtime treat, served with hot coffee or tea as an afternoon pick-me-up, or for a homey after-dinner dessert.

A LESSON ON EVERYDAY CAKES

Butter It Right Most of these cakes are baked in fluted tube pans. This shape works well for large cakes with rich batters. As the central tube warms up in the oven, it radiates heat and helps bake the cake from the center outward. The American Bundt pan, with its decorative swirled sides, is the most familiar of this pan type. It is based on the European kugelhopf pan. The difference is in the pan material. American Bundt pans are often made from cast iron with a nonstick surface, and both of these factors can contribute to a thick, dark crust. The European kugelhopf pans are molded from thinner metals, such as tinned steel, and make a more delicately browned and tastier cake exterior. I have scores of kugelhopf pans at the bakery, and I love coming across unique ones at kitchenware shops or garage sales.

Because the pans are made on both sides of the Atlantic, the diameter of tube pans fluctuates widely. Rather than measure the pans by their diameter, it is better to select based on capacity. A large tube pan will hold 10 to 12 cups of batter; a small tube pan will hold 8 to 10 cups. To determine their capacity, fill the pans to the brim with water, then measure the water.

If you must use a cast-iron pan, after you put the filled pan in the oven, reduce the oven temperature by 25°F. Test the cake about 10 minutes before the estimated baking time, as the batter could bake more quickly than in a thinner pan.

If you have had trouble unmolding cakes from a fluted cake pan, you probably didn't butter and flour the pan properly. The interior, including the center tube, must be evenly coated with butter and flour.

Use very well-softened butter, and apply it with a soft-bristled pastry brush (round brushes work better than rectangular ones). Be sure to get the butter into every crevice. Sprinkle the butter coating with a generous amount of flour, tilting the pan and shaking it to distribute the flour. Invert the pan and tap it to remove any excess flour. Check your handiwork to be sure the pan is evenly coated with a thin layer of butter and flour, and repair as needed.

Getting Ready Creaming the butter and sugar, the first step in making the batter, is the most crucial. The butter and sugar must be beaten together at medium-high speed until they are well combined and the mixture is filled with invisible air bubbles. The amount of bubbles in the creamed mixture will affect the volume and texture of the cake, so don't skimp on the creaming time. And be sure to stop the mixer and scrape down the sides of the bowl often.

For the best results, use a heavy-duty stand mixer fitted with the paddle attachment. These machines will cream the butter and sugar better than any handheld mixer and allow for thorough distribution of the dry ingredients in the batter. You can use a handheld electric mixer, but increase the creaming time by 1 or 2 minutes.

The butter should be softened to "cool" room temperature, no more. (With a heavy-duty mixer, you can use butter right out of the refrigerator, cut into ½-inch cubes. Just mix it on high speed for 1 or 2 minutes, and it will become soft enough to incorporate the sugar.) The butter should be malleable, not squishy or shiny. To speed softening, cut the chilled butter into small cubes, and it should be ready to cream in 15 to 20 minutes.

Making the Batter Creaming is really a three-step process. First, cream the room-temperature butter for about 1 minute on medium-high speed until it looks smooth and creamy. Then gradually beat in the sugar, about 1 tablespoon at a time. (Superfine sugar will give the most tender crumb.) Finally, beat the butter and sugar mixture for 3 to 4 minutes, stopping the mixer and scraping the bottom and sides of the bowl at least three times during the process. If you must use a handheld mixer, increase the creaming time to about 6 minutes. The final creamed mixture will be filled with incorporated air, evidenced by its very pale yellow color.

When adding the eggs, take care that they are not added too quickly, or the creamed mixture will look curdled. After all, a cake batter is an emulsified mixture, and if one ingredient is added more quickly than another, the batter will "break." Many cookbooks say to add the eggs to the creamed butter and sugar one egg at a time, but even that seemingly small amount could cause curdling. For the best results, beat the eggs together. With the mixer running, add the beaten eggs about 1 tablespoon at time to the creamed mixture. Temperature discrepancies will also cause curdling, so be sure to use room-temperature eggs.

The next step, mixing in the dry ingredients, is as important as creaming, as it affects the tenderness of the cake. If the batter is overmixed, the gluten in the flour will strengthen and make a tough cake.

Reduce the mixer speed to low. In three additions, add in the dry ingredients, and mix just until they are incorporated. Some recipes alternate the addition of the dry ingredients with a liquid, but start by adding the dry ingredients first, to make the batter stronger and ready to accept the liquid.

Scrape, scrape, scrape! That's my advice for mixing a smooth batter. Once or twice during mixing, stop the machine and scrape the bottom and sides of the bowl with a long-handled silicone spatula. When the batter is finished, scrape up the mixture from the bottom of the bowl to be positively sure that every bit has been incorporated.

If the recipe calls for beaten egg whites, they must be beaten in a separate bowl. Be sure the whites are at room temperature before beating, as you will get slightly more volume than with chilled whites.

To beat egg whites, beat in a separate bowl with a balloon whisk or a handheld electric mixer. The bowl and beating utensil must be absolutely grease-free. Even a speck of grease or fat in the bowl will stop the whites from forming peaks. (Never use hard rubber or plastic bowls for beating eggs—I use stainless steel for everything in my kitchen—because they can absorb grease that you will never be able to remove.) If I have any doubts about the status of a bowl, I wipe it out with a paper towel moistened with distilled white or cider vinegar. Don't rinse out the bowl. Just like cream of tartar, which is a powdered acid, the tiny amount of residual vinegar provides acidity to help stabilize the beaten whites.

Is It Done? The quickest way to check a cake for doneness is by touch—the cake should spring back when lightly pressed with your fingertips. But, the most reliable way is with a wire cake tester, available at any kitchenware shop. Insert the tester straight into the center of the cake. The tip of the tester should reach the middle of the baking batter. Withdraw the tester (pull it straight up and don't wiggle it). If the cake is done, the tester will be clean with no clinging crumbs. If moist crumbs or batter cling to the tester, continue baking. Some bakers use a bamboo skewer or toothpick instead of a tester because they're handy, but both have their drawbacks. Some skewers are too thick and will deflate delicate desserts or leave large holes on the cake's surface, and toothpicks are too short to reach the middle of the cake, so I don't use them.

Cool the cake on a wire rack for 10 minutes before unmolding. This allows the cake to contract slightly away from the pan. To unmold the cake, place the wire rack on the top of the pan. Holding the pan and the rack together, invert and place on the work surface. Rap the rack lightly on the work surface, and the cake will slip out of the pan (if it hasn't already).

All of the cakes in this book are good "keepers" and will stay fresh for a few days, wrapped tightly in plastic wrap and stored at room temperature.

Mrs. Stein's Chocolate Cake

Makes 10 to 12 servings

·····························

When I was gathering the recipes for this chapter, my daughters, Jennifer and Tina, reminded me of an almost ridiculously chocolate pound cake that I hadn't made in years. How I let this one slip through the cracks, I'll never know. I did some searching, and there it was, tucked away in my treasured recipe book. It was splattered with chocolate batter, a clear indication that it was a favorite that I made again and again. I received the recipe from Mrs. Stein, a Hungarian beauty who was a relative of my father-in-law, Joe Firestone. Welcome back, old friend.

Softened unsalted butter and flour, for the pan

1½ cups whole milk

1 tablespoon fresh lemon juice

2⅓ cups unbleached all-purpose flour

1 cup Dutch-processed cocoa powder

1½ teaspoons baking soda

½ teaspoon fine sea salt

½ ounce (½ square) unsweetened chocolate, finely chopped

10 tablespoons (1¼ sticks) unsalted butter, chilled and cut into ½-inch cubes

1¼ cups superfine sugar

1 teaspoon pure vanilla extract

3 large eggs, at room temperature, beaten

Confectioners' sugar, for garnish, optional

1   Position a rack in the center of the oven and preheat to 350°F. Butter and flour the inside of a 8- to 10-cup fluted tube pan and tap out the excess flour.

2   Combine the milk and lemon juice in a glass measuring cup. Let stand in a warm place (near the preheating oven) while preparing the rest of the batter; the milk will curdle. Sift the flour, cocoa, baking soda, and salt together into a medium bowl.

3   Bring ½ inch of water to a simmer in a small saucepan, and turn off the heat. Place the chocolate in a custard cup or ramekin and set in the hot water. Let stand until the chocolate is melted, then remove from the water, being careful not to splash any water into the chocolate, and stir until smooth. Let stand until tepid.

4 Beat the butter in the bowl of a heavy-duty stand mixer fitted with the paddle attachment on medium-high speed until smooth, about 1 minute. Gradually beat in the sugar, then add the vanilla. Beat until the mixture is very light in color and texture, scraping occasionally, about 4 minutes. Gradually beat in the eggs. Reduce the mixer speed to low. Beat in the cooled chocolate. In thirds, alternating with two equal additions of the milk mixture, add the flour mixture, scraping down the bowl and beating until smooth after each addition. Spoon the batter into the pan and smooth the top with a spatula.

5 Bake until the top of the cake springs back when gently pressed with your finger, and a cake tester inserted into the center of the cake comes out clean, about 1 hour. Cool on a wire rack for 10 minutes. Invert and unmold the cake onto the rack and cool completely. Sift a light coating of confectioners' sugar on top, if using. (The cake can be stored at room temperature, wrapped in plastic wrap, for up to 2 days.)

Margaret's Espresso Cake

Makes 12 servings

....

T his is one of my late mother-in-law Margaret's most-treasured recipes. I've made a few tweaks of my own. First, Margaret kept a kosher kitchen and baked with margarine, but this updated version has my beloved butter. Also, I've substituted full-flavored espresso powder for the generic instant coffee in the original. And Margaret never used a tube pan. Nonetheless, when I make this cake, I think of her and smile. A simple coffee glaze tops it all off.

BAKER'S NOTE: To give the cake its proper deep beige color and coffee flavor, you must use hot brewed coffee plus instant coffee. Instant espresso gives the richest flavor.

Softened unsalted butter and flour, for the pan	*½ teaspoon fine sea salt*
1 cup hot brewed coffee	*16 tablespoons (2 sticks) unsalted butter, chilled and cut into ½-inch cubes*
3 tablespoons instant coffee, preferably instant espresso	
3 cups unbleached all-purpose flour	*2 cups superfine sugar*
	1 teaspoon pure vanilla extract
2½ teaspoons baking powder	*4 large eggs, at room temperature, separated*

Coffee Glaze

2 tablespoons hot brewed coffee	*1 tablespoon whole milk*
½ teaspoon instant espresso powder	*2 cups confectioners' sugar, sifted*

1 Position a rack in the center of the oven and preheat to 350°F. Butter and flour the inside of a 10- to 12-cup fluted tube pan and tap out the excess flour.

2 Combine the brewed coffee and espresso powder in a glass measuring cup; let cool.

3 Sift the flour, baking powder, and salt together into a medium bowl. Beat the butter in the bowl of a heavy-duty stand mixer fitted with the paddle attachment on high speed until smooth, about 1 minute. Gradually beat in the sugar, then add the vanilla, and beat until very light in color and texture, scraping occasionally, about 4 minutes. One at a time, beat in the yolks. Reduce the mixer speed to low. In thirds, starting with the flour mixture, alternating with two equal additions of the cooled coffee, beat in the flour mixture, beating until smooth after each addition.

4   Whip the egg whites in a grease-free medium bowl with a handheld electric mixer on high speed (or use a balloon whisk) until soft peaks form. Using a silicone spatula, stir about one-fourth of the whites into the batter, then gently fold in the remaining whites. Scrape the batter into the prepared pan. Smooth the top with the spatula.

5   Bake until the top of the cake springs back when gently pressed with your finger, and a cake tester inserted into the center of the cake comes out clean, 55 to 60 minutes.

6   Cool on a wire rack for 10 minutes. Invert and unmold the cake onto the rack set over a half-sheet pan. Cool completely.

7   To make the glaze, mix the brewed coffee and espresso powder in a small saucepan to dissolve the espresso. Stir in the milk. Add the confectioners' sugar and whisk until smooth. Place over low heat and whisk constantly until the glaze thins slightly and is warm to the touch.

8   Transfer the glaze to a glass measuring cup. Slowly pour the warm glaze over the cake, letting it flow into the indentations in the cake, and also down the hole in the center of the cake. You will have plenty of glaze. Cool completely. (The cake can be stored at room temperature, wrapped in plastic wrap, for up to 2 days.)

Orange Chocolate Chiffon Cake

Makes 12 servings

....

For many years, the recipe for chiffon cake was the well-guarded secret of a Los Angeles caterer. For the right price, he was eventually convinced to sell the formula, and now many bakers have developed their favorite versions of this lovely, tender cake. I have always been fond of the combination of orange and chocolate, so I've used those flavors in my recipe. This batter isn't temperamental, but it is choosy about its pan. It is baked in a plain (not fluted) tube pan with a removable bottom, commonly known as an angel-food cake pan. Do not use a nonstick pan. Note that the cake pan is not greased (as the batter prefers a tactile, not slick, surface for rising) and that the cake must cool upside down for it to hold its shape.

BAKER'S NOTE: If you have access to high-quality, imported candied orange peel (the average supermarket version is tasteless), decorate the glazed top of the cake with the peel.

2 large oranges

2¼ cups pastry or cake flour (not self-rising)

1½ cups superfine sugar

1 tablespoon baking powder

1 teaspoon fine sea salt

½ cup vegetable oil

5 large eggs, separated, plus 3 large egg whites, at room temperature

¼ cup water

¾ cup (4½ ounces) finely grated semisweet or bittersweet chocolate

Orange Ganache

½ cup heavy cream

5 ounces semisweet or bittersweet chocolate (no more than 62 percent cacao), finely chopped

2 tablespoons orange-flavored liqueur, such as Grand Marnier, or orange juice

2 tablespoons chopped candied orange peel, for garnish, optional

1 Position a rack in the center of the oven and preheat to 350°F.

2 To make the cake, grate the zest from the oranges and set aside. Roll and press the oranges on the counter. Juice the oranges; measure and reserve ½ cup.

3 Sift the flour, sugar, baking powder, and salt together into the bowl of a heavy-duty stand mixer. Make a well in the center of the dry ingredients, and add, in this order, the oil, 5 egg yolks, orange zest and juice, and water. Attach the bowl to the mixer and fit with the paddle attachment. With the mixer on low speed, beat just until the batter is smooth, being sure to scrape down the sides of the bowl with a silicone spatula.

4 Combine the 8 egg whites in a clean, large bowl. Using a handheld electric mixer set on high speed, whip just until stiff peaks form. Stir about one-fourth of the whites into the batter to lighten it, then fold in the remaining whites with a silicone spatula just until the batter is streaky. Add the grated chocolate and fold until combined. Pour into an ungreased 10-inch-diameter tube pan with a removable bottom. Smooth the top of the batter with the spatula.

5 Bake until the cake springs back when gently pressed with your finger, about 50 minutes. Invert the cake pan onto a work surface and let the cake cool completely. (If the upside-down pan does not balance on its own, set the edges of the pan on upturned ramekins.)

6 Run a long metal spatula or thin knife around the inside of the pan and tube to loosen the cake. Remove the cake from the pan, then carefully pull the bottom of the cake away from the insert. Place the cake, smooth side up, on a wire rack set over a half-sheet pan.

7 To make the ganache, bring the cream to a simmer in a medium saucepan over medium heat. Remove from the heat and add the chocolate and liqueur. Let stand for 3 minutes, then stir well with a silicone spatula until the chocolate melts and the ganache is smooth. (Whisking will create bubbles that will mar the surface of the ganache.) Let stand until slightly cooled, about 5 minutes.

8 Pour the ganache over the top of the cake, using a metal spatula to smooth the ganache so it randomly runs down the sides of the cake. Let stand until the ganache sets. Decorate with orange peel, if using. To serve, cut into slices with a serrated knife. (The cake can be stored at room temperature, wrapped in plastic wrap, for up to 2 days.)

Ruby Cake

Makes 10 to 12 servings

....

R uby is a beauty. When we talk about Ruby at the bakery, she's a "she," not an "it." She's that gorgeous and delicious. Ruby has a surprise raspberry-and-chocolate filling running through the center of each slice.

BAKER'S NOTE: Follow the instructions carefully to encase the filling with batter (you'll need two pastry bags). If the filling touches the sides of the pan, it could burn, and Ruby doesn't like that. • The Raspberry Jam on page 276 is very bright red and really "pops" in the batter. Try to use it if you can.

Softened unsalted butter and flour, for the pan

3 cups unbleached all-purpose flour

1½ teaspoons baking powder

½ teaspoon fine sea salt

16 tablespoons (2 sticks) unsalted butter, chilled and cut into ½-inch cubes

2¼ cups superfine sugar

1½ teaspoons pure vanilla extract

3 large eggs, at room temperature, beaten

1½ cups full-fat sour cream

⅓ cup plus 1 tablespoon Raspberry Jam (page 276)

¼ cup finely chopped semisweet or bittersweet chocolate

1   Position a rack in the center of the oven and preheat to 350°F. Butter and flour the inside of a 10- to 12-cup fluted tube pan and tap out the excess flour.

2   Sift the flour, baking powder, and salt together into a medium bowl. Beat the butter in the bowl of a heavy-duty stand mixer fitted with the paddle attachment on medium-high speed until smooth, about 1 minute. Gradually beat in the sugar, then add the vanilla, and beat until very light in color and texture, scraping occasionally, about 5 minutes. Gradually beat in the eggs. Reduce the mixer speed to low. In thirds, starting with the flour mixture, and alternating with two equal additions of the sour cream, beat in the flour mixture, beating after each addition until smooth.

3   Transfer half of the batter to a large pastry bag (you won't need to fit it with a pastry tip if the bag opening is about ¾ inch wide). Pipe a thick layer of batter into the bottom of the pan. Pipe two circles of the batter into the pan, one around the circumference of the tube, and another around the circumference of the pan. Using an offset metal spatula, create a shallow trough between the circles of batter (figure 1). Place the raspberry jam in a second pastry bag, fitted with a ¼-inch-diameter

plain pastry tip, such as Ateco #802, and pipe it into the trough, being sure not to touch the sides of the pan. Sprinkle with the chocolate (figure 2). Place the remaining batter into the bag, pipe it into the pan, and smooth the surface with a silicone spatula (figure 3). Insert a chopstick in the batter and move it in spirals to distribute the raspberry and chocolate fillings in the cake. Do not let the chopstick touch the sides or bottom of the pan.

4 Bake until the top of the cake springs back when gently pressed with your finger, and a cake tester inserted into the center of the cake comes out clean, about 1 hour. Cool on a wire rack for 10 minutes. Invert and unmold the cake onto the rack to cool completely. (The cake can be stored at room temperature, wrapped in plastic wrap, for up to 2 days.)

Three-Seed Cake

Makes 10 to 12 servings

....

One day, a friend of mine brought me a gift that I have treasured ever since. It's a red antique recipe box, with the recipes intact. What a find! Some of the recipes were newspaper clippings, others were recipe brochures, and some were written in the original owner's hand, but they all had something to offer. I zeroed in on this recipe for a three-seed coffee cake immediately. While I made a few minor changes, it's essentially the mystery baker's recipe.

Softened unsalted butter and flour, for the pan

1 teaspoon anise seeds

1 teaspoon caraway seeds

1 teaspoon poppy seeds

3 cups unbleached all-purpose flour

1 tablespoon baking powder

½ teaspoon fine sea salt

10 tablespoons (1¼ sticks) unsalted butter, chilled and cut into ½-inch cubes

2 cups superfine sugar

4 large eggs, at room temperature, separated

Grated zest of ½ lemon

Grated zest of ½ orange

1 cup whole milk, at room temperature

Lemon Glaze

2 cups confectioners' sugar • 3 tablespoons fresh lemon juice

1   Position a rack in the center of the oven and preheat to 350°F. Butter and flour the inside of a 10- to 12-cup fluted tube pan and tap to remove the excess flour.

2   In an electric coffee grinder, pulse the anise and caraway seeds about 10 times, until some of them have been ground to a powder but others remain coarsely ground. Transfer to a medium bowl and stir in the poppy seeds. Sift the flour, baking powder, and salt together onto a piece of parchment or waxed paper, and set aside.

3   Beat the butter in the bowl of a heavy-duty stand mixer fitted with the paddle attachment on medium-high speed until smooth, about 1 minute. Gradually beat in the sugar, and beat until light in color and texture, scraping occasionally, about 5 minutes. One at a time, beat in the egg yolks,

beating well after each addition. Beat in the lemon and orange zests. Reduce the speed to low. In thirds, alternating with two equal additions of the milk, add the flour mixture and mix until smooth, scraping down the sides of the bowl often. Mix in the anise, caraway, and poppy seeds.

4   Whip the egg whites in a grease-free medium bowl with a handheld electric mixer on high speed (or a balloon whisk) until stiff peaks form. Fold the whites into the batter with a silicone spatula. Scrape into the prepared pan and smooth the top.

5   Bake until the top of the cake springs back when gently pressed with your finger, and a cake tester inserted into the center of the cake comes out clean, 50 to 60 minutes. Cool on a wire rack for 10 minutes. Invert and unmold the cake onto a wire rack set over a half-sheet pan and cool completely.

6   To make the glaze, sift the confectioners' sugar into a medium bowl. Gradually whisk in the lemon juice. Transfer to a glass measuring cup. Slowly pour the glaze over the cake, letting it flow into the indentations of the cake and also down the hole in the center of the cake. Let stand until the glaze is set. (The cake can be stored at room temperature, wrapped in plastic wrap, for up to 2 days.)

Chocolate Soufflé Cake

Makes 10 to 12 servings

....

Here's another cake that has only a few ingredients, perfectly combined, to make an extraordinary dessert. It looks a little odd, with its cracked top, but when served with a big dollop of chocolate whipped cream, it more than makes up for looks with its flavor.

BAKER'S NOTE: This cake can also be baked in an 8 by 3-inch springform or loose-bottomed cheesecake pan. In this case, you can serve the cake directly from the bottom of the pan. • Don't overbake this cake. Even though it may seem a little underdone, after it cools, the chocolate will firm up. The consistency of the cooled cake should remind you of a very dense, moist chocolate cheesecake disguised as a candy bar.

12 ounces semisweet or bittersweet chocolate (no more than 62 percent cacao), finely chopped

7 tablespoons unsalted butter, thinly sliced

6 large eggs, at room temperature

¼ cup superfine sugar

1 teaspoon pure vanilla extract

2 tablespoons unbleached all-purpose flour

Chocolate Whipped Cream

1½ cups heavy cream, divided

3 ounces semisweet or bittersweet chocolate (no more than 62 percent cacao), finely chopped

2 tablespoons superfine sugar

Seeds from ½ Plumped Vanilla Bean (page 295) or ½ teaspoon pure vanilla extract

1   To make the cake, bring 1 inch of water to a simmer in a medium saucepan over low heat. Combine the chocolate and butter in a wide, heatproof bowl. Place over the hot water in the saucepan, stirring often until the chocolate and butter are melted and the mixture is smooth. Remove the bowl from the heat and let stand until the mixture is tepid and pourable, about 15 minutes.

2   Position a rack in the center of the oven and preheat to 350°F. Line a half-sheet pan with a silicone baking mat or parchment paper. Lightly butter the inside of an 8 by 3-inch metal cake ring and put it on the pan.

3   Combine the eggs and sugar in the bowl of a heavy-duty stand mixer. Attach the bowl to the mixer and fit with the whisk attachment. Beat on high speed until the mixture is almost quadrupled in vol-

ume, very pale yellow, and fluffy, about 5 minutes. (If you are using a handheld electric mixer, this will take at least 6 minutes.) You'll know that the right consistency has been reached when, if you lift the whisk attachment a few inches above the bowl, the mixture creates a thick ribbon that falls back on itself and holds its shape on the surface of the mixture for about 5 seconds before sinking.

4   Reduce the mixer speed to low. Beat in the vanilla and the cooled chocolate. Add the flour, scraping down the sides of the bowl as needed. Spread evenly in the cake ring.

5   Bake until the top of the cake looks dry and cracked and, when pressed gently with your fingers, feels almost set, about 40 minutes. Let cool for about 15 minutes in the ring. Carefully lift off the ring. Gently slide the bottom of an 8-inch tart pan or cardboard round underneath the cake and transfer to a serving platter. (The cake can be stored at room temperature, wrapped in plastic wrap, for up to 2 days.)

6   To make the chocolate whipped cream, bring ½ cup of the heavy cream to a boil in a small saucepan over medium heat. Remove from the heat and add the chocolate. Let stand until the chocolate softens, about 3 minutes. Whisk until smooth. Scrape into a small bowl and cool until tepid but pourable. Whip the remaining 1 cup heavy cream with the sugar and vanilla in a chilled medium bowl just until soft peaks begin to form. Add the cooled chocolate mixture and beat until soft peaks form (this may take only a few seconds). Refrigerate until ready to serve, up to 2 hours.

7   Slice the cake with a sharp knife (dipped in hot water and wiped dry before each cut), and serve with the whipped cream.

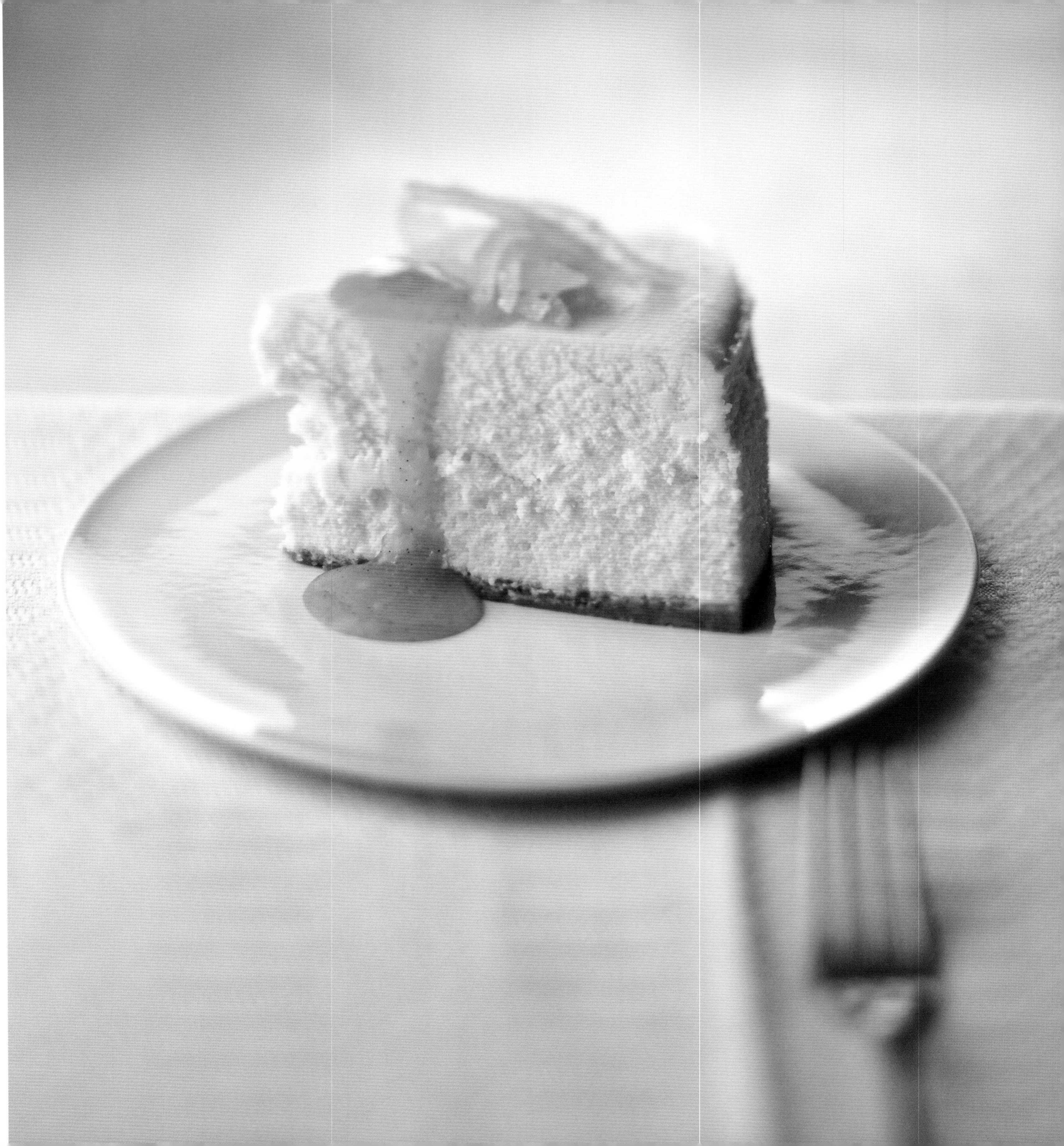

Cheesecake with Orange Marmalade Sauce

Makes 10 to 12 servings

....

As much as I have tried to embrace flavored cheesecakes (we have sold both chocolate and pumpkin at the bakery over the years), I always return to the original vanilla version, where the taste of the cream cheese predominates. This recipe is a wonderful example of the perfect cheesecake.

BAKER'S NOTE: Use a top-quality full-fat cream cheese, but not one labeled "all-natural," or your cheesecake might not set. Be sure that it is thoroughly softened before beating. • A low oven temperature helps guard against cracking. If the cake cracks, it will still be delicious. • In the bakery, we use a metal cake ring placed on a sheet tray. This recipe uses a 9-inch springform pan (preferably one with a tempered glass bottom) instead because the batter could leak if your tray is not perfectly flat.

Softened unsalted butter, for the pan

1 cup crushed Buttery Shortbread (page 225), or use store-bought shortbread cookies

2½ pounds cream cheese, softened at room temperature for at least 2 hours

1 cup superfine sugar

1 cup heavy cream

5 large eggs, at room temperature, beaten

2½ teaspoons unbleached all-purpose flour

Seeds from 1 Plumped Vanilla Bean (page 295)

Grated zest of ¼ lemon

Orange Marmalade Sauce

1 cup orange marmalade, preferably Sarabeth's Orange-Apricot Marmalade

⅓ cup Simple Syrup (page 293)

2 teaspoons fresh lemon juice

Seeds from ½ Plumped Vanilla Bean (page 295)

Crystallized ginger, thinly sliced, for garnish, optional

1 Position a rack in the center of the oven and preheat to 300°F. Butter the inside of a 9-inch springform pan.

2 Sprinkle the crushed crumbs into the pan. Using the bottom of a drinking glass, press the crumbs firmly and evenly in the bottom of the pan.

3   Put the cream cheese in the bowl of a heavy-duty stand mixer. Attach the bowl to the mixer and fit with the paddle attachment. On low speed, beat the cream cheese until it is smooth, scraping down the sides of the bowl often. Increase the speed to medium and gradually add the sugar, then the cream. In five or six additions, add the beaten eggs, beating until they are absorbed into the batter before each addition and scraping down the sides of the bowl often. Add the flour, vanilla seeds, and lemon zest and beat until completely smooth. Pour into the pan.

4   Place the cheesecake on a half-sheet pan and bake until the sides have risen slightly and are barely beginning to color, and the center of the cheesecake looks set, about 50 minutes. Transfer the cheese-cake to a wire rack and let cool completely in the pan.

5   Run a knife around the inside of the pan to loosen the cheesecake. Remove the sides of the pan. Cover the cheesecake with plastic wrap and refrigerate until chilled, at least 4 hours. (The wrapped cheesecake can be stored for up to 2 days.)

6   To make the sauce, process the marmalade, syrup, lemon juice, and vanilla seeds in a food processor fitted with the metal blade until smooth. (The sauce can be made up to 3 days ahead, covered, and stored in the refrigerator.)

7   Slice the cake with a sharp knife (dipped in hot water and wiped dry before each cut). Top each slice with the marmalade sauce and garnish with a sprinkle of crystallized ginger, if using.

Carrot Cake

Makes 6 to 8 servings

....

Every baker should have a good carrot cake in his or her repertoire, and this is the recipe that I turn to again and again. It's moist and spicy, with lots of carrots, and couldn't be easier to make.

BAKER'S NOTE: For the most attractive result, bake the cake in an 8-cup fluted tube pan.

Softened unsalted butter, for the pan	*⅔ cup vegetable oil*
1 cup unbleached all-purpose flour, plus more for the pan	*2 large eggs, at room temperature*
1 teaspoon ground cinnamon	*1½ cups shredded carrots (use the large holes on a box grater)*
1 teaspoon baking powder	*One 8-ounce can crushed pineapple, well drained (½ cup)*
1 teaspoon baking soda	
½ teaspoon fine sea salt	*½ cup (2 ounces) walnuts, toasted and coarsely chopped (page 5)*
1 cup superfine sugar	*½ cup seedless raisins*

1 Position a rack in the center of the oven and preheat to 350°F. Butter and flour the inside of an 8-cup fluted tube pan and tap out the excess flour.

2 Sift the flour, cinnamon, baking powder, baking soda, and salt together into a medium bowl. Combine the sugar, oil, and eggs in the bowl of a heavy-duty stand mixer. Attach the bowl to the mixer and fit with the whisk attachment. Beat on high speed until the mixture has thickened slightly and is light in color and texture, about 3 minutes. Reduce the mixer speed to low. In thirds, add the flour mixture and mix, scraping down the sides of the bowl as needed, just until the batter is smooth. Add the carrots, pineapple, walnuts, and raisins and mix until combined. Pour into the prepared pan and smooth the top with a spatula.

3 Bake until a cake tester inserted into the center of the cake comes out clean, about 45 minutes. Let cool in the pan on a wire rack for 10 minutes. Invert and unmold the cake onto the rack and let cool completely. (The cake can be stored at room temperature, wrapped in plastic wrap, for up to 2 days.)

Sir Francis Crumb Cakes

Makes 8 individual cakes

....

Sporting a thick layer of golden brown streusel on top of tender, buttery pound cake, individual-size crumb cakes are irresistible. Try serving them warm from the oven at a brunch, or as an after-school snack.

BAKER'S NOTE: You'll need eight 3 by 1½-inch metal entremet rings to give the cakes their distinctive round, tall shape.

Crumb Topping

¼ cup unbleached all-purpose flour	6 tablespoons (¾ stick) unsalted butter, melted
⅓ cup plus 1 tablespoon superfine sugar	½ teaspoon ground cinnamon
Softened unsalted butter, for the pans	10 tablespoons (1¼ sticks) unsalted butter, cut into ½-inch cubes, at room temperature
1⅔ cups unbleached all-purpose flour	
1¼ teaspoons baking powder	⅔ cup superfine sugar
¼ teaspoon fine sea salt	2 large eggs, at room temperature, beaten
⅔ cup heavy cream	Seeds from ½ Plumped Vanilla Bean (page 295) or ½ teaspoon pure vanilla extract
⅓ cup plus 1 tablespoon whole milk	

1   Position a rack in the center of the oven and preheat to 350°F. Line a half-sheet pan with parchment paper. Lightly butter the insides of eight 3 by 1½-inch metal entremet rings, and place the rings on the pan.

2   To make the crumbs, stir together the flour, sugar, butter, and cinnamon in a medium bowl until moistened. Compress the mixture in your hands, and then crumble it until it resembles the texture of coarse bread crumbs. Dip the buttered entremet rings into the crumbs and lightly coat the insides. Shake off the excess crumbs. Return the rings to the pan. Press the remaining crumb mixture with your hands until about half of the crumbs are larger, about the size of peas. Set the crumb mixture aside.

3   To make the cakes, sift the flour, baking powder, and salt together. Mix the heavy cream and milk together in a glass measuring cup.

4   Beat the butter in the bowl of a heavy-duty stand mixer fitted with the paddle attachment on high speed until smooth, about 1 minute. Add the sugar and beat until the mixture is light in color and texture, about 3 minutes. Scrape down the sides of the bowl with a silicone spatula. Gradually beat in the eggs, then the vanilla. Reduce the speed to low. In thirds, starting with the flour mixture and alternating with two equal additions of the cream mixture, add the flour mixture, mixing the batter after each addition until smooth, occasionally scraping down the sides of the bowl.

5   Using a 2½-inch-diameter ice-cream scoop, transfer equal amounts of the batter into the entremet rings. Place equal amounts of the crumb mixture over the batter in the rings. Using your fingers, tap the crumbs to help them adhere.

6   Bake until the crumbs are golden brown and a cake tester inserted into the center of a cake comes out clean, 20 to 25 minutes. Cool the cakes in the rings on the pan for 10 minutes. Using a kitchen towel to protect your hands from the heat, if necessary, remove the rings from the cakes. Serve warm or transfer to a wire rack and cool completely. (The cakes can be stored at room temperature, wrapped in plastic wrap, for up to 2 days.)

Black Beauty Cupcakes

Makes 12 cupcakes

....

When chocolate, and only chocolate, will do, make these elegant cupcakes, with a dark-as-midnight bottom crowned with a jaunty ganache topping. Kids will love them, but they have a grown-up, sleek look. The incredibly easy, magical batter uses mayonnaise instead of the typical butter and eggs.

BAKER'S NOTE: The ganache decoration on the cupcakes requires a pastry bag fitted with a plastic coupler so you can change pastry tips. You will need Ateco tips #30 and #4.

Softened unsalted butter, for the pans

½ cup plus 2 tablespoons Dutch-processed cocoa powder, divided

1½ cups plus 2 tablespoons unbleached all-purpose flour, divided

1 cup hot water

1 cup superfine sugar

1½ teaspoons baking soda

¼ teaspoon fine sea salt

¾ cup mayonnaise

Ganache

1⅓ cups heavy cream

12 ounces semisweet or bittersweet chocolate (no more than 62 percent cacao), finely chopped

4 tablespoons (½ stick) unsalted butter, cut into ½-inch cubes, at room temperature

1   Position a rack in the center of the oven and preheat to 350°F.

2   To make the cakes, butter the insides of 12 muffin cups. Sift together 2 tablespoons of the cocoa and 2 tablespoons of the flour. Dust the insides of the molds with the cocoa-flour mixture, and tap out the excess.

3   Combine the remaining ½ cup cocoa powder and the hot water in the bowl of a heavy-duty stand mixer. Whisk to dissolve the cocoa. Whisk in the sugar. Attach the bowl to the mixer and fit with the paddle attachment. Sift the remaining 1½ cups flour, the baking soda, and salt together. With the mixer on low speed, in thirds, add the flour mixture, alternating with two equal addi-

tions of the mayonnaise, and mix, scraping down the sides of the bowl as needed, until the batter is smooth. (The batter will seem a little thinner than usual.) Using a 2½-inch-diameter ice-cream scoop, divide the batter evenly among the muffin cups.

4   Bake until a cake tester inserted in a cake comes out clean, about 20 minutes. Let cool in the pan on a wire rack for 10 minutes. Gently unmold the cakes onto a rack, and let cool completely.

5   To make the ganache, bring the heavy cream to a simmer in a medium saucepan over medium heat. Remove from the heat and add the chocolate. Let stand for 3 minutes, then whisk until smooth. Add the butter, whisking until it has totally melted into the chocolate. Transfer to a bowl and let cool on a wire rack until the ganache thickens to the consistency of pudding and can be piped, about 1 hour.

6   Transfer the ganache to a pastry bag fitted with a coupler and a ⅛-inch-diameter closed-star tip, such as Ateco #30. Pipe strips of ganache in a starburst pattern around the top of each cupcake, leaving a ½-inch-diameter space empty in the center. Change the tip to a ⅛-inch-diameter plain tip, such as Ateco #4, and pipe short spikes in the center of the cupcake. (The cupcakes can be made up to 1 day ahead, covered with a cake dome, and refrigerated. Serve chilled or at room temperature.)

THERE ARE TWO KINDS OF CUSTOMERS AT SARABETH'S. THE FIRST TYPE OF CLIENT CRAVES OUR HOME-STYLE DESSERTS, AND COMES TO US FOR his or her daily chocolate chip cookie. The other shopper thinks of Sarabeth's as the place to buy an extraordinary dessert for a special occasion—the wedding, the anniversary, the dinner at home with the boss. This is my opportunity to be creative.

Party cakes should have a unique element. Often it is the way the cake is decorated, with a layer of perfectly smooth buttercream or a mirror-like glaze. Other times it is indulgent or even slightly decadent ingredients that elevate these cakes. A sheet cake can be rolled into an elegant roulade. While many of these desserts use cake as their springboards, *pâte à choux* can be turned into profiteroles or éclairs, or puff pastry can become a fruit-topped Napoleon.

An impressive party dessert takes a little extra time to create, so you may want to reserve it as a project for a weekend afternoon. Or you can do what I do: Prepare the components (cake layers and fillings) a day ahead, and finish (frostings and decorations) the day of the party.

A LESSON ON LAYER CAKES

Perhaps because it requires a few different components (cake, a filling or two, maybe some fruit, and a frosting or glaze), the classic layer cake is an enduring special occasion dessert. Standing tall and proud, this combination of the architectural and the delicious sends a clear message to the guests that extra effort was made to create a dessert for their pleasure.

Baking and Cutting Cake Layers Building a layered cake can be an exasperating procedure for even the most experienced baker. Baked individually in pans, the cake layers are often domed, which makes for unstable stacking. While the tops can be trimmed, it takes skill and a long serrated knife to do this well.

There is a solution to this dilemma: Skip the traditional pans and bake the batter as a thin sheet cake that can be cut into rounds for stacking. This is the only way we make layer cakes in the bakery. Our method ensures that each cake layer will have the same thickness without the need to trim the tops. Sometimes the layers are stacked with the desired filling in an 8 by 3-inch metal cake ring, then chilled to firm the soft filling. Remove the chilled cake from its ring, and glaze away. Other times the cake is removed from the ring right after assembly, then immediately chilled and then frosted. In either case, the metal ring supports and stabilizes the layers and filling to create a perfectly straight, uniform cake.

To prepare sheet cake layers, line the bottom of an 18 by 13-inch half-sheet pan with a nonstick silicone baking mat. Or if you are using parchment paper, lightly butter the pan first. (I prefer the mat because it will not stick to the baked cake, whereas the parchment must be removed carefully or the somewhat thin cake may tear.) Transfer the batter to the pan. Using a large offset metal spatula, spread it as evenly as possible so the cut-out rounds will all be the same thickness, approximately ¾ inch.

Bake the batter as directed in its recipe, but note that it will take much less time than thicker layer cakes.

When the cake is done, place the pan on a wire rack and let cool completely. To unmold the cake, run a thin knife around the inside edge of the pan to release the cake. Place an 18 by 13-inch sheet of parchment paper over the top of the cake. Place a large cutting board (the same size or larger than the pan) or another half-sheet pan, upturned with the bottom of the pan against the parchment, over the cake. Holding the pan and the board together, invert them. Lift off the pan, then carefully peel off the baking mat (if you have used parchment paper, take extra care not to tear the cake). The cake is now ready to cut into rounds for stacking. Note that the Chocolate Orange Cake on page 148 is quite tender, and must be refrigerated for an hour or so to firm before cutting and stacking.

Using an 8 by 3-inch entremet ring as a template, cut out two 8-inch rounds of cake from opposite corners of the sheet cake. Cut out two half-rounds of cake from the remaining cake, and save the scraps (see page 161, figure 1). The two half-rounds will be put together, with the scraps cut to fill in the gap, to become the center cake layer. When the cake is filled, no one will ever notice the pieced-together layer.

Building Buttercream Layer Cakes Now that your beautifully even layers are baked, it's time to stack them, with the filling, in the metal cake ring. Triple-layer cakes provide a nice proportion of cake to frosting and filling. I prefer an 8 by 3-inch bottomless metal cake ring, but you can also use a springform pan with the same dimensions.

As the cake is built, each layer is brushed with simple syrup mixed with liqueur. (If you wish, use flavoring syrup or coffee instead of the liqueur; for example, substitute hazelnut syrup for Frangelico liqueur.) Génoise is wonderfully spongy and soaks up the syrup, which adds moisture and flavor to the cake. Don't be surprised at the amount of syrup used—without it, the génoise would be a little too dry. With other cakes that are moister, the syrup is simply used to add another flavoring component, and less syrup is needed.

Start by placing the cake ring on a quarter- or half-sheet pan. Insert an 8-inch-diameter cardboard round, white side up, in the bottom of the ring—you may have to trim it slightly for a perfect fit. The cardboard round is optional with a springform pan.

Insert a whole cake layer into the ring. Drizzle and brush the cake layer with about one-third of the syrup. Spread the filling on top with an offset spatula. Next, insert the two partial cake layers, and fill in the gap with pieces of the reserved cake scraps. Top with a smaller cardboard round and press gently to even out the layers and compress them slightly. Remove the cardboard round, and repeat the application of the syrup and filling. Finish with the final whole cake layer, and gently press with the smaller cardboard round and remove the cardboard round. Drizzle and brush on the remaining syrup. Spread a layer of the buttercream over the top of the cake. Slowly and carefully lift up and remove the ring. (If the cake has a very soft filling, as does the Chocolate Truffle Cake on page 151, keep the ring in place until the cake is chilled.)

The stacked and frosted cake is then refrigerated for about one hour to firm up and set the layers. This will make the cake much easier to completely frost later. If you are not planning to serve the cake in the next two hours, loosely cover it with plastic wrap after the frosting is firm.

Frosting the Cake Two tools will make frosting your cake a breeze: a cake-decorating turntable and a large offset metal spatula with an 8-inch blade. The turntable lifts the cake and lets you rotate it to facilitate frosting on all sides. You can improvise with a wide, upside-down bowl or coffee can, but the turntable is much more stable and a good investment for serious bakers. And the offset spatula helps apply the frosting at a more comfortable angle than a straight spatula.

Place the cake with its cardboard round on the turntable. If directed to do so, be sure to reserve some of the buttercream. (More than once, I have used all of the frosting on the cake, then come up short for the final decorating.) Using an offset spatula, start by spreading a thin layer of buttercream on the top of the cake to smooth the surface. Now thinly spread more on the sides of the cake, being sure to fill in gaps between the layers. Don't try to apply it all in one step—spread a few tablespoons at a time, turning the cake for easy access. (This is called a crumb coat. It will hold the crumbs in place when the cake gets its final frosting. The final layer of buttercream will be applied later, after the crumb coat sets.) To smooth the ridge of frosting where the top and sides of the cake meet, lightly swipe the spatula, held just above the top of the cake, from the ridge toward the center of the cake in a series of quick movements around the cake circumference. Refrigerate the cake until the frosting sets, about 15 minutes.

For the final frosting, spread the remaining buttercream over the top and sides of the cake in a thicker layer, and carefully smooth out the ridge on top of the cake as before.

Transfer the cake (slip the offset spatula under the cardboard round to help lift the cake) to the serving platter. Return the cake to the refrigerator and let the buttercream chill and set, about 15 minutes.

The cake is now ready for its final decoration and garnish. This is the moment I enjoy the most, as I decide how to artistically conclude my creation. Every cake has its own personality.

If you plan to decorate with buttercream flourishes, transfer the reserved frosting to a pastry bag fitted with the desired tip. Personally, I am a fan of simple frosting decorations, and use only a small collection of tips to create basic but refined designs (see page 139 for examples). Don't be anxious about decorating; just fill up the bag, experiment, and have a good time. I never took a cake-decorating lesson in my life. Practice by piping onto a piece of parchment paper, then scrape it off and start over again.

Tips to Try Open-star tip with a ⁵⁄₁₆-inch-diameter (such as Ateco #823): Use for individual rosettes and scallops or running borders • Leaf tip (such as Ateco #70): Use to make traditional leaves, or elongate the leaf shape to make an interesting swag • Plain tip with a ⅛-inch diameter (such as Ateco #4): Use for beading • Ribbon tip (such as Ateco #48): Use for borders and ribbons • Multiopening tip (such as Ateco #133): Use for multilinear designs, including tiny mum-like flowers.

My favorite garnishes are fresh flowers. Be sure that they are edible and pollen- and chemical-free.

Vanilla Génoise

Makes one 18 by 13-inch sheet cake, enough for one 3-layer cake

....

A cookbook about fine baking would be incomplete without a recipe for génoise, the workhorse of classic French baking (even though its name suggests that it was probably invented by a Genoese or at least an Italian baker). Most American-style cakes have a base of creamed butter and sugar and are leavened with baking powder or baking soda. Génoise gets its lift purely from beaten eggs. Some bakeries make their génoise on the dry side, but mine has plenty of extra yolks to add flavor and moisture. It is a favorite snack at the bakery; this is as good as génoise gets, even without any buttercream.

BAKER'S NOTE: The fluffy consistency of the beaten egg and sugar mixture is one key to a perfect génoise. Heating the egg mixture over hot water before beating will help the mixture expand to the proper thickness. The correct temperature is 118°F, which can be determined with an instant-read thermometer.

5 tablespoons unsalted butter	Seeds from 1 Plumped Vanilla Bean (page 295) or 1 teaspoon pure vanilla extract
5 large eggs plus 5 large egg yolks	
1 cup superfine sugar	1 cup pastry or unbleached cake flour

1 Position the rack in the center of the oven and preheat to 350°F. Line the bottom of a half-sheet pan with a silicone baking mat, or lightly butter the pan and line the bottom with parchment paper.

2 Melt the butter in a small saucepan over medium heat. Transfer to a small bowl. Let stand until tepid, about 5 minutes.

3 Bring a large saucepan of water to a simmer over high heat. Reduce the heat to very low to maintain the simmer. Whisk the eggs, yolks, and sugar together in the bowl of a heavy-duty stand mixer. Place over the water (the bottom of the bowl should not touch the water) and whisk constantly until the sugar is completely dissolved and the mixture is very warm to the touch (an instant-read thermometer will read 118°F), about 1 minute. Do not overheat the mixture.

4 Attach the bowl to the mixer and fit with the whisk attachment. Add the vanilla. Beat the mixture on high speed until it is almost quadrupled in volume, very pale yellow, and fluffy, about

5 minutes. (If you are using a handheld electric mixer, this will take at least 6 minutes.) You'll know that the right consistency has been reached when, if you lift the whisk attachment a couple of inches above the bowl, the egg mixture creates a thick ribbon that falls back on itself and holds its shape on the surface of the mixture for at least 5 seconds before sinking (figure 1). Remove the bowl from the mixer.

5   Sift the flour through a medium-mesh wire sieve onto a piece of parchment paper. Return the flour to the sieve. In four equal additions, sift the flour over the egg mixture and use a balloon whisk to fold it in (figure 2). Keep the batter as light and fluffy as possible; handle it gently. Transfer about

one-fourth of the batter into a medium bowl; add the butter and fold in with a balloon whisk (figure 3). Pour this mixture back into the remaining batter, and gently fold in with the whisk.

6　Pour the batter into the half-sheet pan and smooth it evenly with an offset metal spatula, being sure that the batter fills the corners of the pan (figures 4, 5, and 6). Bake until the top of the cake is golden brown and it springs back when pressed gently with your finger in the center, 15 to 20 minutes. Transfer to a wire rack and let cool completely in the pan.

7　Run a sharp knife around the inside of the pan to release the cake. Place a cutting board larger than the pan over it. Invert the pan and board together. Remove the pan. Carefully release the baking mat around the perimeter of the cake, then, starting at a short end, roll up the mat and remove it. (The cake can be stored at room temperature, covered with parchment paper and then plastic wrap, for up to 1 day. The parchment paper keeps the cake from sticking to the plastic.) You are ready to assemble the cake.

Hazelnut Génoise

Makes one 15 by 10-inch cake

························

While this is a variation of the vanilla génoise, it has enough substantial changes to necessitate its having its own recipe. It is the cake for the Hazelnut-Espresso Roulade (page 155). Note that this is a smaller recipe than the vanilla génoise, and is baked in a 15 by 10 by 1-inch jelly-roll pan.

BAKER'S NOTE: Use an electric coffee grinder (with a propeller-type blade, not burrs) to grind the toasted hazelnuts into a fine powder. A food processor or blender doesn't chop them finely enough. Also, see the Baker's Note for vanilla génoise (page 143).

4 tablespoons (½ stick) unsalted butter	*4 large eggs plus 4 large egg yolks*
⅓ cup (1¼ ounces) hazelnuts, toasted and skinned (page 5)	*¾ cup plus 1 tablespoon superfine sugar*
¾ cup plus 2 tablespoons pastry or unbleached cake flour, divided	*Seeds from 1 Plumped Vanilla Bean (page 295) or 1 teaspoon pure vanilla extract*

1   Position the rack in the center of the oven and preheat to 350°F. Lightly butter a 15 by 10 by 1-inch jelly-roll pan and line the bottom with parchment paper.

2   Melt the butter in a small saucepan over medium heat. Transfer to a small bowl. Let stand until tepid, about 5 minutes.

3   Grind half of the hazelnuts with 1 tablespoon of the flour in an electric coffee grinder until the mixture is very finely chopped, almost a powder. Transfer to a bowl. Repeat with the remaining hazelnuts and 1 tablespoon of the flour. Transfer to the bowl and stir in the remaining ¾ cup flour.

4   Bring a large saucepan of water to a simmer over high heat. Reduce the heat to very low to maintain the simmer. Whisk the eggs, yolks, and sugar together in the bowl of a heavy-duty stand mixer. Place over the water (the bottom of the bowl should not touch the water) and whisk constantly until the sugar is completely dissolved and the mixture is very warm to the touch (an instant-read thermometer will read 118°F), about 1 minute. Do not overheat the mixture.

5 Attach the bowl to the mixer and fit with the whisk attachment. Add the vanilla. Beat on high speed until the mixture is almost quadrupled in volume, very pale yellow, and fluffy, about 5 minutes. (If you are using a handheld electric mixer, this will take at least 6 minutes.) You'll know that the right consistency has been reached when, if you lift the whisk attachment a couple of inches above the bowl, the egg mixture creates a thick ribbon that falls back on itself and holds its shape on the surface of the mixture for at least 5 seconds before sinking (see page 144, figure 1). Remove the bowl from the mixer.

6 Transfer the flour-nut mixture to a medium-mesh wire sieve. In four equal additions, sift the flour-nut mixture over the egg mixture and use a balloon whisk to fold it in (see page 144, figure 2). The idea here is to keep the batter as light and fluffy as possible, so handle it gently. If any ground hazelnuts remain in the sieve, add them to the egg mixture. Transfer about one-fourth of the batter into a medium bowl; add the butter and fold in with a balloon whisk (see page 144, figure 3). Pour this mixture back into the remaining batter, and gently fold in with the whisk.

7 Pour the batter into the half-sheet pan and smooth it evenly with an offset metal spatula, being sure that the batter fills the corners of the pan (see page 144, figures 4, 5, and 6). Bake until the top of the cake is golden brown and it springs back when pressed gently with your finger in the center, about 20 minutes. Transfer to a wire rack and let cool completely in the pan.

8 Run a sharp knife around the inside of the pan to release the cake. Place a cutting board larger than the pan over it. Invert the pan and board together. Remove the pan. Carefully release the parchment paper around the perimeter of the cake, then, starting at a short end, roll up and remove the paper. You are ready to assemble the roulade.

Chocolate Orange Cake

Makes one 18 by 13-inch sheet cake

....

This unusual cake batter, which has heavy cream as its fat instead of the much more common butter, is based on a recipe from Maida Heatter—a superstar of the baking world. This recipe is used in the Chocolate Truffle Cake (page 151) and Chocolate Orange Tiramisù (page 243).

BAKER'S NOTE: This cake has a very tender crumb that can break when handling. Refrigerate the un-molded sheet cake until the cake is chilled and the cut rounds will be sturdier for stacking.

1¼ cups unbleached all-purpose flour	1½ cups heavy cream
1 cup superfine sugar	Grated zest of ½ orange
½ cup Dutch-processed cocoa powder	¾ teaspoon pure vanilla extract
2 teaspoons baking powder	2 large eggs, beaten
¼ teaspoon fine sea salt	

1   Position a rack in the center of the oven and preheat to 350°F. Line a half-sheet pan with a silicone baking mat, or lightly butter the pan and line the bottom with parchment paper.

2   Sift the flour, sugar, cocoa, baking powder, and salt together. Combine the cream, orange zest, and vanilla in the bowl of a heavy-duty stand mixer. Attach the bowl to the mixer and fit with the whisk attachment. Whip on medium speed until the cream holds its shape, just before soft peaks begin to form. Gradually beat in the eggs—the mixture will thin somewhat. Change to the paddle attachment. On low speed, add the flour mixture, and beat until smooth, scraping down the sides of the bowl, about 1 minute. Because the cream is chilled, the batter thickens to the consistency of very stiff frosting. Distribute the batter in 5 large dollops in the pan, 1 in each corner and 1 in the center. Spread evenly with an offset metal spatula.

3   Bake until the cake springs back when pressed gently with your finger in the center, about 15 minutes. Transfer to a wire rack and let cool completely. Run a knife around the inside of the half-sheet pan to loosen the cake. Place a large piece of parchment paper over the cake, then top with a large cutting board. Invert the pan and board together, and remove the pan and mat. Cover the cake with plastic wrap and refrigerate for at least 1 hour and up to 1 day before using.

Pâte à Choux

Makes about 2 cups dough, enough for 24 profiteroles or 12 éclairs

....

P âte à choux, which American bakers may know simply as cream puff dough, is very unusual. While most of the other doughs in the French baking lexicon are about layering chilled butter with flour, this one is prepared from ingredients that are actually boiled together. It is an important dough to master, as it is used to create the crisp, airy shells for éclairs and profiteroles and other treats, both sweet and savory.

BAKER'S NOTE: *Pâte à choux* means "cabbage pastry" in modern French, but it has nothing to do with vegetables. *Choux* probably derived from *chaud*, or "hot" in French. • Don't be afraid to bake pastries made with *pâte à choux* until they are golden brown, or they will collapse during cooling. Use this dough to make the Éclairs with White Chocolate Cream (page 169) or Butter Pecan Profiteroles (page 261).

½ cup plus 1 tablespoon whole milk	*¼ teaspoon fine sea salt*
½ cup plus 1 tablespoon water	*1¼ cups unbleached all-purpose flour*
7 tablespoons unsalted butter, cut into ½-inch cubes	*4 large eggs, at room temperature, beaten*
1 teaspoon granulated sugar	

1 Combine the milk, water, butter, sugar, and salt in a heavy-bottomed medium saucepan. Bring to a boil over medium heat, stirring often with a wooden spoon to help dissolve the butter. The butter must be completely melted by the time the liquid boils, so adjust the heat as needed.

2 Immediately dump all of the flour at once into the saucepan. Using the wooden spoon, willfully and briskly stir to make the mixture come together into a thick paste. (I say willfully because the mixture will become lumpy if it is stirred slowly or weakly. This isn't a thin sauce—really get in there and stir.) Reduce the heat to medium-low. Continue stirring (and even mashing) the dough for at least 1 minute until it resembles a blob of mashed potatoes (figure 1). A thin film will form on the bottom of the pan, which is okay, but adjust the heat as needed to keep it from scorching. The idea here is to force some of the excess steam from the dough.

3 Transfer the hot dough to the bowl of a heavy-duty stand mixer fitted with the paddle attachment. Beat on low speed for 30 seconds to slightly cool the dough and force out more steam. Increase the

speed to medium. A tablespoon or two at a time, add the beaten eggs, letting each addition absorb into the dough before adding more. With each addition, the dough will break up, and then come together with beating. When all of the eggs have been added, increase the speed to high and beat until the dough has a sheen, about 15 seconds (figure 2). The dough will be warm, elastic, and very sticky. Use the dough immediately, because cooled dough will not puff to its full expansion. It is usually transferred to a pastry bag and piped for the most uniform shapes (figure 3).

Chocolate Truffle Cake

Makes 12 servings

....

An edible masterpiece of chocolate, with a subtle orange flavor, this cake is the perfect finale to a very special dinner. Layers of dark chocolate cake alternate with whipped ganache, then the cake is coated with a shiny glaze.

BAKER'S NOTE: It is important to mask the top of the cake with whipped ganache to give it a smooth surface so the final glaze is equally smooth. After the cake is chilled and the ring is removed, smooth the sides of the cake. • The Valrhona chocolate pearls (see Sources, page 297) make a very elegant finish to this cake. Or use your imagination to come up with alternatives.

Chocolate Orange Cake (page 148)

Orange Syrup

⅔ cup Simple Syrup (page 293) • *1 tablespoon orange-flavored liqueur, such as Grand Marnier*

Whipped Ganache

2¼ cups heavy cream, divided

14 ounces semisweet or bittersweet chocolate (no more than 62 percent cacao), finely chopped

Chocolate Glaze

¼ cup heavy cream

2 tablespoons superfine sugar

2 tablespoons freshly brewed espresso or 1½ teaspoons instant espresso powder dissolved in 2 tablespoons boiling water

8 ounces semisweet or bittersweet chocolate (no more than 62 percent cacao), finely chopped

2 tablespoons light corn syrup

Chocolate pearls, for garnish

1   Assemble the cake at least 1 day before serving so the layers can firm in the refrigerator.

2   To make the orange syrup, stir the simple syrup and liqueur together.

3   To make the whipped ganache, bring ¾ cup plus 2 tablespoons of the cream to a simmer in a medium saucepan over medium heat. Put the chocolate in a heatproof bowl. Add the hot cream and let stand until the chocolate softens, about 3 minutes. Whisk until smooth. Let cool until tepid but still fluid, about 15 minutes.

4   Whip the remaining 1¼ cups plus 2 tablespoons cream in the chilled bowl of a heavy-duty stand mixer fitted with the whisk attachment on medium speed only until the cream holds its shape, just before soft peaks begin to form. Pour the whipped cream over the cooled chocolate mixture and fold together with a silicone spatula. Do not overmix, or the ganache will be grainy. Transfer ½ cup of the ganache to a small bowl and set aside.

5   To assemble the cake, transfer the cake, with its cutting board, to the work surface. Using an 8 by 3-inch metal cake ring as a template, cut out two 8-inch rounds of cake from opposite corners of the chocolate cake. Cut out two half-rounds of cake from the remaining cake, and save the scraps (see page 161, figure 1). The two half-rounds will be put together, with the reserved scraps cut to fill in the gap, to become the center cake layer.

6   Place the cake ring on a half-sheet pan. Insert an 8-inch cardboard round, white side up, inside the ring. Place a whole cake layer in the ring, and drizzle and brush with about 3½ tablespoons of the syrup. Top with half of the whipped ganache filling, and spread evenly. Top with the partial cake layers, and fill in the gap with trimmings of the reserved cake scraps. Top with a smaller cardboard round and press gently to level the layers. Remove the cardboard round. Drizzle and brush the layer with another 3½ tablespoons syrup. Spread with the rest of the filling. Add the final cake layer, cover with the smaller cardboard round, and press gently to level the layers (see page 161, figures 3 and 4). Remove the cardboard round. Drizzle and brush the cake with the remaining syrup (see page 161, figure 5). Using a small offset spatula, spread the reserved ½ cup filling over the top cake layer to make a smooth surface that fills any small holes. Refrigerate the cake until completely chilled, at least 6 hours or overnight.

7   Remove the cake from the refrigerator. Place on the work surface. Rinse a kitchen towel under hot water and wring it out. Wrap the hot, moist towel around the sides of the cake ring, being careful not to get water on the top of the cake. Let stand for about 30 seconds. Lift up on the ring to remove it. (If it doesn't remove easily, moisten the towel again and reapply to the sides.) Place the cake on a small round wire cake rack set on a half-sheet pan. Using a small offset spatula rinsed under hot water and dried, smooth the sides of the cake to even out the exposed ganache between the layers. Refrigerate the cake on the rack until the outer layer of ganache is very firm, about 30 minutes.

8   Meanwhile, make the glaze. Bring the cream, espresso, and sugar just to a simmer in a small saucepan over medium heat. Remove from the heat and add the chocolate. Let stand until the chocolate softens, about 3 minutes. Add the corn syrup and stir well with a silicone spatula until the chocolate is melted and the glaze is smooth. Do not whisk, as this will create bubbles that will mar the surface of the glaze. Strain into a 2-cup glass measuring cup. Let stand until tepid but still liquid and pourable, about 15 minutes.

9   Transfer the cake on its wire cake rack to a room-temperature half-sheet pan. About 1 inch from the top edge of the cake, pour some of the glaze in a circle around the outside edge of the cake. Pour the remaining glaze in the center of the cake. Using a large offset metal spatula, quickly smooth the glaze over the top of the cake, letting the excess run down the sides. If needed, use the spatula to scrape up the glaze on the pan, and pour it back over the top of the cake to fill in any unglazed areas. Transfer the cake on the rack to a clean half-sheet pan. Refrigerate until the glaze sets, at least 1 hour. (The cake can be made up to 1 day ahead, covered with a cake dome, and refrigerated.)

10 Lightly press small handfuls of the chocolate pearls along the bottom edge of the cake. Transfer the cake to the serving dish, and sprinkle more along the top edge of the cake, letting them fall randomly on the plate. Slice the cake with a sharp knife (dipped in hot water and wiped dry before each cut), and serve.

Hazelnut-Espresso Roulade

Makes 10 servings

....

Not all party cakes are baked in layers. Roulades are a nice change, each slice revealing a swirl of cake and buttercream. I am extremely fond of the flavors here, with the toasty nuts complementing the roasted taste of the espresso. The cake has a sophisticated look that is well suited to an afternoon party, especially when served on an attractive oblong serving platter.

Espresso Syrup

½ cup Simple Syrup (page 293)	1½ tablespoons brewed espresso or
1½ tablespoons hazelnut liqueur, such as Frangelico	½ teaspoon instant espresso powder dissolved in 1½ tablespoons boiling water
Hazelnut Génoise (page 146)	Toasted and coarsely chopped hazelnuts (page 5), for garnish
Hazelnut Buttercream (page 284)	

1 To make the syrup, stir the simple syrup, liqueur, and espresso together.

2 Put the hazelnut génoise, with the side where the parchment paper was removed facing down, on an 18 by 13-inch piece of parchment paper. Brush with the syrup. Spread ½ cup of the buttercream over the cake, leaving a ½-inch border along the top edge. Starting at the top, roll the cake, jelly-roll style. Move the roulade, seam side down, to the center of the parchment paper, and fold the parchment paper on top. Hold the edge of a yardstick along the long side of the roulade. Holding the yardstick securely, pull the top layer of the parchment paper under the yardstick to tighten the paper and lightly compress the roulade. Keeping the paper taut, roll up the cake in the parchment and refrigerate for 15 to 20 minutes to chill slightly.

3 Slide the roulade onto an oblong serving platter and remove the parchment. Slip a few strips of clean parchment paper just underneath the roulade to keep the platter clean when applying the buttercream. Transfer about 1 cup of the buttercream to a pastry bag fitted with a $5/16$-inch-diameter open-star pastry tip, such as Ateco #823. Using an offset spatula, spread some of the remaining buttercream in a thin layer over the roulade. Refrigerate until the buttercream is set, about 20 minutes.

4 Spread the remaining buttercream over the roulade, using long strokes next to each other to give the surface a striated appearance. Slide the parchment strips out from under the roulade. Using the buttercream in the pastry bag, pipe alternating swags down the top of the roulade. Sprinkle the chopped hazelnuts on the swags and around the bottom edge of the roulade. Refrigerate again until the buttercream is firm, about 20 minutes. (The roulade can be refrigerated for up to 1 day.) Remove from the refrigerator 1 hour before serving. Slice the cake with a sharp knife (clean between slices), and serve.

Lemon-Raspberry Cake

Makes 8 servings

....

This is the cake that I recommend most frequently when asked to create a wedding cake. It has the lively tang of raspberries and lemon (always refreshing after a big meal), and a lovely pale buttercream frosting. When it comes to cake decorating, each baker has an individual, personal style, and mine falls into the "less is more" category. This cake is finished just with buttercream leaves and a simple arrangement of your favorite flowers. Please be sure that the flowers are edible and pollen- and chemical-free. Candied rose petals or candied violets are a nice alternative to the fresh flowers.

Two 6-ounce containers fresh raspberries   *¼ cup Simple Syrup (page 293)*

Vanilla Génoise (page 143)   *1 cup Lemon Curd (page 287)*

Lemon-Rose Buttercream (page 284)   *Edible flowers, such as freesia, for garnish*

1   One at a time, split and open up each raspberry like a book. Place the raspberries on a paper towel–lined half-sheet pan. (The split raspberries make the filling layer more even.)

2   To assemble the cake, place the rectangular-shaped génoise on a work surface. Using an 8 by 3-inch metal cake ring, cut out two 8-inch rounds of génoise from opposite corners of the rectangle, cutting close to the edge of the rectangle. Cut out two half-rounds from the remaining génoise, and save the scraps (figure 1). The two half-rounds will be put together, with the scraps cut to fill in the gap, to become the center cake layer.

3   Place an 8 by 3-inch metal cake ring on a half-sheet pan. Insert an 8-inch cardboard round, white side up, in the bottom of the ring. Fit a pastry bag with a ⁷⁄₁₆-inch-diameter plain pastry tip, such as Ateco #805. Fill the bag with about ⅔ cup of the buttercream. Place a whole cake layer in the cake ring. Drizzle and brush the cake with about ¼ cup of the simple syrup. Pipe a ring of buttercream around the circumference of the cake. Using a small offset metal spatula, spread ½ cup of the lemon curd in the center of the cake layer, up to the buttercream ring. Layer half of the raspberries, cut sides down, on the lemon curd. Top with the two partial layers, and fill in the center gap with trimmings of the reserved cake scraps. Place a smaller cardboard round on the cake layer and press gently to level the layers. Remove the cardboard round. Drizzle and brush the layer with another ¼ cup of

the syrup, and repeat the filling procedure with another buttercream ring and the remaining lemon curd and raspberries (figure 2). Return any buttercream that is left in the pastry bag to the bowl. Add the final cake layer, cover with the cardboard round, and press gently to level the layers (figures 3 and 4). Remove the cardboard round. Drizzle and brush the top layer with the remaining syrup (figure 5). (Ideally, before you frost it, the top of the cake will almost reach the top edge of the ring.) Place about 1 cup of the buttercream onto the cake (figure 6). Using a large offset metal spatula, spread so that it is even with the top edge of the ring, and sweep off the excess so that it is very smooth and even (figure 7). Carefully lift off the metal cake ring (figures 8 and 9). Refrigerate the cake on the pan until the buttercream is firm, about 1 hour.

4   Place the cake on a cake-decorating stand. Spread another thin layer of buttercream on the top of the cake, then frost the sides. Refrigerate until the buttercream is set, about 15 minutes. Apply a final, thicker coat on the top and sides of the cake. To smooth the ridge of frosting where the top and sides of the cake meet, lightly swipe the spatula, held just above the top of the cake, from the ridge toward the center of the cake, in a series of quick movements around the cake circumference. Refrigerate the cake until the buttercream is set, about 20 minutes.

5   Stir the remaining buttercream well with a silicone spatula. Transfer the buttercream to a pastry bag fitted with a leaf tip, such as Ateco #70. Pipe a ring of leaves, alternating the direction of the leaves from left to right, around the upper edge of the cake. Transfer the cake to a serving dish and repeat the leaf design on the lower edge of the cake where it meets the serving dish. Garnish the cake with the flowers. (The cake can be served immediately, or refrigerated, uncovered, for up to 1 day. Let stand at room temperature for 1 hour before serving.) Slice the cake with a sharp knife (wipe clean between slices), and serve.

Raspberries and Cream Charlotte

Makes 10 servings

....

Acharlotte is one of the best reasons I know for baking ladyfingers. This French dessert, a creamy mousse encased in light ladyfingers, is the perfect ending to a special dinner party. Raspberries make a particularly enticing mousse for the charlotte, with a bright hot pink color adding to the visual appeal of the dessert.

BAKER'S NOTE: A mound of fresh raspberries tops the charlotte, but you can also use a mixture of any summer berries (such as raspberries, blueberries, strawberries, and blackberries) or a mélange of sliced peaches and berries. • For a gorgeous finishing touch, tie a 2½-inch-wide ribbon around the charlotte and make a bow. You will need at least 1 yard of ribbon.

24 Ladyfingers (page 213)

Filling

Five 6-ounce containers fresh raspberries	*1 cup superfine sugar, divided*
2 teaspoons fresh lemon juice	*1⅔ cups heavy cream*
5 teaspoons unflavored gelatin powder	*Seeds from ¼ Plumped Vanilla Bean (page 295) or*
¼ cup cold water	*¼ teaspoon pure vanilla extract*

Topping

Five 6-ounce containers fresh raspberries • *Confectioners' sugar, for garnish*

1 Line a half-sheet pan with parchment paper. Place an 8 by 3-inch metal cake ring on the pan. Insert an 8-inch cardboard round, white side up, in the bottom of the ring.

2 On a clean work surface, evenly line up the ladyfingers next to one another with their sides touching. Cut one rounded end from each ladyfinger so the cookies are 3 inches long, reserving the trimmings. Stand a ladyfinger, rounded tip up, inside the ring, with the rounded side facing out and the flat side of the ladyfinger facing toward the center. To help the ladyfinger stand, place one of the small cookie trimmings against the bottom end to support it, and repeat with each ladyfinger. Continue with enough ladyfingers to line the sides of the pan. Line the bottom of the pan with the remaining ladyfingers, cut to fit, and the trimmings.

3   To make the filling, coarsely puree the raspberries and lemon juice in a food processor. Rub the puree through a fine-mesh sieve into a bowl. Discard the seeds. You should have 2½ cups puree.

4   Sprinkle the gelatin over the water in a small bowl and let stand until the gelatin absorbs the water, about 5 minutes. Bring the puree and ½ cup sugar to a simmer in a medium saucepan over medium heat, stirring often. Remove from the heat. Add the softened gelatin to the hot puree and stir until the gelatin is completely dissolved, about 1 minute.

5   Transfer the puree to a medium stainless steel bowl set in a larger bowl filled with ice cubes and water. Let stand, stirring occasionally, until the puree is cold and begins to hold its shape. Remove the bowl from the ice bath before the puree sets too much.

6   Combine the cream, the remaining ½ cup sugar, and the vanilla in the chilled bowl of a heavy-duty stand mixer. Attach the bowl to the mixer and fit with the whisk attachment. Whip just until soft peaks form. Stir about one-fourth of the whipped cream into the raspberry puree to lighten it, then fold in the remaining cream. Pour the raspberry filling into the lined ring and smooth the top. Cover with plastic wrap and refrigerate the charlotte until it is set, at least 6 hours or overnight.

7   Remove the pan from the refrigerator. Lift up on the ring to remove it. Arrange some of the raspberries in a single layer on the filling, then top with the remaining berries. Sift confectioners' sugar over the top. Slice the charlotte with a knife (wipe clean between slices), and serve chilled.

Coconut and Mango Cake

Makes 8 to 10 servings

....

Coconut cake is one of the most beloved of all American desserts. My version is more sophisticated than most, with the fragrant, tropical flavor of mango balancing the flaky texture of the coconut. It is constructed of génoise layers, soaked with mango liqueur syrup, and stacked with fresh mango and buttercream. Of course, it's finished with a generous coating of coconut.

Mango-Orange Syrup

¼ cup Simple Syrup (page 293) • 1 tablespoon fresh orange juice • 1 tablespoon mango liqueur

Vanilla Génoise (page 143)	*Mango Buttercream (page 284)*
2 ripe mangoes, pitted, peeled, and cut into very thin slices	*1½ cups sweetened coconut flakes*

1 To make the syrup, combine the simple syrup, orange juice, and liqueur in a small bowl.

2 To assemble the cake, place the rectangular-shaped génoise on a work surface. Using an 8 by 3-inch metal cake ring, cut out two 8-inch rounds of génoise from opposite corners of the rectangle, cutting close to the edge of the rectangle. Cut out two half-rounds from the remaining génoise, and save the scraps (see page 161, figure 1). The two half-rounds will be put together, with the scraps cut to fill in the gap, to become the center cake layer.

3 Place an 8 by 3-inch metal cake ring on a half-sheet pan. Insert an 8-inch cardboard round, white side up, in the bottom of the ring. Fit a pastry bag with a ⁷⁄₁₆-inch-diameter plain pastry tip, such as Ateco #805. Fill the bag with about ⅔ cup of the buttercream. Place a whole cake layer in the cake ring. Drizzle and brush the cake layer with about ¼ cup of the syrup. Spread with about ½ cup of the buttercream on the top. Pipe a thin ring of frosting around the circumference of the cake. Arrange half of the mango slices, overlapping them slightly, over the buttercream. Top with the two partial cake layers, and fill in the center gap with trimmings of the reserved cake scraps. Place a smaller cardboard round on the cake layer and press gently to level the layers. Remove the cardboard round. Drizzle and brush the layer with another ¼ cup of the syrup, and repeat the filling

procedure by spreading another ½ cup of buttercream on top, pipe another ring of buttercream, and top with the remaining mango slices (see page 161, figure 2). Add the final cake layer, cover with the cardboard round, and press gently to level the layers (see page 161, figures 3 and 4). Remove the cardboard round. Return any buttercream that is left in the pastry bag to the bowl. Brush the top layer with the remaining syrup (see page 161, figure 5). (Ideally, the top of the cake will almost reach the top edge of the ring.) Place about 1 cup of the buttercream onto the cake (see page 161, figure 6). Using a large offset metal spatula, spread the buttercream so it is even with the top edge of the ring, and sweep off the excess frosting so the buttercream is very smooth and even (see page 161, figure 7). Carefully lift off the metal cake ring (see page 161, figures 8 and 9). Refrigerate the cake on the pan until the buttercream is firm, about 1 hour.

4   Place the cake on a cake-decorating stand. Apply a final, thicker coat of buttercream on the top and sides of the cake. To smooth the ridge of frosting where the top and sides of the cake meet, lightly swipe the spatula, held just above the top of the cake, from the ridge toward the center of the cake, in a series of quick movements around the cake circumference.

5   Generously sprinkle the coconut on the top of the cake, and gently press handfuls of the coconut against the buttercream on the sides to coat, letting the coconut that doesn't adhere fall onto the work surface. Gather up the fallen coconut and continue pressing it onto the buttercream until all of the coconut is used. (The cake can be served immediately, or refrigerated, uncovered, for up to 1 day. Let stand at room temperature for 1 hour before serving.) Slice the cake with a very sharp, thin knife (clean between slices), and serve.

Mille-Feuille with Summer Berries

Makes 6 servings

....

Mille-feuille translates to "thousand leaves" in French, and refers to the multiple, tissue-thin layers in puff pastry. In this version, the pastry is baked into golden brown rectangles, and stacked with a colorful assortment of juicy summer berries and vanilla-flecked pastry cream.

BAKER'S NOTE: This pastry is weighted with a second pan to create a crisp but not puffy pastry for layering with the filling and fruit. To fit all of the pastry squares on the half-sheet pan, flip the pan over and arrange them on the underside of the pan. They will barely fit at first, but they will shrink when baked.

Unbleached all-purpose flour, for rolling the dough

½ recipe Puff Pastry (page 20)

Two 6-ounce containers fresh raspberries

One 6-ounce container fresh blackberries

1 cup fresh blueberries

1 ripe kiwi, peeled, cut in half lengthwise, and sliced ¼ inch thick

Pastry Cream (page 286)

1 cup heavy cream

Confectioners' sugar, for garnish

1   On a lightly floured work surface, roll the puff pastry into an 18 by 13-inch sheet. Using a yardstick and a pizza wheel, neatly trim the edges. Fold into thirds and refrigerate to chill and relax the dough, about 15 minutes.

2   Unfold the pastry onto a lightly floured work surface. Pierce it well with a fork. Using the yardstick and the pizza wheel, cut it lengthwise into thirds. Then cut it crosswise into sixths to make 18 rectangles. Overlap the rectangles on a half-sheet pan, and refrigerate for 30 minutes.

3   Meanwhile, position a rack in the center of the oven and preheat to 400°F. Line the underside of a half-sheet pan with parchment paper.

4   Arrange the pastry rectangles very closely on the pan. Bake for 15 minutes. Top the pastries with a piece of parchment paper and a second half-sheet pan to weigh them down. Continue baking until the rectangles are crisp and golden brown, about 15 minutes more. Remove the second half-sheet pan and the parchment paper. Cool completely. Using a serrated knife, trim the edges of the baked pastries to expose the flaky layers.

5   Carefully combine the raspberries, blackberries, blueberries, and kiwi in a bowl. Refrigerate until ready to serve.

6   Put the pastry cream in a medium bowl. Whip the heavy cream in a chilled medium bowl with a handheld electric mixer on high speed (or use a balloon whisk). Stir about one-fourth of the whipped cream into the pastry cream to lighten it, then fold in the remaining whipped cream.

7   For each serving, place a puff pastry strip on a dessert plate. Top with a dollop of the pastry cream and a spoonful of fruit. Top with a second pastry strip, more pastry cream, and more fruit. Finish with a third pastry strip. Sift confectioners' sugar over the top. Serve at once.

Éclairs with White Chocolate Cream

Makes 12 éclairs

....

There was a time when every bakery made éclairs, the crisp, airy strips of *pâte à choux* stuffed with pastry or whipped cream and topped with chocolate glaze. My version uses two kinds of chocolate—white in the filling, and dark for the glaze. Every éclair lover has a particular way of attacking the pastry. Do you pick it up with your fingers, or do you carefully cut it into pieces with a fork and knife? What gets eaten first—the filling or the top shell?

Pâte à Choux (page 149)

White Chocolate Cream

1½ cups heavy cream, divided • 6 ounces white chocolate, finely chopped

Chocolate-Espresso Glaze

¼ cup heavy cream

1 tablespoon granulated sugar

1 teaspoon instant espresso powder dissolved in 2 teaspoons boiling water

1 tablespoon water

4 ounces semisweet or bittersweet chocolate (no more than 62 percent cacao), finely chopped

1 tablespoon light corn syrup

1 Position racks in the center and top third of the oven and preheat to 400°F. Line two half-sheet pans with parchment paper.

2 Fit a large (at least 14 inches) pastry bag with an ¹¹⁄₁₆-inch-diameter plain pastry tip, such as Ateco #809. Fill the bag with the freshly made warm *pâte à choux* dough. Pipe twelve 5-inch-long strips of dough on the two pans, spacing them at least 2 inches apart. Exert a good amount of pressure on the bag of dough so the strips are wide and thick. Smooth any pointed tips of dough with a finger dipped in water.

3 Bake until crisp and golden brown, 25 minutes. Do not underbake, or the éclairs will fall when they come out of the oven. Remove from the oven. Using a small paring knife, pierce a small slit into the crease on the side of each éclair. Return the éclairs to the oven and continue baking until a bit

more crisp and golden brown, about 10 minutes. Don't let them burn, of course, but don't be afraid to get them good and crisp. Turn off the oven and prop the door open with a wooden spoon. Let the éclairs cool completely in the oven.

4   To make the white chocolate cream, heat ½ cup of the cream in a small saucepan over medium heat until simmering. Remove from the heat. Add the white chocolate and let stand until softened, about 3 minutes. Whisk until smooth. Let cool until tepid.

5   Whip the remaining 1 cup cream in the chilled bowl of a heavy-duty stand mixer fitted with the whisk attachment on medium-high speed just until soft peaks form. Add the cooled white chocolate mixture and whip until the cream holds its shape. Remove from the bowl. If you would like it a bit stiffer, whisk by hand with a balloon whisk. Refrigerate until ready to use.

6   To make the glaze, bring the cream, sugar, dissolved espresso, and water to a simmer in a medium saucepan over medium heat. Remove from the heat. Add the chocolate and let stand until softened, about 3 minutes. Add the corn syrup and whisk until smooth. Pour into a bowl large enough to fit an éclair. Use the glaze while it is still warm.

7   Using a serrated knife, cut each éclair in half lengthwise. Remove any stringy, uncooked dough from the inside of each éclair to make a crisp pastry shell. Set the top and bottom of each éclair side by side on a half-sheet pan to keep each pair together. One at a time, hold the top half of each éclair, cut side up, and dip into the glaze to coat the exterior. Let any excess glaze drip back into the bowl. Place, glazed side up, next to its matching bottom half. Repeat with the remaining éclairs.

8   Transfer the whipped white chocolate cream to a pastry bag fitted with a ⁷⁄₁₆-inch-diameter open-star tip, such as Ateco #825. Pipe swirls of the cream onto the top surface of the bottom shells. Place the top glazed halves on their matching bottom halves. Refrigerate until the glaze sets, about 15 minutes. (The éclairs are best the day they are made.)

Chapter Six

Pies and Tarts

OF COURSE YOU'VE HEARD THE SAYING "IT'S AS EASY AS PIE." THAT'S A BIT OVERSIMPLIFIED, BECAUSE FRANKLY, PIES AREN'T ALL THAT EASY to make. While we have a great American tradition of home-baked pies, I have worked hard to make the bakery's pies and tarts a bit different and even better than what Grandma left cooling on the windowsill.

The bakery's fruit-crumb pies are baked in individual portions, like an Americanized tart (or a "Frenchified" pie). The banana cream pie has a creamy filling with an almond crust. Our pumpkin pie tastes more like pumpkin than sugar, and has just a hint of spices. The crust is the backbone of every pie and tart. It should be tasty enough to eat by itself, like a cookie. A single recipe for crust is not enough for a truly fine baker because the crust should be matched to the filling—just as you wouldn't use one frosting for all of your cakes. I use a tender crust dough (fine-crumbed and not too sweet), a sweet tart dough (to complement sweet fillings like pecan), and an almond pastry dough (just the thing for cream pies).

A LESSON ON PIES AND TARTS

Making the Dough For its buttery flavor and crisp texture, a European-style short crust can't be beat. American bakers often emphasize flakiness in their pie dough, a texture that is attained only by using pork lard or vegetable shortening, ingredients that, in my opinion, have very aggressive flavors. Short crust dough is always made with butter, known for its superior flavor and for producing a crisp, crumbly crust (*short* means "crumbly" in old English) that resembles a not-too-sweet shortbread cookie.

My favorite pie dough comes from my dear friends Wendy and Michael London. It is tasty, sturdy, and easy to work with. The butter in it is creamed, and the aeration contributes to the delicacy of the baked pastry. My tart dough, with sugar and eggs for richness, also uses creamed butter. The technique is a little different for my almond pastry dough. Because the ground nuts in the dough make it a bit heavier, the butter is cut into the dry ingredients with a pastry blender. As the dough bakes, the butter creates steam, which makes the dough separate into thin, flaky layers.

Remember one of the most important rules for pie and tart dough—once the flour is added, don't overhandle the dough, or you'll activate the gluten in the flour and get a tough crust. This is especially important because these recipes use unbleached all-purpose flour, which has a higher gluten content and fuller flavor than pastry flour. When adding the flour to the butter mixture, mix it just until the ingredients are combined and clump together; not until they form a smooth dough.

The dough must be chilled to firm up the butter and allow the gluten to relax. Gather it up and transfer to a lightly floured work surface. Gently knead the dough a few times to smooth it out and combine the ingredients.

It takes the same amount of time to make a large amount of dough (enough for two pies or tarts, a double-crust pie, or many tartlets) as it does for the pastry for one shell. So, my versatile Tender Pie Dough and Sweet Tart Dough on pages 176 and 177 reflect this philosophy. After making the dough, divide it into two halves. Form each half into a disk about 1 inch thick. Wrap it in plastic wrap and re-frigerate until it is chilled through but still supple enough to roll out easily, about 1 hour. If the dough is chilled until it is hard, let it stand at room temperature for about 30 minutes to soften slightly. When you need only one pastry shell, freeze the remaining dough for another time.

Rolling the Dough When rolling out dough, keep two things in mind. You want to roll it to an even thickness, and you don't want it to stick to your work surface. If the dough is the right temperature and texture (chilled and malleable, not cold and hard), it won't crack, and if it does, you can always patch it together with your fingertips.

Lightly flour a work surface. Unwrap the dough and rap the entire circumference around its edge on the work surface (to help avoid cracking during rolling). Place the dough on the surface and sprinkle the top with flour. Using the rolling pin, gently tap the top of the dough a few times, first horizontally and then vertically, to soften the dough slightly.

Starting at the center of the disk, roll the dough away from you. Give it a quarter turn, and roll out again from the center. Keep rolling, turning the dough a quarter turn after each roll, and it will even-tually widen into a circle. Be sure that the dough isn't sticking to the work surface. If necessary, run a long metal spatula under the dough to free it, and scatter flour under the dough as a buffer. Once the dough is 8 or 9 inches in diameter, you can stop turning it after every roll and just roll it to an even thickness—⅛ inch. Unless you are an experienced baker and know this measurement by sight and feel, don't guess—use a ruler.

Fitting the Dough into the Pan When the dough is the right thickness, roll it up onto the rolling pin. For a pie, unroll the dough over the pan. Fit the dough into the pan, pressing it gently into the corners. If necessary, trim any excess dough, leaving a ¾- to 1-inch overhang. Fold over the overhang so the fold is flush with the edge of the pan. To flute the dough, use the end of a thin wooden spoon or a chopstick and press it around the edge of the pie at ½-inch intervals, supporting the dough with one hand while you use the other to do the fluting.

For a tart, unroll the dough over a tart pan with a removable bottom. There is no need to butter the pan—the dough has plenty of butter. Gently ease the dough into the pan, letting the excess hang over the edge of the pan. Press the dough firmly against the sides of the pan, being sure to form a distinct right angle where the sides meet the bottom. Run the meaty part of your palm around the circumfer-ence of the pan to press and remove the excess dough, reserving the fallen dough. Using your forefinger, quickly and firmly press the dough into the grooves around the sides of the pan, taking care not to press too hard or the dough will be too thin and burn during baking. This may sound like a minor detail, but it helps strengthen the sides of the crust. (If you have pressed too hard and can see the pan through the dough, use some of the reserved dough to patch the area.) Go around the pan again, pressing the dough against the sides of the pan, letting the dough peek about 1/16 inch above the edge of the pan. This final adjustment makes the dough stand a smidge taller, and will compensate for the shrinkage that will occur when the pastry is baked. If the dough is to be prebaked, pierce the bottom of the shell with a fork in a uniform pattern. Do not pierce the sides, as this will only weaken the shell.

For tartlets, use a 6-inch metal entremet ring (or a saucer and knife) to cut out rounds of dough, and follow the instructions for lining the pans.

For both pie and tart shells, the dough-lined pan should be frozen for 15 minutes to chill and firm the dough, which helps it keep its shape during baking. There's no need to wrap the pan in plastic if you are going to bake within 15 minutes or so. If you need more time, cover the dough. The dough-lined pans can be wrapped tightly in plastic and frozen overnight. Do not thaw the dough, but add a few more minutes for baking.

Baking the Dough Always bake pies and tarts on a half-sheet pan—it gives the dough a hot, flat surface for baking, helping to crisp the bottom crust. Positioning the oven rack on the bottom third brings the pie closest to the source of heat, which also prevents soggy crusts.

Some recipes require that the shell be partially or fully baked before adding the filling. Line the dough with a round of parchment paper that extends 1 inch above the top of the pan. (Avoid using aluminum foil—parchment paper is less likely to stick to sweet dough, and doesn't leave marks in the dough.) Fill the paper with a single layer of aluminum pastry weights or dried beans, making sure they are pressing against the dough where it goes up the sides of the pan.

Place the pie or tart pan on a half-sheet pan. Bake until the dough looks set, about 15 minutes. Remove the weights and paper. For a partially baked shell, continue baking until the pastry is barely beginning to color, about 5 minutes more. For a fully baked shell, bake until the crust is golden brown, another 5 minutes, for a total of approximately 25 minutes. If the pastry puffs up (and even though you've pricked the shell, it might), try not to prick it again; just press it down with your fingers.

To remove a tart from its pan, first check to be sure that any filling that has boiled over isn't sticking to the pan. If it is, use the tip of a sharp knife to carefully release the pan. Place the tart on a ramekin, and the ring should fall away. Cool completely. If you wish, the tart can be removed from the bottom round and transferred to a platter. Slide a long, sharp knife between the bottom crust and the bottom round of the pan. Using a thin, wide spatula as an aid, carefully slide the tart from the round to the platter.

Tender Pie Dough

Makes two 9-inch single-crust pies, one double-crust pie, or 6 individual deep-dish pies

....

Fellow bakers and dear friends Wendy and Michael London of Mrs. London's Bakery and Café, a beloved shop in Saratoga Springs, New York, shared this unusual pastry dough with me. I have used it for many of my pies ever since. It is different from traditional American pie dough. Instead of using the typical technique of cutting chilled butter into flour, this has a creamed butter and milk base. Expect a tender, delicious, buttery pastry, but not an especially flaky one.

BAKER'S NOTE: This makes a large batch of dough. Divide it in half and use both halves, or freeze one portion to use another time. This is the dough to use for Rustic Apple Streusel Pie (page 180), Individual Deep-Dish Peach Crumb Pies (page 189), and Thanksgiving Pumpkin Pie (page 199).

14 tablespoons (1¼ sticks) unsalted butter, at cool room temperature, cut into tablespoons

⅓ cup whole milk

2½ cups unbleached all-purpose flour

1 tablespoon plus 1 teaspoon superfine sugar

¼ teaspoon fine sea salt

1 Beat the butter in the bowl of a heavy-duty stand mixer fitted with the paddle attachment at high speed until the butter is smooth, about 2 minutes. With the mixer running, slowly dribble in the milk, occasionally stopping the mixer and scraping down the sides of the bowl with a silicone spatula. The butter mixture should be fluffy, smooth, and shiny, like a buttercream frosting.

2 Mix the flour, sugar, and salt together in a small bowl. With the mixer speed on low, gradually add the flour mixture and incorporate just until the dough forms a mass on the paddle and the sides of the bowl are clean. Turn out the dough onto a lightly floured surface. Knead a few times until it is smooth and supple. Divide the dough in half. Shape each portion into a disk, about 1 inch thick. Wrap each disk in plastic wrap.

3 Refrigerate until chilled but not hard, 30 minutes to 1 hour. (The dough can be refrigerated up to 1 day, but it will be very hard, and should stand at room temperature for about 30 minutes before rolling out. The dough can also be frozen, double wrapped in plastic, for up to 2 weeks. Defrost in the refrigerator overnight.)

Sweet Tart Dough

Makes two 9-inch tarts or eight 3 ¾-inch tartlets

....

Unlike pies, which are served from their baking dishes, tarts are removed from their pans, and therefore require a crisp, strong crust to contain the filling. This tart dough is not overly sweet and perfectly complements many different fillings.

BAKER'S NOTE: This makes a large batch of dough. Divide it in half and use both, or freeze one portion to use another time. This is the dough to use for Lemon Cream Tart with Strawberries (page 193), Lemon Meringue Tartlets (page 195), and Pecan and Bourbon Tart (page 200).

12 tablespoons (1½ sticks) unsalted butter, at cool room temperature, cut into tablespoons

6 tablespoons superfine sugar

1 large egg plus 1 large egg yolk, beaten

½ teaspoon pure vanilla extract

2¼ cups unbleached all-purpose flour

¼ teaspoon fine sea salt

1 Beat the butter in the bowl of a heavy-duty stand mixer fitted with the paddle attachment on high speed until smooth, about 1 minute. Add the sugar and beat, occasionally scraping down the bowl, until very light in color and texture, about 3 minutes. Gradually dribble in the eggs and vanilla. Reduce the mixer speed to low and add the flour and salt. Mix just until the dough clumps together and the sides of the bowl are almost clean.

2 Gather up the dough and transfer to a lightly floured work surface. Knead a few times until smooth and supple. Divide the dough in half. Shape each portion into a disk, about 1 inch thick, and wrap each disk in plastic wrap. Refrigerate until chilled but not hard, 30 minutes to 1 hour. (The dough can be refrigerated up to 1 day, but it will be very hard, and should stand at room temperature for about 30 minutes before rolling out. The dough can also be frozen, double wrapped in plastic, for up to 2 weeks. Defrost in the refrigerator overnight.)

Almond Pastry Dough

Makes enough for one 9-inch pie

....

This delicious, buttery crust bakes into a crisp, nut-flavored shell. Use a single batch for my signature Banana Cream Pie (page 185), and a double batch for the luscious Apple Bretonne Tartlets (page 183).

BAKER'S NOTE: When making the tartlets, you will have leftover dough, which can be made into cookies. Roll out the dough ¼ inch thick. Cut into shapes with a cookie cutter and bake at 350°F until light golden brown, about 12 minutes.

3 tablespoons sliced natural almonds, toasted (page 5)	*8 tablespoons (1 stick) unsalted butter, cut into ½-inch cubes, chilled*
1 cup plus 1 tablespoon unbleached all-purpose flour, divided	*1 large egg yolk*
	1 tablespoon ice water, plus more as needed
3 tablespoons superfine sugar	*Seeds of ½ Plumped Vanilla Bean (page 295)*
⅛ teaspoon fine sea salt	*¼ teaspoon almond extract*

1 Grind the almonds in a coffee grinder with 1 tablespoon of the flour until powdery. Combine the remaining 1 cup flour, the ground almond mixture, sugar, and salt in a medium bowl. Add the butter cubes and toss to coat with the flour mixture. Using a pastry blender, cut in the butter until the mixture looks like coarse meal with some pea-size pieces of butter, about 2 minutes (figures 1 and 2). Using a fork, mix the egg yolk, 1 tablespoon ice water, vanilla seeds, and almond extract together in a small bowl. Drizzle the yolk mixture all over the flour mixture and, using a wooden spoon, combine just until the dough clumps together. If the dough is too dry, add more ice water, a little at a time (figure 3).

2 Transfer the dough to a lightly floured work surface and shape into a 1-inch-thick disk (figures 4, 5, and 6). Wrap in plastic wrap. Refrigerate until chilled but not hard, 30 minutes to 1 hour. (The dough can be refrigerated up to 1 day, but it will be very hard, and should stand at room temperature for about 30 minutes before rolling out. The dough can also be frozen, double wrapped in plastic, for up to 2 weeks. Defrost in the refrigerator overnight.)

Rustic Apple Streusel Pie

Makes 8 servings

....

When the weather turns brisk and apples are at the peak of their season, we add these icons of autumn baking to the offerings at the bakery. This is apple pie with a difference. Instead of using two crusts to create a top and a bottom to encase the cinnamon-flavored apple filling, I roll a single, large disk of dough that can be folded and pleated around the fruit. The exposed filling in the center of the pie is then covered with streusel.

BAKER'S NOTE: Be sure to slice the apples thin so that they cook in the amount of time needed to bake the crust—this isn't a chunky filling. • Peel the apples, one at a time. Stand an apple on the work surface. Using a large knife, cut each apple in half. Place each half, flat side down, and slice lengthwise into ¼-inch slices. Now trim the core off each slice. You will have perfect half-moons, without the ugly hole from an apple corer.

½ recipe Tender Pie Dough (page 176)

Apple Filling

4 pounds Granny Smith apples, peeled, cut into ¼-inch-thick slices, and trimmed (see Baker's Note)

⅔ cup superfine sugar

3 tablespoons unbleached all-purpose flour, plus more for rolling out the dough

2 teaspoons pure maple syrup, preferably Grade B

2 teaspoons fresh lemon juice

½ teaspoon ground cinnamon

Seeds from ¼ Plumped Vanilla Bean (page 295) or ¼ teaspoon pure vanilla extract

1 large egg, well beaten with a hand blender • Streusel (page 189)

1   Position a rack in the bottom third of the oven and preheat to 350°F. Line a half-sheet pan with parchment paper.

2   To make the filling, gently toss the apples, sugar, flour, maple syrup, lemon juice, cinnamon, and vanilla in a medium bowl until well combined.

3   Lightly flour a work surface. Unwrap the dough and rap the entire circumference around its edge on the work surface. Dust the top of the dough with flour. Roll out into a 15-inch round. Transfer the dough to a 9-inch pie pan, centering it in the pan, and let the excess dough hang over the sides. Heap the apples in the crust, mounding them high in the center. Bring up the edges of the dough, pleating the dough as needed around the circumference of the dish—the center of the filling will be visible. Brush the exposed crust with the egg. Place the streusel over the exposed filling to cover it, then sprinkle any remaining streusel over the crust.

4   Place the pie on the half-sheet pan. Bake, rotating the pan halfway through, until the crust is golden brown and any juices that escape are thick, about 1 hour. If the crust is browning too quickly, tent it with parchment paper. Remove from the oven and cool on a wire rack for 1 hour. Serve warm or at room temperature.

Apple Bretonne Tartlets

Makes 8 tartlets

....

Never heard of a Bretonne? I hadn't either until one of my bakers, who had worked in Belgium, made one for me. These are individual, almond-topped apple tarts, with small cubes of fruit in a custardy filling—don't forget a scoop of ice cream.

BAKER'S NOTE: The apples must be peeled and cut into uniform ⅓-inch cubes. One at a time, stand an apple on the work surface. Using a large knife, cut a ½-inch-thick slice from one side of the apple. Make another thick slice, stopping just short of the tough core. Stack the slices in their natural formation and keep them together. Turn the apple 90 degrees, and cut off two more slices in the same manner. Repeat twice, turning the apple 90 degrees after each double-cut. Repeat with the remaining apples. Discard the core trimmings. • Cut the stacks lengthwise into ⅓-inch-wide strips. Cut across the strips at ⅓-inch intervals to create ⅓-inch cubes. Repeat with the remaining apple quadrants.

2 recipes Almond Pastry Dough (page 178)

Apple Filling

4 medium Granny Smith apples, peeled and cut into ⅓-inch cubes (see Baker's Note)

¾ cup superfine sugar

1 teaspoon fresh lemon juice

1 tablespoon unbleached all-purpose flour

Seeds from ½ Plumped Vanilla Bean (page 295)

Vanilla Cream

3 large egg yolks (save the whites for the almond topping)

¼ cup confectioners' sugar, sifted

Seeds from ½ Plumped Vanilla Bean (page 295)

4 tablespoons (½ stick) unsalted butter, at soft room temperature

¼ cup unbleached all-purpose flour

Almond Topping

3 large egg whites, at room temperature

½ cup superfine sugar

2 cups (8 ounces) sliced natural almonds, toasted (page 5)

Confectioners' sugar, for garnish • Whipped Cream (page 292) or Vanilla Bean Ice Cream (page 250), for serving

1   Position a rack in the bottom third of the oven and preheat to 375°F.

2   On a lightly floured work surface, roll out the dough ⅛ inch thick. Following the instructions on page 173, line eight 3¾ by ¾-inch tartlet pans with removable bottoms with the dough. Pierce the bottom of each tartlet in a uniform pattern with a fork. Freeze for 15 minutes.

3   Place the tartlet pans on a half-sheet pan. Line each with a round of parchment paper and fill with pie weights or dried beans. Bake until the pastry is set and dry but not beginning to brown, about 15 minutes. Remove from the oven. Remove the parchment paper and the weights. Let cool.

4   Meanwhile, mix the apples, sugar, and lemon juice in a medium bowl. Set aside for 30 minutes. Transfer the apples to a large colander set over a medium bowl and drain the excess juice. Return the apples to their bowl. Stir in the flour and vanilla seeds.

5   To make the vanilla cream, using a handheld electric mixer on high speed, beat the egg yolks, confectioners' sugar, and vanilla seeds in a small bowl until thickened and light in color, about 2 minutes. Add the butter, then the flour, and beat until very pale and fluffy, about 2 minutes. Set aside.

6   To make the almond topping, whisk the egg whites in a medium bowl until foamy. Whisk in the sugar. Add the almonds and mix gently with your hands (which work better than a spoon for this job) until the almonds are well coated; take care not to break the almonds. Set aside.

7   For each tartlet, using a tablespoon, place the vanilla cream in the cooled shells. Spread evenly with a small offset spatula. With an ice-cream scoop, add apple filling to each tartlet, leaving the filling mounded. Using your hands, spread the almond topping thinly and evenly over the apples, masking the apples as best you can. Place the tartlets on a half-sheet pan lined with parchment paper to catch any drips that might occur.

8   Bake, rotating the pan halfway through, until the crusts are golden brown and the tartlets feel firm when gently pressed with your finger in the center, about 30 minutes. The apple juices may bubble over the sides of the tartlet pans.

9   Let cool in the pans for 10 minutes, no longer. Remove the sides of the pans. Cool completely on a wire rack. Remove the bottoms of the pans. Lightly sift confectioners' sugar on top. Serve at room temperature, with whipped cream or ice cream.

Banana Cream Pie

Makes 8 servings

....

More than one happy person has deemed this the ultimate banana cream pie. The almonds in the crust are a perfect match for the bananas. But it's the filling that is really special—instead of the usual thick pastry cream, it's a lighter version made with whipped cream and a bit of gelatin.

Almond Pastry Dough (page 178)

Cream Filling

2 teaspoons unflavored gelatin powder	*1½ cups whole milk*
2 tablespoons cold water	*Seeds from ½ Plumped Vanilla Bean (page 295) or ½ teaspoon pure vanilla extract*
4 large egg yolks	
⅓ cup superfine sugar	*3 ripe medium bananas, cut lengthwise in half, then into ⅓-inch slices*
1½ tablespoons cornstarch	*¾ cup heavy cream, chilled*

Topping

1½ cups heavy cream, chilled	*Seeds from ½ Plumped Vanilla Bean (page 295) or ½ teaspoon pure vanilla extract*
3 tablespoons superfine sugar	
	2 tablespoons sliced almonds, toasted (page 5), for garnish

1   Position a rack in the bottom third of the oven and preheat to 375°F. Following the instructions on page 173, line a 9-inch pie pan with the dough. Pierce the bottom of the dough in a uniform pattern with a fork. Freeze for 15 minutes.

2   Line the dough with a round of parchment paper and fill with pastry weights or dried beans. Bake on a half-sheet pan for 15 minutes, until the pastry is set. Remove the parchment paper and the weights and continue baking until the pastry is golden brown, about 10 minutes more. Cool completely.

3   To make the filling, sprinkle the gelatin over the water in a small bowl. Set aside until the gelatin softens, about 5 minutes. Whisk the yolks, sugar, and cornstarch in a heatproof medium bowl until combined; set aside. Place a heatproof bowl with a medium-mesh wire sieve near the stove.

4   Heat the milk in a heavy-bottomed medium saucepan over medium heat until very hot. Gradually whisk the hot milk into the egg yolk mixture. Pour the mixture back into the saucepan. Whisking constantly, being sure to reach into the corners of the saucepan, cook over medium heat until the filling thickens and comes to a full boil. Reduce the heat to low and whisk for 1 minute. Remove from the heat, add the gelatin mixture, and whisk until the gelatin is completely melted (the pastry cream will thin slightly—don't worry). Strain through the medium-mesh wire sieve into the clean medium bowl. Stir in the vanilla. Place a piece of plastic wrap directly on the surface (this discourages a skin from forming), and pierce a few holes in the plastic wrap with the tip of a sharp knife. Let stand on a wire rack until completely cooled and thickened but not set. Remove the plastic wrap and fold in the bananas.

5   Using a whisk or a handheld electric mixer, beat the cream in a small bowl just until it forms soft peaks. Fold the whipped cream into the banana mixture. Fill the cooled pastry shell and smooth the top. Cover with plastic wrap and let the filling set in the shell in the refrigerator, about 1 hour.

6   To make the topping, beat the heavy cream, sugar, and vanilla just until it forms stiff peaks. Transfer to a pastry bag fitted with a ⅜-inch-diameter open-star tip, such as Ateco #824. Pipe swirls of whipped cream to completely cover the top of the pie. Refrigerate until the pie is chilled, at least 1 hour. Just before serving, top with the toasted almonds. Serve chilled.

Individual Deep-Dish Peach Crumb Pies

Makes 6 small pies

....

These streusel-topped pies never fail to impress. They have an old-fashioned flavor and a sophisticated look. Use any filling that appeals to you, taking advantage of whatever fresh fruit is available. Don't be nervous about unmolding the pies from the ramekins. The freestanding pies look wonderful, but if you prefer, serve the pies in the ramekins, and they'll still look pretty terrific.

BAKER'S NOTE: While some bakers loosen the peach skins by blanching (boiling the peaches for 30 to 60 seconds, draining, and rinsing under cold running water), I think that this cooking affects the flavor and texture of the peach. To skin the peach, cut it in half vertically, twisting the halves apart to reveal the pit. Remove the pit, which now gives each half a nice indentation to hold the peach steady while peeling. Pare away the skin, trying not to take away too much of the flesh. You can also use a vegetable peeler to remove the skin. • If you make these pies often, use a 6-inch metal entremet ring to cut the dough rounds, as it cuts cleanly. Otherwise, make do with a saucer and sharp knife.

Tender Pie Dough (page 176) • *Softened unsalted butter and flour, for the ramekins*

Peach Filling

5 ripe medium freestone peaches, pitted, peeled, and cut into ½-inch cubes (about 4 cups; see Baker's Note)

⅓ cup packed light brown sugar

2 teaspoons cornstarch

Seeds from 1 Plumped Vanilla Bean (page 295) or 1 teaspoon pure vanilla extract

Streusel

⅓ cup plus 1 tablespoon unbleached all-purpose flour

1 tablespoon superfine sugar

1 tablespoon light brown sugar

⅛ teaspoon ground cinnamon

2½ tablespoons unsalted butter, melted

⅛ teaspoon pure vanilla extract

1   Position a rack in the bottom third of the oven and preheat to 350°F. Line a half-sheet pan with parchment paper. Generously butter the insides of six 6-ounce (¾-cup) ramekins. Dust the insides well with flour, being sure they are completely coated, and tap out the excess flour. Set aside.

2   To make the filling, combine the peaches, brown sugar, cornstarch, and vanilla in a medium bowl. Let stand while preparing the crumb pies.

3   To make the streusel, combine the flour, superfine sugar, brown sugar, and cinnamon in a small bowl. Stir the melted butter and vanilla together in another small bowl. Gradually stir the butter mixture into the flour mixture, just until evenly moistened (you may not need all of the butter). Squeeze the mixture in your hands until thoroughly combined. Crumble the mixture in the bowl to make fine crumbs with some small lumps. Set the streusel aside.

4   On a lightly floured work surface, roll out the first disk of pie dough, ⅛ inch thick. Using a 6-inch metal entremet ring or a saucer as a template, cut out three rounds of dough. Stack the rounds on a half-sheet pan, separating them with parchment paper, and place in the refrigerator. (The dough softens easily and must remain cold.) Repeat with the second disk of pie dough. Working quickly, fit the rounds into the prepared ramekins, pressing evenly into the corners (figures 1 and 2). Let the excess dough hang over the sides and gently form a ruffle. Place the ramekins on a half-sheet pan and refrigerate for 5 minutes.

5   Scoop the filling into the shells, piling it just above the edge of the ramekin (figure 3). One at a time, pleat the pastry over the filling—the center of the filling will be exposed (figures 4 and 5). Gently press the streusel over the top of the dough and filling (figure 6).

6   Bake until the tops are nicely browned, 50 to 60 minutes. To check the pies for doneness, use the rounded tip of a dinner knife to separate the top edge of the crust from the side of a ramekin and take a peek—the side crust should be golden brown. If not, bake a few minutes longer. If you are concerned about the tops overbrowning, tent them with aluminum foil. Transfer the ramekins to a wire rack and cool, about 20 minutes. (Do not let the pies cool completely, or they may stick to the ramekins and be difficult to remove. If this happens, remember that the pies are just as tasty if eaten directly from the ramekins.)

7   To unmold the pies, use your fingers to gently loosen the top edge of the crust from the ramekin. (If you wish, you may carefully run a knife around the inside of the ramekin to loosen the crust, but take care not to cut the crust.) Using a kitchen towel, pick up a ramekin. Cup your other hand and invert the pie into the cupped hand to unmold the pie. Place right side up onto the wire rack. Repeat with the remaining pies. Serve warm or at room temperature.

Blueberry Crumb Pies: Substitute 2 pints fresh blueberries, picked over for stems, for the peaches.

Lemon Cream Tart with Strawberries

Makes 8 servings

....

For tartlets, I use my intense lemon curd. But for a full-size tart, this curd can get a little too puckery, so I soften its tartness with whipped cream to make a light but still-lemony mousse. While this tart is perfectly nice as it is, a topping of fresh strawberries is a spectacular finish.

½ recipe Sweet Tart Dough (page 177)

½ teaspoon unflavored gelatin powder

1 tablespoon cold water

1 cup Lemon Curd (page 287)

¾ cup heavy cream, divided

1½ pints fresh strawberries, hulled and cut lengthwise into quarters

Apricot Glaze (page 293), warm

1 Position a rack in the bottom third of the oven and preheat to 350°F. On a lightly floured work surface, roll out the dough into a ⅛-inch-thick circle. Following the instructions on page 173, line a 9-inch tart pan with a removable bottom with the dough. Pierce the bottom of the dough in a uniform pattern with a fork. Freeze for 15 minutes.

2 Line the dough with a 13- to 14-inch round of parchment paper and fill with pastry weights or dried beans. Place the pan on a half-sheet pan. Bake for 15 minutes. Remove from the oven and remove the parchment and the weights. Continue baking until the pastry is golden brown, 10 to 15 minutes more. Transfer to a wire rack and cool completely.

3 Sprinkle the gelatin over the water in a ramekin. Let stand until the gelatin absorbs the water, about 5 minutes. Bring ½ inch of water to a simmer in a small saucepan. Place the ramekin in the water and stir constantly with a small silicone spatula until the gelatin is completely dissolved, at least 1 minute. Remove the ramekin from the water.

4 Place the lemon curd in a large bowl. Stir 1 tablespoon of the cream into the gelatin. Whip the remaining cream in a chilled medium bowl with a handheld electric mixer at high speed until the cream is well thickened but hasn't formed peaks. With the mixer running, pour the gelatin mixture near the beaters so it is quickly and evenly distributed into the cream. Continue beating until the cream forms soft peaks. Stir one-quarter of the whipped cream into the lemon curd to lighten it, then fold in the remaining cream.

5 Spread the lemon filling in the cooled pastry shell. Cover with plastic wrap, with the wrap barely touching the surface. Refrigerate until chilled and set, at least 1 hour.

6 Remove the plastic wrap. Arrange the strawberries, cut sides down, in concentric circles on the filling. Brush with the warm glaze. Remove the sides of the pan and serve at once.

Lemon Meringue Tartlets

Makes 8 tartlets

....

Traditional lemon meringue pie filling is like a pudding and lacks the sweet-tart character that I love. Lemon curd is the way to go, as it has the proper pucker and citrus flavor. Tartlets are the perfect size to allow for just the right amount of curd and a towering topping of meringue.

Sweet Tart Dough (page 177) • 1 cup Lemon Curd (page 287)

Meringue

5 large egg whites, at room temperature • ¾ cup superfine sugar

1 Position a rack in the bottom third of the oven and preheat to 350°F.

2 On a lightly floured work surface, roll out the two disks of dough, ⅛ inch thick. Following the instructions on page 173, line eight 3¾ by ¾-inch tartlet pans with removable bottoms with the dough. Pierce the bottom of each tartlet in a uniform pattern with a fork. Freeze for 15 minutes.

3 Place the pans on a half-sheet pan. Line each with a round of parchment paper and fill with pie weights or dried beans. Bake until the pastry is set and dry but not beginning to brown, about 15 minutes. Remove from the oven, and remove the parchment paper and the weights. Return to the oven and continue baking until the tartlet shells are golden brown, about 10 minutes more. Keep the oven on. Transfer to a wire cooling rack and let cool completely. Remove the tartlets from the pans. Carefully place the tartlets on a half-sheet pan lined with parchment paper.

4 To make the meringue, choose a saucepan that will snugly hold the bowl of a heavy-duty stand mixer. Add about 1 inch of water to the saucepan (the bottom of the bowl should not touch the water). Bring the water to a boil over high heat, then reduce the heat so the water is at a simmer. Whisk the egg whites and sugar together in the bowl of the mixer with a balloon whisk until the sugar dissolves. Place the bowl over the water in the saucepan and stir constantly with a silicone spatula, frequently scraping down the sides of the bowl, until the mixture is hot and opaque (an instant-read thermometer will read 160°F), about 5 minutes. Keep checking the temperature, being careful not to overcook the egg mixture. Attach the bowl to the mixer and fit with the whisk attachment. Whip

with the mixer on high speed until the meringue is cool (place your hand on the bottom of the bowl to judge the temperature) and forms stiff, shiny peaks, 5 to 7 minutes. Transfer the meringue to a large pastry bag fitted with a 5/16-inch-diameter open-star tip, such as Ateco #823.

5   Spread about 2 tablespoons lemon curd into each cooled shell. Pipe tall swirls of meringue over the curd, making sure that the meringue touches the edge of the pastry. Bake at 350°F until the meringue is tinged golden brown, about 8 minutes. Let cool completely.

Thanksgiving Pumpkin Pie

Makes 8 servings

....

The bakery must have made tens of thousands of these pies over the years. It's less sweet and spicy than the traditional recipe, so the pumpkin flavor really comes through. (By the way, don't bother to use fresh pumpkin puree—the canned version is quite good.) To avoid forming air in the filling, whisk the filling very gently, just until combined; otherwise it will puff high in the oven and crack when cooled. If, even after your best efforts, the top cracks, just mask it with whipped cream.

½ recipe Tender Pie Dough (page 176)

One 15-ounce can solid-pack pumpkin

3 tablespoons superfine sugar

2 tablespoons light brown sugar, rubbed through a coarse-mesh wire sieve

½ teaspoon ground cinnamon

A few gratings of fresh nutmeg

¼ teaspoon fine sea salt

2 large eggs, at room temperature

1½ cups heavy cream

1 tablespoon maple syrup, preferably Grade B

1   Position a rack in the bottom third of the oven and preheat to 400°F. Following the instructions on page 173, line a 9-inch pie pan with the dough. Pierce the bottom of the dough in a uniform pattern with a fork. Freeze for 15 minutes.

2   Whisk the pumpkin, superfine sugar, brown sugar, cinnamon, nutmeg, and salt together in a medium bowl just until combined. Whisk the eggs until combined in another bowl, then add the cream and maple syrup and whisk again. Add to the pumpkin mixture and whisk just until evenly mixed. Pour into the pie shell.

3   Place the pie pan on a half-sheet pan. Bake for 15 minutes. Reduce the heat to 350°F and continue baking for about 30 more minutes, or until the filling looks evenly puffed and it moves as a unit when the pie is gently shaken. Do not test with a knife, because the resulting slit will expand into a huge crack during cooling.

4   Cool completely on a wire rack. If desired, cover and refrigerate until chilled, or serve at room temperature.

Pecan and Bourbon Tart

Makes 8 servings

....

Here's a very upscale version of that down-home American classic pecan pie. The filling is much lighter than most, and a hint of bourbon works to offset its sweetness without being overpowering. Serve the tart warm with whipped cream.

½ recipe Sweet Tart Dough (page 177)

¼ cup dark corn syrup

1 cup packed light brown sugar

6 tablespoons (¾ stick) unsalted butter, cut into tablespoons

2 large eggs plus 1 large egg yolk, at room temperature

1 tablespoon bourbon, preferably Wild Turkey

2 cups (8 ounces) coarsely chopped pecan pieces

1 Position a rack in the bottom third of the oven and preheat to 350°F. On a lightly floured work surface, roll out the dough into a ⅛-inch-thick circle. Following the instructions on page 173, line a 9-inch tart pan with a removable bottom with the dough. Pierce the bottom of the dough in a uniform pattern with a fork. Freeze for 15 minutes.

2 Line the dough with a round of parchment paper and fill with pastry weights or dried beans. Place the tart pan on a half-sheet pan. Bake until the pastry looks set, about 15 minutes. Remove from the oven and remove the parchment and the weights. Continue baking the tart until the crust is barely browned, about 5 minutes longer. Remove from the oven.

3 Bring the corn syrup, brown sugar, and butter to a boil in a medium saucepan over medium heat, stirring often. Remove from the heat and cool slightly. Beat the eggs and yolk together in a heatproof bowl. Slowly whisk the hot syrup into the egg mixture, then whisk in the bourbon. Strain through a wire sieve into another bowl to remove the chalazae (the white cords attached to the egg yolks) in the filling. Add the pecans and mix well.

4 Pour the pecan mixture into the pastry. Smooth the top with an offset metal spatula so the nuts are flat and evenly distributed—if some nuts are higher than others, they could burn. Bake just until the filling has puffed evenly, about 35 minutes. If the edges of the crust are browning too deeply, cover them with a strip of aluminum foil. Cool in the pan for 10 minutes. Remove the sides of the tart pan, transfer to a wire rack, and cool until warm or room temperature.

Chapter Seven

Plain and Fancy Cookies

REMEMBER WHEN EVERY KITCHEN HAD A COOKIE JAR? WHAT USED TO BE A COMMON SIGHT IN YESTERDAY'S KITCHEN IS OFTEN NOW AN EXPENSIVE collectible. A beautiful antique cookie jar is wonderful to look at, but it becomes even more lovable when it performs its original function, filled to the brim with homemade cookies. I think every one of today's kitchens should include a shiny new cookie jar and, of course, cookies.

At Sarabeth's Bakery, we stick pretty close to childhood favorites that have pleased generations of cookie lovers. It is our goal to make each cookie the very best example of its type: the fudgiest brownies, the chewiest oatmeal-raisin cookies, and the most buttery and tender shortbread. Our Chocolate Marmalade Cookies and Linzer Hearts (pages 211 and 215), elegantly shaped into sweet little sandwiches, are more at home next to a pot of freshly brewed tea than a glass of cold milk.

Some bakers like cookies because they are easy to make—mix, drop onto a half-sheet pan, and bake. Unless you are making rolled cookies, they are instant gratification personified. True, cookies are easy to make, but they are also easy to make badly. With a little extra attention, you'll avoid the most common problems, such as burned bottoms or cookies that run together during baking.

A LESSON ON COOKIES

Must-Have Cookie Utensils When I opened Sarabeth's Bakery, I wanted cookies with homemade flavor that looked as good as they tasted. With just a few well-chosen tools, your cookies will have that balance of nostalgic flavor and good looks.

For perfectly shaped balls of dough that will bake into evenly shaped cookies, stainless steel scoops can't be beat. If all of your cookie dough balls are exactly the same size, they will cook in the same time and look uniform—and that's your goal. The scoops I use for drop cookies measure 1½ and 2 inches in diameter. They hold about 1½ and 3 tablespoons of dough respectively.

The better the cookie sheet, the better the cookie. Flimsy cookie sheets encourage burned cookies and will eventually warp. I've said it before, but I'm repeating it here: The only baking sheet worth buying is the heavy-duty aluminum rimmed half-sheet pan, measuring about 18 by 13 inches.

Forget about nonstick cookie sheets—parchment paper or silicone baking mats are much more efficient. (Read more about these indispensable baker's helpers on page 10.) The biggest problem with nonstick cookie sheets is that they often have dark-colored surfaces, which absorb the oven heat and lead to burned cookie bottoms. Although some bakers swear by double-thick insulated cookie sheets, they should be avoided because they discourage the proper crisping and browning of cookie bottoms.

Mixing the Dough Most cookies are made by the creaming method. The tips that apply to everyday cakes (page 111) also apply to cookie dough. Heavy-duty stand mixers work best, but make sure to stop the mixer and scrape the butter-and-sugar mixture a few times during creaming. When adding the ingredients, be careful not to overmix. With certain cookies, overmixing can toughen the dough or create too much air, resulting in puffy cookies.

As much as I like heavy-duty stand mixers, it is difficult to mix chunky ingredients (such as nuts and chocolate chips) in them in such a way that they are distributed evenly throughout the dough—they never seem to make it to the bottom of the bowl. My solution: Add these ingredients to the bowl and mix briefly with a sturdy spoon. Dump the dough out onto the work surface, and work in the "chunkies" with your hands. This is also a great way to feel the texture of the dough so the next time you make it you will have a tactile as well as visual way to be sure it's just right.

Chilling and Rolling Some cookie dough needs to be chilled before rolling out. The dough should be formed so it chills quickly and facilitates easy rolling. For example, if the chilled dough will be rolled into a ⅛-inch-thick rectangle, it should be shaped into a 1-inch-thick rectangle.

For drop cookies, I use only ice-cream scoops, which create cookies that are the same size and shape. Drop cookie dough doesn't need refrigeration, but it shouldn't stand at room temperature for too long before baking, or the butter will soften and the cookies will spread too much when baked.

Baking the Cookies Cookies should be evenly spaced on the half-sheet pans to promote even baking. Every recipe suggests how far apart to place the cookies, as some spread more than others during baking. If you aren't sure, err on the side of having the cookies too far apart so they don't melt together and "marry." Never place cookie dough on a hot pan that has been used to make a previous batch. Let the pan cool naturally. If you try to hurry the process by running cold water over the pan, the pan could warp.

For the best results, bake the cookies, one pan at a time, in the center of the oven, keeping the remaining pans of cookies in a cool place. This may not be practical for some home bakers. To bake two pans at a time, position racks in the center and upper third of the oven, and preheat the oven. Halfway through baking, switch the position of the pans from top to bottom and front to back—again to promote even baking. Every oven has hot spots, and this rotating will help the situation. Even when baking one pan at a time, rotate the pan from front to back halfway through baking.

Cooling the Cookies Don't be in a hurry to remove the cookies from the pans—hot cookies will fall apart. It's fine to let the cookies completely cool on the pans. I rarely cool cookies on a wire rack, but some home cooks prefer that method because it frees up the pan to bake subsequent batches. If you have enough half-sheet pans (most serious bakers have at least four), then it will not be a problem.

Chocolate Chubbies

Makes about 2 dozen cookies

....

I n my opinion, these are the moistest, most intensely chocolate chocolate chip cookies in the world. These are based on a recipe given to me many years ago from the SoHo Charcuterie, a restaurant that helped establish that Manhattan neighborhood as the place to go for anything chic and trendy, from art to food. For the best-looking cookies, a 2-inch ice-cream scoop is a must.

8 tablespoons (1 stick) unsalted butter, cut into ½-inch cubes

9 ounces semisweet or bittersweet chocolate (no more than 62 percent cacao), finely chopped

3 ounces unsweetened chocolate, finely chopped

½ cup unbleached all-purpose flour

½ teaspoon baking powder

¼ teaspoon fine sea salt

3 large eggs, at room temperature

1¼ cups superfine sugar

2 teaspoons pure vanilla extract

2 cups (12 ounces) semisweet chocolate chips

1½ cups (5½ ounces) coarsely chopped pecans

1¼ cups (4½ ounces) coarsely chopped walnuts

1   Position racks in the center and top third of the oven and preheat to 350°F. Line two half-sheet pans with parchment paper.

2   Bring 1 inch of water to a simmer in a medium saucepan over low heat. Put the butter in a wide heatproof bowl, and melt the butter over the hot water in the saucepan. Add the semisweet and unsweetened chocolate, stirring often, until melted and the mixture is smooth. Remove the bowl from the heat and let stand, stirring occasionally, until cooled slightly but still warm, about 5 minutes.

3   Sift the flour, baking powder, and salt together into a medium bowl. Whip the eggs in the bowl of a heavy-duty stand mixer fitted with the whisk attachment on medium-high speed until the eggs are foamy and lightly thickened, about 30 seconds. Increase the speed to high and gradually add the sugar, then the vanilla. Whip until the eggs are very thick and pale yellow, about 3 minutes. Reduce the mixer speed to medium and beat in the tepid chocolate, making sure it is completely incorporated. Change to the paddle attachment and reduce the mixer speed to low. Gradually add the flour mixture. Remove the bowl from the mixer. Using a wooden spoon, stir in the chocolate

chips, pecans, and walnuts, making sure the chunky ingredients are evenly distributed at the bottom of the bowl. (Do not turn the dough out onto the work surface, as I recommend on page 203, because the chocolate dough makes a mess.) The dough will be somewhat soft.

4   Using a 2-inch-diameter ice-cream scoop, portion the batter onto the prepared pans, placing the cookies about 1½ inches apart. Bake the cookies immediately—if you wait, they won't be shiny after baking. Bake, switching the position of the pans from top to bottom and front to back about halfway through baking, until the cookies are set around the edges (if you lift a cookie from the pan, the edges should release easily, even if the center of the cookie seems underdone), 17 to 20 minutes. Do not overbake. Cool completely on the baking pans. (The cookies can be stored in an airtight container at room temperature, with the layers separated by parchment paper, for up to 3 days.)

Pecan Moons

Makes about 6 dozen cookies

....

Delicate, with a melt-in-your-mouth texture, these moon-shaped pecan shortbreads are one of my most popular creations. Yes, the recipe makes a lot, but they are quite small and disappear quickly.

BAKER'S NOTE: You will need a 2-inch moon-shaped cookie cutter to make these.

½ cup (2 ounces) pecan halves

3 ¼ cups unbleached all-purpose flour, divided

¼ teaspoon fine sea salt

¾ pound (3 sticks) unsalted butter, at room temperature, cut into ½-inch cubes

½ cup superfine sugar

½ cup confectioners' sugar, sifted, plus additional for garnish

1 teaspoon pure vanilla extract

1 In a food processor fitted with the metal blade, process the pecans and 1 cup of the flour until the pecans are finely ground, about 30 seconds. Add the remaining flour and salt and pulse to combine.

2 Beat the butter in the bowl of a heavy-duty stand mixer fitted with the paddle attachment on medium-high speed until smooth, about 1 minute. Beat in the superfine sugar and confectioners' sugar, then the vanilla. Continue beating, occasionally stopping the mixer to scrape the bottom and sides of the bowl, until the mixture is pale yellow, about 3 minutes. Reduce the speed to low. In thirds, add the pecan-flour mixture. Mix well, scraping down the sides of the bowl, until the dough cleans the sides of the bowl.

3 Line two half-sheet pans with parchment paper. Place the dough on a lightly floured work surface and knead briefly until smooth. Dust the work surface and the top of the dough with flour, and roll out into a ¼-inch-thick rectangle. Using a 2-inch moon-shaped cookie cutter, cut out the cookies. Transfer them to the pans, placing them ½ inch apart. Gather up the scraps, roll, and cut out more cookies until all of the dough has been used. Refrigerate the cookies, about 30 minutes.

4 Meanwhile, position racks in the center and top third of the oven and preheat to 350°F. Bake, switching the position of the pans from top to bottom and front to back halfway through baking, until lightly browned around the edges, 12 to 15 minutes. Cool completely on the pans. Sift with confectioners' sugar. (Store in an airtight container for up to 5 days.)

Chocolate Clouds

Makes about 3 dozen cookies

....

Many years ago, I retired these crunchy chocolate chip cookies from our menu, but upon loud protests from their fans, I had to put them back. There are a lot of people who love their crisp, light, meringue-like texture

BAKER'S NOTE: Place the dough about 3 inches apart on the half-sheet pans—they spread.

1⅓ cups superfine sugar

1⅓ cups packed light brown sugar

16 tablespoons (2 sticks) unsalted butter, at room temperature, cut into ½-inch cubes

¾ teaspoon pure vanilla extract

2 large eggs, at room temperature, beaten

2 cups unbleached all-purpose flour

¼ teaspoon baking soda

¼ teaspoon fine sea salt

2 cups (8 ounces) toasted sliced almonds (page 5)

2 cups (12 ounces) semisweet chocolate chips

1 Position racks in the center and top third of the oven and preheat to 350°F. Line three half-sheet pans with parchment paper. Rub the superfine sugar and brown sugar together through a coarse-mesh wire sieve into a medium bowl; set aside. Beat the butter in the bowl of a heavy-duty stand mixer fitted with the paddle attachment on high speed until smooth, about 1 minute. Gradually add the sugar mixture, then the vanilla. Beat, occasionally scraping the bottom and sides of the bowl, until the mixture is pale yellow and light-textured, about 5 minutes. Gradually beat in the eggs.

2 Sift the flour, baking soda, and salt together into a medium bowl. With the mixer speed on low, add the dry ingredients in three additions, mixing just until each addition is incorporated. Add the almonds and chocolate chips and mix just until combined. Empty the dough onto the work surface, and use your hands to thoroughly distribute the almonds and chocolate chips in the dough.

3 Using a 2-inch-diameter ice-cream scoop, portion the batter onto the prepared pans. Using the heel of your palm, slightly flatten each ball of dough. Bake two of the pans with the cookies, switching the position of the pans from top to bottom and front to back about halfway through baking, until the cookies are evenly golden brown, 15 to 18 minutes. During the last 3 minutes, rap each pan on the rack. The cookies will deflate and their signature cracks will appear on the tops. Repeat with the third pan. Cool on the pans. (Store in an airtight container for up to 5 days.)

Chocolate Marmalade Cookies

Makes about 2 dozen sandwich cookies

....

Sandwich cookies are always a labor of love. These go one step beyond the norm with a chocolate coating. The combination of buttery cookie, fruity marmalade, and chocolate is sublime and worth the extra effort. Make these a day ahead of serving to allow the cookies to soften and the marmalade to set; otherwise they will slide apart when dipped in the chocolate. These are on the top of my list as the very best melt-in-your-mouth creations.

BAKER'S NOTE: Tempering chocolate is a specific way of melting the chocolate so it sets with a glossy finish. Untempered chocolate will streak and stick to your fingers when you touch it. You will need a digital thermometer to help gauge the precise temperatures. It is difficult to temper less than 12 ounces of chocolate, and there will be leftover chocolate after dipping. If you spread the melted chocolate on parchment paper to set, it can be retempered and reused at another time.

10 tablespoons (1¼ sticks) unsalted butter, at room temperature, cut into ½-inch cubes

½ cup superfine sugar

2 large egg yolks, at room temperature

Grated zest of ¼ lemon

⅛ teaspoon fine sea salt

1½ cups plus 1 tablespoon unbleached all-purpose flour

½ cup orange marmalade, preferably Sarabeth's Orange-Apricot Marmalade, finely chopped

12 ounces semisweet or bittersweet chocolate (no more than 62 percent cacao), finely chopped, divided

1 Beat the butter in the bowl of a heavy-duty stand mixer fitted with the paddle attachment on high speed until smooth, about 1 minute. Gradually add the sugar. Beat, occasionally scraping down the sides of the bowl, until light in color and texture, about 3 minutes longer. Beat in the yolks, lemon zest, and salt. Reduce the speed to low. In thirds, add the flour, and mix just until the dough comes together and the sides of the bowl are almost clean.

2 Turn out the dough onto a lightly floured work surface. Gather and shape the dough into a smooth ball. Roll the dough under your hands into a 14-inch-long log that is about 1½ inches in diameter. Place an 18 by 13-inch sheet of parchment paper on the work surface, with the long side facing you. Transfer the dough log to the center of the parchment paper. Fold the parchment paper over the log.

Hold the edge of a yardstick securely along the long side of the log, pull the top layer of the parchment paper under the yardstick to tighten the paper and lightly compress the log. The log should now be about 16 inches long. Unwrap the log. To remove the visible seam in the dough, roll it lightly on the paper to smooth it out. Reroll the paper around the log. Do not twist the ends closed, as this dough is soft. Refrigerate until the dough is chilled and firm, at least 1 hour.

3 Position racks in the center and top third of the oven and preheat to 350°F. Line two half-sheet pans with parchment paper.

4 Unwrap the log. Using a thin, sharp knife, cut the log crosswise into ⅜-inch-thick rounds, keeping the rounds in sequence. Place the cookies, about 1 inch apart, on the pans, arranging them in pairs so they will fit together nicely when sandwiched. Bake, switching the position of the pans from top to bottom and front to back halfway through baking, until the edges of the cookies are lightly browned, about 12 minutes. Cool completely on the baking pans.

5 Turn the cookies over so the undersides face up. Spoon a rounded ½ teaspoon of marmalade onto one of each pair of cookies, and sandwich their flat sides together. Let the cookies stand overnight at room temperature to set the marmalade.

6 To temper the chocolate, bring 1 inch of water to a simmer in a medium saucepan. Reduce the heat to very low. Place 8 ounces of the chocolate in a wide, heatproof bowl. Transfer the bowl to the saucepan, being sure the bottom of the bowl does not touch the water. Let stand, stirring occasionally, until the chocolate reaches 110° to 112°F on a digital instant-read thermometer. Remove the bowl from the heat and place on a kitchen towel. Add the remaining 4 ounces chocolate and stir until melted. Let stand, stirring every minute or so, until the chocolate reaches 88°F.

7 Line a half-sheet pan with fresh parchment paper. One at a time, dip a cookie in the chocolate, letting the chocolate come about one-third up the sides of the cookie. Give the cookie a gentle shake to remove excess chocolate, then carefully place the cookie on the pan. Push each cookie with your finger to move it about ⅛ inch from its position on the pan to dislodge and remove the "foot" of chocolate that has formed. Let the cookies stand until the chocolate sets. (The cookies can be stored in an airtight container, with the layers separated by parchment paper, for up to 5 days.)

Ladyfingers

Makes about 2 dozen cookies

....

Ladyfingers are truly a cookie classic. Their simple, unadorned flavor, with just a hint of vanilla, makes them perfect for nibbling. Or use as a component in a mousse-filled charlotte, such as the Raspberries and Cream Charlotte on page 163.

3 large eggs, separated, at room temperature

¼ cup plus 3 tablespoons superfine sugar, divided

Seeds from ¼ Plumped Vanilla Bean (page 295) or ¼ teaspoon pure vanilla extract

⅛ teaspoon fine sea salt

⅔ cup pastry or unbleached cake flour, sifted twice

Confectioners' sugar, for sifting

1 Position racks in the center and top third of the oven and preheat to 400°F. Line two half-sheet pans with parchment paper.

2 Put the egg whites in a grease-free medium bowl. Whip on high speed with a handheld electric mixer until soft peaks form. One tablespoon at a time, beat in ¼ cup of the superfine sugar and whip until the whites form stiff, shiny peaks. Set the whipped whites aside.

3 Combine the yolks, vanilla, salt, and the remaining 3 tablespoons superfine sugar in another medium bowl. Whip the yolk mixture on high speed until thick and pale yellow, about 3 minutes. Turn off the mixer and lift the beaters 2 inches above the beaten yolk mixture—the mixture should form a thick ribbon that falls back on itself and remains on the surface for a few seconds before sinking. Add about one-fourth of the whites to the egg mixture and stir to lighten with a silicone spatula. Add the remaining whites to the batter and fold together until just combined. In five additions, sift the flour over the egg mixture, and use a large balloon whisk or silicone spatula to gently fold in each addition. Transfer the batter to a large (at least 16 inches long) pastry bag fitted with a ⅜-inch-diameter plain pastry tip, such as Ateco #804. Pipe 4-inch-long strips of the batter onto the pans, spacing them about 1 inch apart. Sift confectioners' sugar over the tops of the ladyfingers.

4 Bake until the ladyfingers are golden brown (you may see some crackles on top), 10 to 12 minutes. These cookies are delicate, so don't switch the position of the pans, or the ladyfingers could deflate. The pan on the top rack could be done a little sooner than the one on the center rack. Cool completely on the pans. Carefully remove the ladyfingers from the parchment paper with a metal spatula. (Store in an airtight container, with the layers separated by parchment paper, for up to 3 days.)

Linzer Hearts

Makes about 3 dozen sandwich cookies

....

These classic cookies are a little time-consuming to make, but the results are so beautiful and delicious that you won't mind the extra effort. The cinnamon-scented hazelnut dough is cut out into heart shapes, then baked and sandwiched with raspberry preserves. This lovely cookie is reminiscent of the finest Linzertorte (Linz is an Austrian town that is famous for this kind of tart/cake). The dough is on the soft side, so handle it with care.

BAKER'S NOTE: These cookies bake up crisp but soften when they come in contact with the preserves, and soften even more if stored in an airtight container. You will need a 2¼-inch heart-shaped cookie cutter (measured across its widest point) to make these beautiful jewels.

¾ cup (3 ounces) hazelnuts

2½ cups pastry or unbleached cake flour, sifted, divided, plus additional for sprinkling

1¼ teaspoons ground cinnamon

½ teaspoon baking powder

⅛ teaspoon fine sea salt

12 tablespoons (1½ sticks) unsalted butter, at room temperature, cut into ½-inch cubes

½ cup plus 1 tablespoon superfine sugar

1 large egg, at room temperature, beaten

Approximately ½ cup raspberry preserves

Confectioners' sugar, for decoration

1   Position a rack in the center of the oven and preheat to 350°F. Spread the hazelnuts on a half-sheet pan and bake until the skins are cracked, about 10 minutes. A handful at a time, place the warm hazelnuts in a kitchen towel and rub together in the towel to remove the skin (some skin may remain on the nuts). Cool completely.

2   In a food processor fitted with the metal blade, process the cooled nuts with ½ cup of the flour until finely ground. Mix the remaining 2 cups flour, the cinnamon, baking powder, and salt with the nut mixture in a medium bowl.

3   Beat the butter and superfine sugar in the bowl of a heavy-duty stand mixer fitted with the paddle attachment on medium-high speed until light in color and texture, about 5 minutes, occasionally scraping down the sides of the bowl with a silicone spatula. Gradually beat in the egg. Reduce the

speed to low and add the flour mixture. The dough will be very moist. Place the dough on a large piece of plastic wrap. Wrap loosely in the plastic and shape into a 1-inch-thick rectangle. Refrigerate until chilled, 1 to 2 hours.

4 Position racks in the center and top third of the oven and preheat to 350°F. Line three half-sheet pans with parchment paper.

5 Cut the chilled dough in half. Place one half of the dough on a lightly floured work surface, and sprinkle the top with flour. Roll out the dough into a ⅛-inch-thick rectangle. Using a 2¼-inch heart-shaped cookie cutter dipped in flour, cut out the cookies. Transfer to the prepared pans. (The dough is delicate, and you will probably find it easiest to move the hearts with a floured offset metal spatula.) Gather up the scraps and set aside. Repeat rolling and cutting out the cookies with the remaining half of dough. Place the pans in the refrigerator (there is no need to cover them). Combine all of the remaining scraps into a ½-inch-thick rectangle and wrap in plastic wrap. Refrigerate the dough until lightly chilled, about 10 minutes. Repeat the rolling and cutting procedure until all of the dough has been cut into hearts and placed on the pans. Refrigerate the hearts on the pans until well chilled, about 30 minutes.

6 Bake the first two pans of cookies, switching the position of the baking pans from top to bottom and front to back, until the edges of the cookies are lightly browned, 15 to 17 minutes. Repeat with the last pan of cookies. Cool completely on the pans.

7 Arrange half of the cookies on a half-sheet pan lined with parchment paper, with the undersides facing up. Spoon about ½ teaspoon of the raspberry preserves onto the centers of the cookies. Top each with one of the remaining cookies, flat sides facing, to make a sandwich. Cover with parchment and let stand at least 8 hours or overnight to set. (The cookies can be stored in an airtight container, with the layers separated by parchment paper, for up to 5 days.) Just before serving, sift confectioners' sugar over the cookies.

Oatmeal-Raisin Cookies

Makes about 2 dozen cookies

....

Every baker must have a great oatmeal cookie recipe. This one gets a delicious nutti-ness from the sunflower seeds—an ingredient that you don't find in many cookies but which is a perfect complement for the oatmeal.

⅔ cup superfine sugar

⅔ cup packed light brown sugar

1½ cups unbleached all-purpose flour

¼ teaspoon baking soda

¼ teaspoon fine sea salt

1½ cups old-fashioned (rolled) oats

16 tablespoons (2 sticks) unsalted butter, at room temperature, cut into ½-inch cubes

1 teaspoon pure vanilla extract

2 large eggs, at room temperature, beaten

1½ cups seedless raisins

½ cup hulled sunflower seeds

1 Position racks in the center and top third of the oven and preheat to 350°F. Line two half-sheet pans with parchment paper.

2 Rub the superfine sugar and brown sugar together through a coarse-mesh sieve into a medium bowl. Sift the flour, baking soda, and salt into another bowl, then add the oats and stir well to combine.

3 Beat the butter in the bowl of a heavy-duty stand mixer fitted with the paddle attachment on high speed until smooth, about 1 minute. Gradually add the sugar mixture, then the vanilla. Beat, occa-sionally scraping the bottom and sides of the bowl, until the mixture is pale yellow and very light-textured, about 3 minutes. Gradually beat in the eggs. Reduce the mixer speed to low. In thirds, beat the dry ingredients into the creamed mixture, beating just until each addition is incorporated. Mix in the raisins and sunflower seeds. Do not overmix.

4 Using a 2-inch-diameter ice-cream scoop, portion the batter onto the prepared pans, placing the cookies about 1½ inches apart. Bake, switching the position of the pans from top to bottom and front to back about halfway through baking, until the cookies are light golden brown, 15 to 18 minutes. Cool completely on the pans. (The cookies can be stored in an airtight container at room tempera-ture for 5 days.)

Palmiers

Makes about 2½ dozen palmiers

....

We bake hundreds of these melt-in-your-mouth cookies every day; they are an amazing combination of flaky pastry and crunchy caramelized sugar. The trick is getting the sugar to melt into a thin amber glaze. The solution? Freeze the sugar-coated dough for a week to absorb a little moisture from the freezer.

BAKER'S NOTE: Palmiers are baked a week to a month after you make and freeze the dough strip.

Unbleached all-purpose flour, for rolling	*⅔ cup superfine sugar, divided*
½ recipe (about 1 pound) Puff Pastry (page 20), chilled	*Additional ⅓ cup superfine sugar, for dipping (to be used later, when the palmiers are baked)*

1 At least 1 week before baking the palmiers, very lightly flour a work surface. Place the pastry on the surface with the open seam facing you. Roll out the dough into a 17 by 13-inch rectangle, about ⅛ inch thick. Transfer to a half-sheet pan and refrigerate, uncovered, for about 30 minutes.

2 Clean the flour from the work surface. Sprinkle ⅓ cup of the sugar over an area equal to the size of the pastry sheet. Place the pastry on the sugar. Sprinkle another ⅓ cup sugar over the pastry. Roll a large, heavy rolling pin over the pastry to press in the sugar, but do not enlarge it. Using a yardstick and a pizza wheel, trim the sides of the pastry to 16 by 12 inches, with the long side at the top.

3 Fold the top edge of the dough down 2 inches. Fold the bottom edge of the pastry up 2 inches (figure 1). Repeat, folding the top edge down and the bottom edge up (figures 2 and 3). The edges of the folded pastry should not meet but leave a ¼-inch gap in the center of the pastry. Lightly roll over the length of the dough with the rolling pin. Fold the pastry in half horizontally at the gap to make a long strip (figure 4). Using the side of your hand, lightly rap the length of the strip to barely compress the layers (figure 5). Gently roll over the top of the pastry strip to elongate it to 24 inches (figure 6). Discard any excess sugar on the work surface.

4 Cut in half vertically and wrap each piece in parchment paper, then tightly in plastic wrap. Place the wrapped pastry on sturdy cardboard to support it in the freezer. Freeze for at least 1 week or up to 1 month. When ready to bake, defrost in the refrigerator overnight.

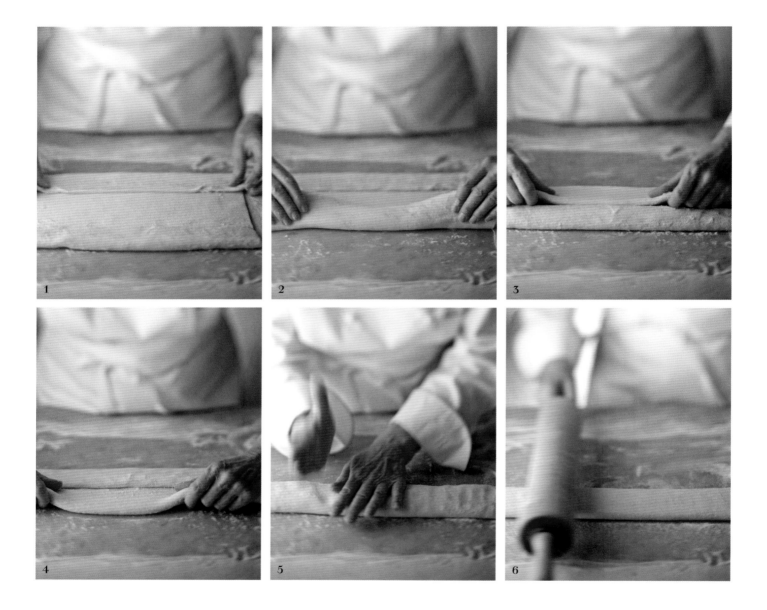

5 Position racks in the center and top third of the oven and preheat to 350°F. Line two half-sheet pans with parchment paper. Unwrap the pastry strips. Using a very sharp, thin knife, cut the strip vertically into ½-inch-wide pieces. Put the additional ⅓ cup sugar in a small bowl. One at a time, dip the pastries in the sugar to coat, then place them 1 inch apart, cut sides up, on the pans.

6 Bake for 20 minutes. Remove the pans from the oven, and turn over the palmiers. Return to the oven, switching the position of the pans from top to bottom and front to back. Continue baking until the palmiers are crisp, golden brown, and sheathed in a caramelized sugar coating, about 10 minutes more. Cool completely on the pans. (Store in an airtight container for up to 3 days.)

Rugelach

Makes 3 dozen cookies

....

Rugelach are roll-up cookies that every Jewish grandmother makes, or wants to make. They can be filled with preserves or nuts or more exotic fare. My version uses a special nut mixture with raspberry preserves in a flaky cream cheese dough.

BAKER'S NOTE: Be sure that the cream cheese is well softened before creaming it with the butter. Let it stand at room temperature for at least 2 hours. Use full-fat cheese.

16 tablespoons (2 sticks) unsalted butter, at room temperature, cut into ½-inch cubes

8 ounces cream cheese, softened, cut into ½-inch cubes

2 tablespoons superfine sugar

½ teaspoon pure vanilla extract

⅛ teaspoon fine sea salt

2¼ cups unbleached all-purpose flour

Approximately ½ cup raspberry or apricot preserves

Confectioners' sugar, for serving

Filling

¼ cup (1 ounce) finely chopped walnuts

1 tablespoon superfine sugar

1 tablespoon light brown sugar

½ teaspoon Dutch-processed cocoa powder

½ teaspoon ground cinnamon

1 Beat the butter and cream cheese in the bowl of a heavy-duty stand mixer fitted with the paddle attachment on medium-high speed until evenly combined, stopping the mixer once or twice to scrape down the sides and bottom of the bowl, about 2 minutes. Beat in the superfine sugar, vanilla, and salt. Reduce the speed to low. Add 1¼ cups of the flour and mix just until incorporated, then repeat with the remaining 1 cup of flour. Do not overmix.

2 Turn out the dough onto a lightly floured work surface. Flour your hands well and gently knead to be sure that the ingredients are evenly distributed, about 10 seconds. Divide the dough into thirds. Shape each portion into a 1-inch-thick disk and wrap each in plastic wrap. Refrigerate until chilled and firm, about 2 hours.

3 To make the filling, combine the walnuts, superfine sugar, brown sugar, cocoa, and cinnamon in a small bowl; set aside.

4   Position racks in the center and top third of the oven and preheat to 350°F. Line two half-sheet pans with parchment paper.

5   Working with one disk of dough at a time, unwrap and place on a lightly floured work surface. Sprinkle the top of the dough with flour, and roll out into a 13-inch-diameter circle. Using a small offset metal spatula, spread with about 2 tablespoons of the preserves, leaving a 2-inch-diameter space in the center of the dough, and a 1-inch border around the edge. Sprinkle the jam with about 2 tablespoons of the filling mixture. Using a sharp pizza wheel or large knife, cut the dough into quarters, then cut each quarter into 3 wedges, to give a total of 12 wedges. One at a time, starting at the wide end, fold the corners in about ¼ inch and then roll up. Do not roll the rugelach too tightly or the jam and filling will ooze out. Keep the outside of each cookie free of the jam and filling, or they'll tend to burn. Wipe your fingers clean after making each rugelach, or you will transfer the sticky interior of the last cookie to the exterior of the next one. Place each rugelach on the pans about 1 inch apart, with the point of each facing down. Curve the ends of the rugelach slightly toward the point to make a crescent. Repeat this process with the other two disks of dough.

6   Bake until lightly browned, about 30 minutes. Cool completely on the pans. (The cookies can be stored in an airtight container at room temperature for 5 days.) Just before serving, sift with confectioners' sugar.

Buttery Shortbread

Makes about 2 dozen cookies

....

Shortbread cookies are quite easy to make. They traditionally have just a few ingredients, so the buttery flavor really comes through. Sugar sprinkled over the hot baked cookies as they come out of the oven gives them an extra crunch. These cookies were the first sweet my grandchildren ever ate and are still their favorite.

16 tablespoons (2 sticks) unsalted butter, at room temperature, cut into ½-inch cubes

½ cup superfine sugar

½ teaspoon pure vanilla extract

Grated zest of ½ lemon

2 cups unbleached all-purpose flour

⅛ teaspoon fine sea salt

½ cup granulated sugar, for sprinkling

1   Position racks in the center and top third of the oven and preheat to 350°F. Line two half-sheet pans with parchment paper.

2   Beat the butter in the bowl of a heavy-duty stand mixer fitted with the paddle attachment on medium-high speed until the butter is smooth, about 1 minute. Gradually add the superfine sugar, then the vanilla and lemon zest, mixing until light in color and texture, about 3 minutes. Reduce the mixer speed to low. In thirds, add the flour and salt. Mix, scraping down the sides of the bowl to be sure the dough is well combined, until the dough cleans the sides of the bowl.

3   Place the dough on a lightly floured work surface and knead briefly until smooth. Dust the work surface and the top of the dough with flour, and roll out the dough into a ¼-inch-thick rectangle. Using a 2½-inch round fluted cookie cutter, cut out the cookies, and place them 1 inch apart on the half-sheet pans. Gather up the scraps, roll out, and cut out more cookies until all of the dough has been used. Refrigerate the cookies until chilled, about 30 minutes.

4   Bake, switching the position of the pans from top to bottom and front to back halfway through baking, until the edges are very lightly browned, about 15 minutes. Remove from the oven and immediately sprinkle the cookies lightly with the granulated sugar (the sugar will not stick if the cookies aren't hot). Cool completely on the pans. (The cookies can be stored in an airtight container at room temperature for 5 days.)

Brownies

Makes 1 dozen brownies

....

These moist brownies are always popular items in our dessert case. Brownies may be one of the easiest sweets to make, but pay attention to the details. For fudgy brownies, slightly underbake, and refrigerate overnight.

1¼ cups unbleached all-purpose flour

¼ teaspoon baking soda

¼ teaspoon fine sea salt

8 ounces semisweet or bittersweet chocolate (no more than 62 percent cacao), finely chopped

8 tablespoons (1 stick) unsalted butter, cut into tablespoons, plus more for the pan

⅓ cup plus 1 tablespoon hot water

3 large eggs, at room temperature

1 cup superfine sugar

1½ teaspoons pure vanilla extract

1¼ cups (8 ounces) semisweet chocolate chips

1 Make the brownies at least 1 day before serving. Position a rack in the center of the oven and preheat to 350°F. Lightly butter a 9 by 13-inch rimmed baking pan and line the bottom with parchment paper. Sift the flour, baking soda, and salt together into a medium bowl, and set aside. Bring 1 inch of water to a simmer in a medium saucepan over low heat. Combine the chopped chocolate, butter, and ⅓ cup plus 1 tablespoon hot water in a wide, heatproof bowl. Place over the simmering water in the saucepan, stirring often, until the chocolate and butter are melted and the mixture is smooth. Remove the bowl from the heat and let stand, stirring occasionally, until tepid.

2 Beat the eggs, sugar, and vanilla in the bowl of a heavy-duty stand mixer with the whisk attachment until the eggs have tripled in volume, about 3 minutes. Change to the paddle attachment. Add the cooled chocolate and mix on low speed until combined. Add the flour mixture and mix just until combined, scraping down the sides of the bowl as needed. Stir in the chocolate chips. Spread the batter evenly in the prepared pan. Bake until a cake tester inserted into the center of the brownies comes out with a moist crumb, about 25 minutes. Do not overbake. Transfer to a wire cooling rack and let cool completely in the pan. Cover with plastic wrap and refrigerate overnight.

3 Run a knife around the inside of the pan. Place a cutting board over the pan. Invert the pan and board together to unmold the pastry. Peel off the parchment paper. Cut the upside-down pastry into 12 brownies. (The brownies can be refrigerated in an airtight container for up to 3 days.)

Chapter Eight

Spoon Desserts

THE ITALIANS HAVE A NAME FOR THIS FAMILY OF PUDDINGS AND CUS-TARDS: SPOON DESSERTS. TENDER ENOUGH TO EAT WITH A SPOON, THIS category includes some of the most popular desserts in the world, such as crème caramel, crème brûlée, and tiramisù. Their yielding textures provide an element of comfort in every bite, the culinary equivalent of putting on a favorite old sweater or wrapping yourself up in a soft blanket.

Eggs, sugar, and cream work in tandem to give spoon desserts their delicacy. When cooking eggs, the key is heat control. Overcooked eggs act up—yolks curdle, custards break and weep, whites turn rubbery. A water bath insulates baked custards to help keep overcooking at bay, but a low oven temperature is the more important factor. Constant stirring and an eye on the thermometer discourage curdling the crème anglaise in my rice pudding. You may think of spoon desserts as baby food, which is fine with me because perhaps it will remind you to "baby" the eggs in the recipes.

Although these desserts will seem familiar, just like the other classic sweets in this book, these are truly unique. The tiramisù is flavored with orange and chocolate; the bread puddings are studded with raspberries and baked in individual servings; the rice pudding is actually a combination of a sweet risotto and crème anglaise. When you serve these spoon desserts, your guests will enjoy truly extraordinary versions of timeless recipes.

Crème Brûlée

Makes 8 servings

....

There's nothing halfhearted about crème brûlée. If you want to make it well, there are no substitutes for the decadence of heavy cream and egg yolks, just as there is no shortcut for slowly cooking the custards in a water bath. But the custard in crème brûlée shares top billing with a co-star: the glassy sugar topping, which I create with a tool you may not be familiar with, an iron salamander.

BAKER'S NOTE: To give crème brûlée its thin, caramelized sugar topping, most cooks are content with a butane culinary torch. To my taste, nothing beats the classic caramel salamander. This cast-iron implement, which looks like a metal hockey puck on a long handle, is frankly low-tech, and once you try it, you won't use anything else to brûlée your crème. (See Sources on page 297 for where to buy one.) Be sure to heat the salamander thoroughly for at least 30 minutes before applying to the sugar. The sugar will smoke dramatically; have the exhaust fan in your range hood turned onto its highest setting. • If you prefer, use a butane culinary torch to caramelize the sugar topping on the crème brûlée. Cover each of the custards with the sugar mixture. Wave the flame from the torch about an inch above each custard (making sure that it barely touches the sugar) until the sugar has melted and caramelized into a thin pool. When cool, it will harden into its signature topping. • When it comes to baked custards like crème brûlée and crème caramel, I actually prefer vanilla extract to vanilla beans, because the tiny seeds sink to the bottoms of the custards and the vanilla flavor is concentrated in one spot.

1 quart heavy cream	*8 large egg yolks, at room temperature*
½ cup superfine sugar	*2 teaspoons pure vanilla extract*

Topping

½ cup packed light brown sugar • ½ cup superfine sugar

1   At least 6 hours before serving, position a rack in the center of the oven and preheat to 300°F.

2   Combine the cream and sugar in a heavy-bottomed medium saucepan. Place the egg yolks in a heat-proof medium bowl near the stove. Bring the cream mixture to a simmer over medium-low heat, stirring often. Gradually whisk the hot cream mixture into the yolks. Whisk in the vanilla. Strain the mixture through a wire sieve into a heatproof 1-quart or larger liquid measuring cup or pitcher.

3   Divide the cream mixture evenly among eight 6-ounce (¾-cup) ramekins. Using a small spoon, skim any bubbles from the surface of the custard. Place the ramekins in a shallow roasting pan. Slide the oven rack partially out of the oven. Place the pan on the rack. Taking care not to splash any water into the ramekins, pour enough hot tap water to come about ½ inch up the sides of the ramekins. Gently slide the rack with the pan into the oven.

4   Bake until the custards are set (the mixture will move as a unit when a ramekin is shaken, with a dime-size center portion that still looks uncooked), about 45 minutes. Using rubber gloves, carefully remove the ramekins from the water and transfer to a wire rack. Let cool completely.

5   Cover each custard with plastic wrap. Refrigerate until well chilled, at least 4 hours or overnight.

6   Heat the "puck" end of a cast-iron salamander directly in the flames of a gas burner, or on the coils of an electric burner on high heat, for 30 minutes.

7   To make the topping, combine the brown sugar and superfine sugar and rub through a medium-mesh wire sieve. Return the sugar mixture to the sieve. Turn your range hood's exhaust fan on high. Uncover the custards and place on a half-sheet pan. Rub the sugar mixture through the sieve to apply a ⅛-inch-deep, even layer over the top of each custard. With the bottom of a ramekin, gently flatten the sugar on each custard, cleaning the bottom of the ramekin after each pressing. Place the half-sheet pan under the range hood. One at a time, gently touch the hot puck onto the sugar to melt it—it will take only a second or two to caramelize. Expect a lot of smoke. (If you don't have a strong exhaust fan, use the butane torch, as it creates considerably less smoke than the salamander.) Serve immediately.

Orange Blossom Crème Caramel

Makes 8 servings

....

Crème caramel, a quivering custard with an amber cap sitting in a pool of slightly bitter caramelized sugar syrup, is one of the best desserts for make-ahead entertaining, as you must allow time for the custards to chill and set. A touch of orange gives these a surprising flavor that complements the traditional vanilla.

BAKER'S NOTE: The caramel will set up quickly when poured into the ramekins, making it difficult to properly coat the interiors. Warming the ramekins in the oven first solves this problem.

Caramel

1¼ cups superfine sugar · 3 tablespoons water

2¾ cups whole milk	*4 large eggs plus 3 large egg yolks, at room temperature*
¼ cup heavy cream	*½ cup superfine sugar*
Zest of ½ orange, removed from the orange with a vegetable peeler	*1 teaspoon pure vanilla extract*
	1 teaspoon orange blossom water

1   Position a rack in the center of the oven and preheat to 325°F. Place eight 6-ounce (¾-cup) ramekins in a roasting pan.

2   To make the caramel, bring the sugar and water to a boil in a heavy-bottomed medium saucepan over high heat, stirring just until the sugar is dissolved. Boil the syrup, occasionally swirling the pan by the handle, until it is caramelized, about the color of a penny, and smoking lightly, about 5 minutes. The caramel must be fairly dark and have a slightly bitter aroma, or it won't have enough flavor. You must judge this point with your eyes and nose. A candy thermometer isn't much help here, as the syrup is too shallow to get an accurate reading.

3   During the last few minutes of making the caramel, place the ramekins in the roasting pan in the oven for about 3 minutes to warm them. Remove the ramekins from the oven.

4   Working quickly, pour equal amounts of the caramel syrup into the warm ramekins. Using a kitchen towel to protect your hand, tilt each ramekin to coat the inside as best as you can. It doesn't have to be an even coating as long as the bottom is covered. Return the ramekins to the shallow roasting pan.

5   To make the custard, bring the milk, cream, and orange zest to a simmer in another medium saucepan. Whisk the eggs, yolks, and sugar together in a heatproof medium bowl. Gradually whisk in the hot milk mixture. Strain the custard through a medium-mesh wire sieve into a large, heatproof pitcher. Discard the zest. Stir in the vanilla and orange blossom water.

6   Divide the custard equally among the ramekins. Slide the oven rack partially out of the oven. Place the pan on the rack. Taking care not to splash any water into the ramekins, pour enough hot tap water to come about ½ inch up the sides of the ramekins. Cover the pan with aluminum foil. Gently slide the rack with the pan into the oven.

7   Bake until a knife inserted near the edge of the custard comes out clean (be careful when opening the foil, as steam will escape), even if the center seems slightly unset, about 30 minutes. Remove from the oven and discard the foil. Using rubber gloves, carefully remove the ramekins from the pan and let cool completely on a wire rack. Cover each ramekin with plastic wrap. Refrigerate until well chilled, at least 2 hours and up to 2 days.

8   When ready to serve, run a nonserrated dinner knife around the inside of each ramekin, taking care not to cut into the custard. To unmold, place a dessert plate, upside down, over a ramekin. Holding the ramekin and plate together, invert them, and give them a few sharp shakes to dislodge the custard. Lift off the ramekin. Serve chilled.

Triple-Chocolate Chocolate Pudding

Makes 6 servings

....

Who says that chocolate pudding is for kids? My version has two kinds of chocolate and is bolstered with cocoa to make it a triple threat for chocolate lovers. At the bakery, we pour the pudding into small Mason jars for serving.

3 tablespoons unsalted butter	*⅛ teaspoon fine sea salt*
4½ ounces semisweet or bittersweet chocolate (no more than 62 percent cacao), finely chopped	*3 large eggs plus 1 large egg yolk, at room temperature*
1 ounce unsweetened chocolate, finely chopped	*¼ cup heavy cream*
3 cups whole milk	*1 tablespoon dark rum*
1 cup granulated sugar, divided	*1 teaspoon pure vanilla extract*
¼ cup Dutch-processed cocoa powder	*Whipped Cream (page 292)*
3 tablespoons cornstarch	*Chocolate shavings, made with a vegetable peeler*

1 Bring 1 inch of water to a simmer in a medium saucepan over low heat. Place the butter in a wide, heatproof bowl and melt the butter over the hot water. Add the semisweet and unsweetened chocolates and let stand, stirring often, until melted and smooth. Remove the bowl from the heat.

2 Heat the milk and ⅓ cup of the sugar in a medium saucepan over low heat until steaming. Whisk the remaining ⅔ cup sugar with the cocoa, cornstarch, and salt in a heatproof medium bowl. Add the eggs, yolk, and cream and whisk until well combined. Gradually whisk in about half of the hot milk mixture. Pour the cocoa mixture into the medium saucepan. Bring to a full boil over medium heat, whisking often, being sure to reach into the corners of the saucepan. Reduce the heat to low and let boil for 30 seconds. The cornstarch and cocoa keep the eggs from curdling.

3 Remove from the heat. Add the melted chocolate mixture, rum, and vanilla and whisk until combined. Pour into six 8-ounce glass jars or individual bowls. Cover each with a piece of plastic wrap, letting the plastic touch the surface of the pudding, and pierce a few times with the tip of a small sharp knife. (If you like a skin on your pudding, do not cover it.) Let cool until tepid, about 1 hour. Refrigerate until chilled, at least 2 hours. (The puddings can be refrigerated for up to 3 days.)

4 To serve, top each pudding with whipped cream and chocolate shavings.

Creamy Rice Pudding

Makes 10 servings

....

For many of our customers, this rice pudding is the ultimate dessert—the treat they turn to when they want to reward themselves, or when they need a pick-me-up. Most rice puddings are rustic, even slapdash, but my goal wasn't to make the easiest rice pudding, just the best. It combines risotto and crème anglaise to give a mix of the lusciously creamy and the pleasantly starchy.

BAKER'S NOTE: I know you will think that this recipe is too large, but trust me. It will disappear before your eyes. So, make it when you need to serve a crowd, or share it with your friends, who will thereafter remain devoted to you for life. • Arborio rice is the most common Italian rice used for risotto, but there are other varieties that are equally good. It is important to use rice with high starch content, such as Arborio, Vialone Nano, Carnaroli, or Baldo.

Crème Anglaise

1 cup heavy cream	½ Plumped Vanilla Bean (page 295)
1 cup whole milk	6 large egg yolks
⅔ cup granulated sugar	

Sweet Risotto

2 quarts whole milk	1⅔ cups Italian rice for risotto (see Baker's Note)
1 cup granulated sugar	⅔ cup seedless raisins
½ Plumped Vanilla Bean (page 295)	

Whipped Cream (page 292), for serving

1   At least 8 hours before serving the rice pudding, make the crème anglaise. Combine the cream, milk, and sugar in a heavy-bottomed medium saucepan. Squeeze the seeds from the plumped vanilla bean into the mixture. Split the bean lengthwise, and add to the saucepan. Place the egg yolks in a heatproof medium bowl near the stove. Whisk well and keep the whisk in the bowl. Also, near the stove, place a medium-mesh wire sieve over a second heatproof bowl placed in a larger bowl filled with an ice bath.

2   Heat the cream mixture over medium heat, stirring almost constantly with a silicone spatula to dissolve the sugar, until the mixture is very hot but not simmering. Gradually whisk the hot cream mixture into the yolks. Return this mixture to the saucepan and reduce the heat to medium-low.

3   Cook, stirring constantly with the spatula, being sure to reach the corners of the saucepan, until the custard is thick enough to nicely coat the spatula. (A finger run through the custard on the spatula will cut a swath, and an instant-read thermometer will read 180°F.) Immediately strain the custard through the sieve into the bowl that is in the ice bath. (This removes any bits of cooked egg white.) Discard the vanilla bean. Let cool, stirring often, until the custard is chilled and thickened, at least 1 hour. Cover the bowl of custard and refrigerate until ready to use, up to 1 day.

4   Meanwhile, prepare the sweet risotto. Combine the milk and sugar in a heavy-bottomed large saucepan. Squeeze the seeds from the plumped vanilla bean into the mixture. Split the bean lengthwise, and add to the saucepan. Stir in the rice. Bring to a simmer over medium heat, stirring almost constantly. Reduce the heat to low so the liquid is at a steady simmer. Cook the rice mixture, stirring every 10 minutes or so, until the rice is tender and has absorbed almost all of the milk but is not dry, about 40 minutes. Do not stir the rice mixture too often, or you will release too much starch from the rice into the milk. Adjust the heat as necessary so the mixture simmers without scorching. And don't be concerned if you see a thin skin form on the surface of the milk. The final texture should remind you of a savory risotto, with tender rice in a loose, creamy "sauce." The mixture will thicken upon cooling. Remove and discard the vanilla bean.

5   Spread the risotto into a half-sheet pan. Cover with a large sheet of plastic wrap, pressing the wrap directly onto the surface of the risotto. Pierce the plastic all over with the tip of a small sharp knife. Let stand at room temperature until cooled, at least 2 hours.

6   Transfer the risotto to a large bowl. Add the crème anglaise and raisins. Using clean hands, combine the rice and crème anglaise, gently separating the rice grains with your fingers. Spoon into ten 1-cup glass jars, and cover with the lids. Or, spoon into individual bowls and cover with plastic wrap. Refrigerate until chilled, at least 2 hours. (The puddings can be refrigerated for up to 2 days.)

7   To serve, remove the lids and top each pudding with whipped cream. Serve chilled.

Raspberry Bread Pudding
Makes 8 servings

....

The usual procedure for bread pudding is to bake the entire recipe in a single pan. I prefer individual bread puddings for a more tailored, elegant look. Don't be alarmed at the low baking temperature, as this ensures that the puddings remain creamy and do not curdle. This signature dessert is served at all of the Sarabeth's restaurants. The raspberry sauce is a must, so be sure to make it.

BAKER'S NOTE: You will need eight 3-inch-diameter by 2⅜-inch-tall entremet rings for the puddings.

Softened unsalted butter, for the entremet rings

1 large loaf (1½ pounds) firm white sandwich bread, such as Pain de Mie (page 101), preferably unsliced

One 6-ounce container fresh raspberries

Crème Anglaise

3 cups heavy cream

3 cups whole milk

1½ cups granulated sugar

2 Plumped Vanilla Beans (page 295)

16 large egg yolks

Confectioners' sugar, for garnish • Raspberry Sauce (page 291)

1 Position racks in the center and top third of the oven and preheat to 325°F. Lightly butter the insides of eight 3-inch-diameter by 2⅜-inch-tall metal entremet rings. Line a half-sheet pan with parchment paper. Place the rings on the pan.

2 Cut the entire loaf of bread into ⅓-inch-thick slices and discard the ends. Using one of the entremet rings like a cookie cutter, cut out 8 circles of bread, and set aside. Remove the crust from the remaining slices, and cut the bread into ⅓-inch cubes. You should have about 7 cups of bread cubes.

3 Spread the cubes on two additional half-sheet pans. Bake, stirring the cubes occasionally, until lightly toasted, about 15 minutes. (Keep your eye on them; they burn easily.) Transfer the cubes to a large bowl. Reduce the oven temperature to 250°F.

4 To make the crème anglaise, pour the cream and milk into a heavy-bottomed large saucepan, and add the sugar. Squeeze the seeds from the plumped beans into the mixture. Split the beans lengthwise and add them to the saucepan. Whisk the egg yolks in a large, heatproof bowl and place near the stove. Place a fine-mesh wire sieve over a second heatproof bowl placed in a larger bowl filled with an ice bath.

5 Heat the cream mixture over medium heat, stirring often with a silicone spatula to dissolve the sugar, until the mixture is very hot but not simmering. Gradually whisk about half of the cream mixture into the yolks. Pour this mixture back into the saucepan. Cook over medium-low heat, stirring constantly with the spatula, until the crème anglaise is thick enough to nicely coat the spatula. (A finger run through the custard on the spatula will cut a swath, and an instant-read thermometer will read 180°F.) Immediately strain the custard through the sieve into the bowl in the ice bath to remove any bits of cooked egg white. Discard the vanilla bean. Cool for 15 minutes.

6 Measure 1¼ cups of the crème anglaise into a glass measuring cup; cool completely, cover, and refrigerate. Reserve as the sauce for the puddings.

7 Pour 4 cups of the remaining warm crème anglaise over the bread cubes and stir gently. Let stand until the bread has soaked up the custard, about 20 minutes. If the mixture looks dry, add more of the crème anglaise as needed.

8 Fit a bread round into the bottom of each entremet ring; it should make a tight fit. Pour about 2 tablespoons of the crème anglaise into each ring to cover the round (figure 1). Let stand until softened, about 5 minutes.

9 Using a 2-inch-diameter ice-cream scoop, carefully fill each entremet ring halfway with the bread cube mixture (figure 2). Use your fingers to evenly spread out the mixture, taking care that there are no air pockets. Put a tablespoon of crème anglaise in each ring. Place 4 to 5 raspberries in the center of each pudding (figure 3). Fill with the remaining bread cube mixture (figures 4 and 5). Carefully pour enough of the remaining crème anglaise to cover the cubes. Gently poke your fingers into each pudding to distribute the anglaise between the cubes (figure 6). Each ring should be filled to the top. Depending on the consistency and soaking power of the bread, you may have leftover crème anglaise.

10 Carefully transfer the pan of puddings to the oven. Bake until the puddings bounce back when lightly pressed in the centers, about 50 minutes. Let cool until tepid, about 1½ hours. Slip off the rings.

11 For each serving, place a pudding on a dessert plate. Sift a light coating of confectioners' sugar on top. Spoon about 2½ tablespoons of the reserved crème anglaise around the pudding. Using a dessert spoon, drop seven or eight ¼ teaspoonfuls of the raspberry sauce, spaced at equal distances, in the crème anglaise around the pudding. Drag the tip of a small sharp knife through the drops of raspberry sauce to make heart shapes. Serve at once.

Chocolate Orange Tiramisù

Makes 10 servings

....

I love classic tiramisù (made with ladyfingers) as much as the next person. But here's a version with a pudding-like mascarpone filling, layered with orange-scented chocolate cake that makes an extraordinary dessert for a crowd. Build the tiramisù in your prettiest transparent glass bowl so everyone can admire the interplay of the contrasting colors of the chocolate and mascarpone.

BAKER'S NOTE: While there is American-made mascarpone, the Italian cheese is smoother and richer.

Chocolate Orange Cake (page 148)

Coffee Syrup

⅓ cup hot brewed strong coffee, preferably French or Italian roast

2 tablespoons superfine sugar

⅓ cup orange-flavored liqueur, preferably Grand Marnier

Mascarpone Filling

¾ cup heavy cream

6 large egg yolks

½ cup superfine sugar

One 17.3-ounce (500-gram) container mascarpone, at room temperature

1 Keep the chocolate orange cake refrigerated until you are ready to assemble the tiramisù (see step 6). It is easier to handle when chilled.

2 To make the syrup, stir the coffee and sugar in a small bowl. Add the liqueur and let cool.

3 To make the filling, whip the cream in a chilled medium mixing bowl with a handheld electric mixer on high speed (or use a balloon whisk) just until stiff peaks begin to form. Do not overbeat. Refrigerate the whipped cream until ready to use.

4 Choose a saucepan that will snugly hold the bowl of a heavy-duty stand mixer. Add about 1 inch of water to the saucepan (the bottom of the bowl should not touch the water). Bring the water to a boil over high heat, then reduce the heat so the water is at a simmer. Whisk the yolks and sugar together in the mixer bowl with a balloon whisk until the sugar dissolves. Place the bowl over the water in the saucepan and stir constantly with a silicone spatula, frequently scraping down the sides of the pan, until the mixture is thickened and hot (an instant-read thermometer will read 160°F), about 5 minutes. Keep checking the temperature, being careful not to overcook the egg mixture. Attach the bowl to the mixer and fit with the whisk attachment. Whip with the mixer on high speed until the mixture is fluffy, tripled in volume, and cool to the touch, about 5 minutes. Remove the bowl from the mixer.

5 Whisk the mascarpone in a large bowl until smooth. Gradually fold the mascarpone into the egg mixture. Stir one-quarter of the whipped cream into the mascarpone mixture to lighten it, then fold in the remaining cream.

6 To assemble the tiramisù, remove the chocolate orange cake from the refrigerator. Cut a round of cake to fit the bottom of a glass bowl with a minimum 2-quart capacity. Drizzle the cake with half of the coffee mixture. Spread with half of the mascarpone mixture. Cut a second round of cake to fit over the mascarpone layer. Reserve the leftover cake for the topping. Drizzle with the remaining coffee mixture and finish with the remaining mascarpone filling, and smooth the top. Cover and refrigerate for at least 4 hours or overnight.

7 Just before serving, crumble the remaining chocolate cake to measure about ½ cup. Rub through a medium-mesh wire sieve directly over the tiramisù to cover the top. Serve chilled.

I N ADDITION TO SELLING BAKED GOODS AT OUR RETAIL SHOP, SARABETH'S BAKERY ALSO ACTS AS A COMMISSARY FOR ALL OF THE BAKED ITEMS AND desserts at the various Sarabeth's restaurants around the New York area. Although we don't serve ice cream at the bakery, I still make it often for my restaurants. Here are my most-requested ice creams and sorbets, all using the very best ingredients, from ripe, fresh berries to imported chocolate and vanilla beans.

The best ice cream is made with crème anglaise, a thin custard that can be flavored and churned in an ice-cream maker. Eggless Philadelphia-style ice cream and Italian gelato (with fewer eggs and less cream than ice cream) have their proponents, but I prefer the French-style ice cream, with generous amounts of egg yolks and cream. They give my ice cream a silky creaminess that is immediately discernible on the first lick. I have also included a couple of dairy-free sorbets that are packed with fruit flavor.

To showcase your handcrafted ice cream, you might want to serve it in a freshly baked tuile cookie or a homemade ice-cream cone. These crunchy accompaniments take the already wonderful ice cream one step further, which is what the desserts at Sarabeth's are all about.

A LESSON ON ICE CREAM

Ice-Cream Machines At the bakery, we have a super-duper professional ice-cream maker that makes a few quarts at a time in just a few minutes. I am very familiar with this machine, but for testing the recipes in this book, I wanted to get to know the various ice-cream machines available to the home cook. So, I bought and borrowed various machines, and came up with a clear winner.

The job of an ice-cream machine is to provide an extremely cold environment that will freeze a liquid mixture in its metal canister into a semisolid state. A turning paddle churns the ice cream, which incorporates air during the freezing process and lightens the mixture.

The machine should work quickly to freeze the custard, as quick chilling creates small ice crystals that keep the ice cream smooth; gritty ice cream happens when the base liquid takes too long to freeze and large crystals form. If you are unhappy with the texture in your present homemade ice cream, it is probably because the machine isn't freezing the base quickly enough.

I tested three common styles of ice-cream machines. The most basic one uses ice and salt (the salt actually lowers the temperature of the ice cubes) to supply the necessary freezing environment. (One piece of advice: Err on the side of using too much salt.) Some modern machines use easy-to-find ice cubes and table salt, but there are still old-fashioned models that require crushed ice and rock salt, so know what you're buying unless you specifically want the antique version for some reason. An advantage to the ice-and-salt machine is size, as some have large-capacity canisters that hold up to two quarts, as opposed to the modern machines that usually cap at one quart. So if you know you will regularly make ice cream for a crowd, these traditional machines could be a good bet.

Modern ice-cream makers use Freon as the chilling agent. The most expensive models house the

Freon in a countertop unit and use electric-run compressors to bring the Freon to the freezing stage. I had high hopes for this kind of pricey machine, but the ice cream was consistently soft and grainy because it just never got cold enough.

The hands-down winner was the ice-cream machine with a Freon insert. At first glance, these machines may seem inconvenient, as the insert must be frozen for 24 hours before use. If you have a large freezer, space won't be an issue; otherwise, you will have to make room for the insert. This machine froze the custard in less than 20 minutes, which gave the ice cream a silky smoothness without noticeable ice crystals. Electric models turn the paddle for you, but there are also manual machines.

Making Ice Cream and Sorbets Carefully follow each recipe to create the basic mixture for the ice cream. Flavors such as vanilla or coffee can be added through steeping while the liquid is heating. In other cases, the flavorings (such as fruit purees, nuts, or chocolate) are added after the custard is cooked.

Sorbets usually are created from fruit purees, which means they have a high water content. When making sorbet, steps are taken to keep large ice crystals from forming. One way is using invert sugar. This liquid sugar is created by heating regular sugar (sucrose) to break it down into components of fructose and glucose, thereby reducing its crystal size and the chance of crystallization. Simple syrup and corn syrup are both invert sugars, so they are often used to sweeten sorbets.

Be sure the liquid base is thoroughly chilled before putting it in the machine. Warm custard will raise the temperature of the machine's chilling agent to the point where it will never get low enough for freezing. Chill a heated ice cream or sorbet base in a heatproof bowl set in a larger bowl filled with an ice bath, stirring often, and adding fresh ice as needed, until the mixture is very cold, at least 30 minutes. For custard-based mixtures, if you have the time, refrigerate the cooled custard overnight. The additional chilling will thicken the custard a bit more and make ice cream with an even creamier texture.

The base mixture is now ready to be churned. Just follow the instructions for your machine. The ice cream is ready when it is thickened and frozen to the point that the machine begins to strain, indicated by a deepening in the machine's sound. So you can hear this change, keep the machine within hearing range. If the machine isn't turned off when it reaches this point, it could break from the exertion of churning ice cream that is too thick. (Some machines will turn off automatically.)

Storing Ice Cream and Sorbets Just-churned ice cream will have a semisolid texture, like frozen custard from a dispensing machine. Even if you want to eat the ice cream at this state, it will melt into liquid very quickly. The ice cream needs a second freezing in your refrigerator's freezer compartment to firm to a scooping texture. Transfer the ice cream from its canister to an airtight container. Cover and freeze to firm up for at least 4 hours before serving. Even ice cream or sorbet that has been perfectly made will eventually form ice crystals in the freezer, so serve your homemade frozen desserts within two days of making them.

Ice-Cream Cones

Makes 10 cones

....

Being a professional baker, it was only a matter of time before I discovered home-made ice-cream cones, and now I'm spoiled. These delicate but crunchy cones far outshine anything that you can buy. The thin batter is baked on an electric cone maker, then wrapped while warm around a cone form. Once you get the hang of it, you'll be able to whip out a stack of cones in no time.

BAKER'S NOTE: You need an electric ice-cream cone maker that makes 7-inch-diameter cookies. The machine comes with a roller for shaping the cones, but I find that it is a bit too big. Look for a pizzelle or ice-cream cone shaping mold 1½ to 2 inches in diameter at the widest point. • If you find that the batter is too thick, which can happen if it stands, thin it with fresh orange juice or water.

1¼ cups confectioners' sugar, sifted	*4 large egg whites*
1 cup unbleached all-purpose flour	*2 teaspoons fresh lemon juice*
¼ teaspoon fine sea salt	*Seeds from ½ Plumped Vanilla Bean (page 295) or ½ teaspoon pure vanilla extract*
8 tablespoons (1 stick) unsalted butter, melted and cooled	

1 Preheat an electric ice-cream cone maker according to the manufacturer's instructions.

2 Combine the confectioners' sugar, flour, and salt in the bowl of a heavy-duty stand mixer. Attach the bowl to the mixer and fit with the paddle attachment. With the mixer on low speed, gradually pour in the melted butter and egg whites, occasionally scraping down the sides of the bowl, and mix until completely smooth. Add the lemon juice and vanilla and mix until combined.

3 Using a 2-inch-diameter ice-cream scoop (about 2½ tablespoons), place the batter into the center of the ice-cream cone maker. Close the lid and cook until the batter stops steaming and the cookie is golden brown, about 2 minutes. Remove the cookie from the maker and quickly wrap the hot cookie around the cone mold to shape. The cookie will be hot, so use a kitchen towel to help roll it up. Work quickly before the cookie cools and hardens. Repeat with the remaining batter, removing the cones from the mold as they cool. (The cones can be made up to 1 day ahead and stored in an airtight container.)

Vanilla Bean Ice Cream

Makes about 1 quart

....

I f you want to check a pastry chef's skill at making ice cream, taste his or her vanilla ice cream, because with only five ingredients, it is impossible to hide any flaws. Is the ice cream rich with eggs? Is the texture smooth? Does it have a distinct vanilla flavor? Give extra points if vanilla beans are used and you can see the tiny seeds in the ice cream. An instant-read thermometer is a must for cooking the custard to the correct temperature.

1½ cups heavy cream	*2 Plumped Vanilla Beans (page 295)*
1½ cups whole milk	*8 large egg yolks*
¾ cup granulated sugar	

1   Pour the cream and milk into a heavy-bottomed medium saucepan, and add the sugar. Squeeze the seeds from the plumped beans into the mixture. Split the beans lengthwise and add them to the saucepan. Whisk the egg yolks in a heatproof medium bowl and place near the stove. Also near the stove, place a fine-mesh wire sieve over a second heatproof bowl placed in a larger bowl filled with an ice bath.

2   Heat the cream mixture over medium heat, stirring almost constantly with a silicone spatula to dissolve the sugar, until the mixture is very hot but not simmering. Gradually whisk the hot cream mixture into the yolks. Return the yolk mixture to the saucepan and immediately reduce the heat to medium-low.

3   Cook, stirring constantly with the spatula, being sure to reach the corners of the saucepan, until the custard is thick enough to nicely coat the spatula. (A finger run through the custard on the spatula will cut a swath, and an instant-read thermometer will read 180°F.) Immediately strain the custard through the sieve into the bowl in the ice bath. (This removes any bits of cooked egg white that would affect the smoothness of the finished ice cream.) Discard the vanilla bean. Let cool, stirring often, until the custard is chilled, about 30 minutes. If you wish, transfer the custard to a covered container and refrigerate for up to 1 day.

4   Transfer the chilled custard to an ice-cream maker and process according to the manufacturer's instructions. Pack into a covered container and freeze for at least 4 hours before serving.

Blueberry Bombe: With just a few ingredients, you can make a simple and elegant showpiece dessert. I use blueberry jam most often, but just about any of my spreadable fruits will work, too. Spread about 1½ cups softened vanilla bean ice cream in a 5-cup steamed pudding mold with a lid. Spoon about ¼ cup of Billy's Blueberry Jam (page 276), or any of the preserves in this book, and spread it evenly. Repeat with 1½ cups ice cream and ¼ cup jam. Top with the remaining ice cream and smooth the top. Cover the mold with its lid and freeze until solid, at least 4 hours or overnight. Remove the lid. Cut a round of Vanilla Génoise (page 143) to fit the top of the mold, and cut out a hole for the center tube in the mold and replace the lid. Run hot water quickly over the closed mold, then wipe dry. Uncover the mold again. Place the cake round in the mold, then cover with an upside-down serving platter. Invert the mold and the platter together to unmold the ice cream bombe. Return to the freezer until ready to serve. Cut into wedges and serve with fresh blueberries.

Strawberry Ice Cream

Makes about 1 quart

....

Strawberries and cream is a match made in heaven, and when the combination is taken one step further and churned into ice cream, you approach perfection. I have learned that you can't just stir pureed berries into custard and expect great ice cream. Instead, macerate the berries overnight with sugar to break them down and release their juices; otherwise, you'll end up with bits of icy, frozen fruit instead of the smooth ice cream of your dreams. And hold out until you can get wonderful local berries before making this.

1 pound fresh, ripe strawberries, hulled and coarsely chopped	*1½ cups whole milk*
	1 Plumped Vanilla Bean (page 295) or
1 cup granulated sugar, divided	*1 teaspoon pure vanilla extract*
1½ cups heavy cream	*8 large egg yolks*

1   Combine the strawberries and ½ cup of the sugar in a medium bowl. Stir together and cover with plastic wrap. Refrigerate, stirring occasionally, until the berries give off their juices, at least 8 and up to 12 hours.

2   Combine the cream, milk, and the remaining ½ cup sugar in a heavy-bottomed medium saucepan. Squeeze the seeds from the plumped bean into the mixture. Split the bean lengthwise and add to the saucepan. Whisk the egg yolks in a heatproof medium bowl near the stove. Also near the stove, place a fine-mesh wire sieve over a second heatproof bowl and place in a larger bowl filled with an ice bath.

3   Heat the cream mixture over medium heat, stirring almost constantly with a silicone spatula to dissolve the sugar, until the mixture is very hot but not simmering. Gradually whisk the hot cream mixture into the yolks. Return the yolk mixture to the saucepan and immediately reduce the heat to medium-low.

4   Cook, stirring constantly with the spatula, being sure to reach the corners of the saucepan, until the custard is thick enough to nicely coat the spatula. (A finger run through the custard on the spatula will cut a swath, and an instant-read thermometer will read 180°F.) Immediately strain the custard through the sieve into the bowl in the ice bath. (This removes any bits of cooked egg white that would affect the smoothness of the finished ice cream.) Discard the vanilla bean. If using vanilla extract, stir it into the custard now. Let cool, stirring often, until the custard is chilled, about 30 minutes. If you wish, transfer the custard to a covered container and refrigerate for up to 1 day.

5   Using a slotted spoon, transfer about half of the chopped strawberries to a small bowl. Puree the remaining strawberries and their juices in a food processor fitted with the metal blade or a blender. Add the puree and reserved chopped strawberries to the custard and stir well.

6   Transfer the chilled custard to an ice-cream maker and process according to the manufacturer's instructions. Pack into a covered container and freeze for at least 4 hours before serving.

Chocolate Velvet Ice Cream

Makes about 5 cups

....

Chocolate is one of the very few foods that melt at a point lower than body temperature, and this is the main reason why the best chocolate desserts have that smooth, luscious texture. Some cooks use cocoa powder for their ice cream, but not me—it is chocolate that gives this frozen treat its velvety body, along with honey, an invert sugar that discourages ice crystallization. Use your favorite eating chocolate here, but don't use one with higher than 62 percent cacao content, as it might not melt smoothly into the custard. This is the most intense chocolate ice cream you will ever eat.

11 ounces semisweet or bittersweet chocolate (no more than 62 percent cacao), finely chopped

2 cups heavy cream

1 cup whole milk

¼ cup granulated sugar

⅓ cup plus 1 tablespoon orange blossom honey, or use another mild honey

1 Plumped Vanilla Bean (page 295) or 1 teaspoon pure vanilla extract

8 large egg yolks

1   Bring 1 inch of water to a simmer in a medium saucepan over low heat. Put the chocolate in a wide, heatproof bowl. Place the bowl over the hot water in the saucepan and stir often until the chocolate is melted. Remove the bowl from the heat and set aside.

2   Pour the cream and milk into a heavy-bottomed medium saucepan, and add the sugar and honey. Squeeze the seeds from the plumped bean into the mixture. Split the bean lengthwise and add it to the saucepan. Whisk the egg yolks in a heatproof medium bowl near the stove. Also near the stove, place a fine-mesh wire sieve over a second heatproof bowl, and place in a larger bowl filled with an ice bath.

3   Heat the cream mixture over medium heat, stirring almost constantly with a silicone spatula to dissolve the sugar, until the mixture is very hot but not simmering. Gradually whisk the hot cream mixture into the yolks. Return the yolk mixture to the saucepan and immediately reduce the heat to medium-low.

4   Cook, stirring constantly with the spatula, being sure to reach the corners of the saucepan, until the custard is thick enough to nicely coat the spatula. (A finger run through the custard on the spatula

will cut a swath, and an instant-read thermometer will read 180°F.) Immediately strain the custard through the sieve into the bowl in the ice bath. (This removes any bits of cooked egg white that would affect the smoothness of the finished ice cream.) Discard the vanilla bean. If using vanilla extract, stir it into the custard now. Immediately add the melted chocolate, then whisk until smooth. Let stand, stirring often, until the custard is chilled, about 30 minutes. If you wish, transfer the custard to a covered container and refrigerate for up to 1 day.

5   Transfer the chilled custard to an ice-cream maker and process according to the manufacturer's instructions. Pack into a covered container and freeze for at least 4 hours before serving.

Espresso Ice Cream

Makes about 5 cups

....

Thjs ice cream is yet another way to indulge in the satisfying flavor of deeply roasted beans and milk (well, actually cream). For an over-the-top treat, stir a cup or two of your favorite cookies, coarsely chopped, into the finished ice cream before its final freezing.

1½ cups heavy cream	*½ Plumped Vanilla Bean (page 295)*
1½ cups whole milk	*8 large egg yolks*
¼ cup granulated sugar	*2 tablespoons brewed espresso or*
½ cup French or Italian roast coffee beans, very coarsely ground	*1½ teaspoons instant espresso powder dissolved in 2 tablespoons boiling water*

1   Pour the cream and milk into a heavy-bottomed medium saucepan, and add the sugar and coffee beans. Squeeze the seeds from the plumped vanilla bean into the mixture. Split the bean lengthwise and add to the saucepan. Place the egg yolks in a heatproof medium bowl near the stove. Also near the stove, place a fine-mesh wire sieve over a second heatproof bowl.

2   Heat the cream mixture over medium-low heat, stirring almost constantly with a silicone spatula to dissolve the sugar, until very hot but not simmering. Remove from the heat and let stand 5 minutes. Strain the cream mixture into the bowl and discard the coffee beans and the vanilla bean. Gradually whisk the hot cream mixture into the egg yolks. Wash the empty bowl and sieve. Put the sieve back in the clean bowl, and place them in a larger bowl filled with an ice bath.

3   Pour the yolk mixture into the saucepan. Cook on medium-low, stirring constantly with the spatula, being sure to reach the corners of the saucepan, until the custard is thick enough to nicely coat the spatula. (A finger run through the custard on the spatula will cut a swath, and an instant-read thermometer reads 180°F.) Immediately strain the custard through the sieve into the bowl in the ice bath. (This removes any bits of cooked egg white that would affect the smoothness of the finished ice cream.) Stir in the brewed espresso. Let cool, stirring often, until the custard is chilled, about 30 minutes. If you wish, transfer the custard to a covered container and refrigerate for up to 1 day.

4   Transfer the chilled custard to an ice-cream maker and process according to the manufacturer's instructions. Pack into a covered container and freeze for at least 4 hours before serving.

Butter Pecan Ice Cream

Makes about 5 cups

....

After vanilla, butter pecan is my favorite ice cream. I love silky-smooth ice cream, so this chunky treat is a sharp detour from my usual preference. Perhaps it is the luxurious flavor of browned butter that puts it on my short list, as one of my mantras is "more butter is better."

1¼ cups (5 ounces) coarsely chopped pecans

4 tablespoons (½ stick) unsalted butter

1 cup heavy cream

2 cups whole milk

1 cup granulated sugar

*1 Plumped Vanilla Bean (page 295) or
1 teaspoon pure vanilla extract*

8 large egg yolks

1. Position a rack in the center of the oven and preheat to 350°F. Spread the pecans on a half-sheet pan. Bake, stirring occasionally, until the pecans are toasted, about 10 minutes. Remove from the oven and set aside.

2. Bring the butter to a boil in a small saucepan over medium-low heat. Cook until the milk solids in the bottom of the saucepan have turned a nutty brown, resembling the color of walnut shells. Pour the browned butter into a small bowl. Place the warm nuts in a medium bowl. Transfer 2 table-spoons of the browned butter to the pecans and stir well. Let the buttered pecans cool completely.

3. Pour the cream and milk into a heavy-bottomed medium saucepan. Add the sugar and remaining browned butter. Squeeze the seeds from the plumped bean into the mixture. Split the bean length-wise and add it to the saucepan. Place the egg yolks in a heatproof medium bowl near the stove. Also near the stove, place a fine-mesh wire sieve over a second heatproof bowl placed in a larger bowl filled with an ice bath.

4. Heat the cream mixture over medium heat, stirring almost constantly with a silicone spatula to dissolve the sugar, until the mixture is very hot but not simmering. Gradually whisk the hot cream mixture into the yolks. Return the yolk mixture to the saucepan and immediately reduce the heat to medium-low.

5   Cook, stirring constantly with the spatula, being sure to reach the corners of the saucepan, until the custard is thick enough to nicely coat the spatula. (A finger run through the custard on the spatula will cut a swath, and an instant-read thermometer will read 180°F.) Immediately strain the custard through the sieve into the bowl in the ice bath. (This removes any bits of cooked egg white that would affect the smoothness of the finished ice cream.) Discard the vanilla bean. If using vanilla extract, stir it into the custard now. Let cool, stirring often, until chilled, about 30 minutes. If you wish, transfer the custard to a covered container and refrigerate for up to 1 day.

6   Transfer the chilled custard to an ice-cream maker and process according to the manufacturer's instructions. During the last few minutes of churning, add the cooled buttered pecans. Pack the ice cream into a covered container and freeze for at least 4 hours to firm it before serving.

Butter Pecan Profiteroles

Makes 8 servings

....

The standard profiterole is a small cream puff stuffed with vanilla ice cream and topped with chocolate sauce. That's all well and good, but, as a long-standing fan of butter pecan ice cream and butterscotch sauce, here is my chocolate-free version. The touch of salt in the pecan garnish is a great surprise.

BAKER'S NOTE: Cook the caramelized sugar for the butterscotch sauce until it is the deep amber/copper color of an old penny. If the caramel isn't smoking with a distinct bitter aroma, it isn't ready, and the finished sauce will lack depth of flavor.

Pâte à Choux (page 149) • *Butter Pecan Ice Cream (page 258)*

Buttered Pecans

2 tablespoons unsalted butter

½ cup toasted, coarsely chopped pecans (page 5)

¼ teaspoon fleur de sel or coarse kosher salt

Butterscotch Sauce (page 288)

1   To make the profiteroles, place a rack in the center of the oven and preheat to 400°F. Line a half-sheet pan with parchment paper.

2   Fit a large (at least 14 inches) pastry bag with a ½-inch-diameter plain pastry tip, such as Ateco #806. Transfer the warm, freshly made *pâte à choux* dough to the bag and twist the top closed. Pipe 24 balls of dough, each about 1¼ inches wide and 1 inch tall, spacing them about 1½ inches apart, on the half-sheet pan. As you finish piping each ball, move the bag in a right-to-left movement, and use the end of the pastry tip to shear off the pointed tip of dough. If any tips remain, tamp them down with a finger dipped in water.

3   Bake until the profiteroles are well puffed and golden brown, about 25 minutes. Do not underbake, or the profiteroles will collapse when cooled. Remove the pan from the oven. Pierce the side of each profiterole with the tip of a small sharp knife. Return to the oven and bake until the profiteroles are well crisped, about 10 minutes longer.

4   Turn off the oven and prop the door open with a wooden spoon. Let the profiteroles cool completely in the oven. Using a serrated knife, cut each profiterole in half crosswise. Remove any stringy, uncooked dough in the center of each puff to create a crisp shell. Set the top and bottom of each profiterole side by side on a half-sheet pan to keep track of the respective halves. (The profiteroles can be prepared up to 8 hours ahead and stored, uncovered, at room temperature.)

5   Meanwhile, use a 1½-inch-diameter small ice-cream scoop to portion out 24 balls of ice cream onto a half-sheet pan. Cover with parchment paper. Freeze for up to 2 hours, until ready to serve.

6   To make the buttered pecans, just before serving, bring the butter to a boil in a small saucepan over medium-low heat. Cook until the milk solids in the bottom of the saucepan have turned a nutty brown, the color of a walnut shell, about 1 minute. Add the pecans and stir well. Remove from the heat and let cool slightly. Sprinkle with the salt and stir again.

7   When ready to serve, stuff each profiterole with a frozen ice-cream ball. Place 3 filled profiteroles in the center of a dessert plate. Drizzle a tablespoon or two of the butterscotch sauce over the profiteroles. Sprinkle the warm buttered pecans around the profiteroles. Serve at once.

Maple Ice Cream

Makes about 1 quart

....

Maple syrup sweetens this superior ice cream with its unique flavor. This is a wonderful dessert to make in the winter, when there isn't a surplus of fresh seasonal fruit suitable for adding into ice cream. Try a scoop with a slice of Carrot Cake (page 133), or the Rustic Apple Streusel Pie (page 180).

BAKER'S NOTE: Maple syrup is graded by color and depth of flavor, not by quality. Grade B has a rich flavor and darker color that makes it especially suitable for dessert making, and is easily found at natural food stores and many markets. Grade A is more delicate and lighter, and shines when poured over pancakes and other breakfast treats, but when used in baking has less maple flavor. • The maple flavor will be stronger if this ice cream is allowed to soften slightly before serving.

1¼ cups maple syrup, preferably Grade B	*8 large egg yolks*
1 Plumped Vanilla Bean (page 295)	*3 cups heavy cream*

1   Pour the maple syrup into a heavy-bottomed medium saucepan. Squeeze the seeds from the plumped bean into the mixture. Split the bean lengthwise and add to the saucepan. Place the egg yolks in a heatproof medium bowl near the stove. Also near the stove, place a medium-mesh wire sieve over a second heatproof bowl placed in a larger bowl filled with an ice bath.

2   Heat the syrup mixture over medium heat, stirring often with a silicone spatula, until the mixture is very hot but not simmering. Whisk the egg yolks well. Gradually whisk about half of the hot syrup mixture into the yolks. Whisk the egg mixture back into the saucepan and reduce the heat to medium-low. Using a silicone spatula, stir constantly until the mixture is very thick but not simmering, similar to a crème anglaise. Strain through the sieve into the bowl in the ice bath. Discard the vanilla bean. Let stand, stirring often, until chilled, about 30 minutes. Gradually whisk in the cream.

3   Transfer the chilled custard to an ice-cream maker and process according to the manufacturer's instructions. Pack into a covered container and freeze for at least 4 hours before serving.

Frutti di Bosco Sorbet

Makes about 1½ quarts

....

In Italian cooking, *frutti di bosco*, or "fruits of the forest," refers to the irresistible combination of strawberries, blueberries, and raspberries. Pureeing the fruit is simplicity itself, and before long your reward will be a lovely magenta sorbet with a luscious smoothness. If you closed your eyes, you would think you were sitting in a cafe in Florence. *Buon appetito!*

1 pint fresh strawberries, hulled and sliced (about 3 cups)

1 pint fresh blueberries (about 3 cups)

Two 6-ounce containers fresh raspberries

1 tablespoon fresh lemon juice

1 cup granulated sugar

¼ cup water

3 tablespoons light corn syrup

1   Puree the strawberries, blueberries, and raspberries together in a food processor fitted with the metal blade. Rub the puree through a medium-mesh wire sieve placed over a bowl. Discard the seeds and skins in the sieve. You should have about 3¼ cups strained puree. Stir in the lemon juice.

2   Combine the sugar, water, and corn syrup in a heavy-bottomed small saucepan. Bring just to a boil over high heat, stirring constantly. Stop stirring, reduce the heat to medium-low, and cook for 30 seconds. Taste the mixture—it should be very sweet. If needed, add more sugar and stir well to dissolve. Pour the syrup into a heatproof bowl placed in a larger bowl filled with an ice bath and let cool completely. Stir the cooled syrup into the fruit puree.

3   Transfer the mixture to an ice-cream maker and process according to the manufacturer's instructions. Pack the sorbet into a covered container and freeze for at least 4 hours before serving.

Tuiles

Makes about 10 tuiles

....

These paper-thin cookies are called tuiles (meaning "tiles") because they are often molded into a curved shape resembling clay roof tiles. I prefer to shape them over jelly jars so they become edible bowls for homemade ice cream or sorbet. The thin batter is spread into rounds, baked just until golden, and quickly transferred to its mold while still warm. If the cookies cool, they won't be pliable enough to mold, but a quick return trip to the oven will soften them and make them cooperative again.

BAKER'S NOTE: Don't make these on a rainy day, or the molded cookies will lose their shape. Store in an airtight container, as they will soften if left uncovered. Be careful handling them; they are fragile. • Upside-down ½-pint glass jars, topped with 6-ounce (¾-cup) ramekins, make the perfect molds for the tuiles. You will need only three of each, because the tuiles cool and set quickly.

⅓ cup unbleached all-purpose flour	*4 large egg whites*
¾ cup plus 1 tablespoon confectioners' sugar, sifted	*Seeds from 1 Plumped Vanilla Bean (page 295)*
4 tablespoons (½ stick) unsalted butter, melted	

1 Combine the flour and confectioners' sugar in a food processor fitted with the metal blade. Pulse to mix. With the machine running, add the butter. Immediately add the egg whites in a steady stream. Do not overmix. Stop the machine and add the vanilla seeds. Strain through a fine-mesh wire sieve into a bowl. Strain again into a second bowl. Cover and refrigerate for at least 4 hours or overnight.

2 Position racks in the center and top third of the oven and preheat to 375°F. Butter and flour two half-sheet pans, tapping out the excess flour. Place three ½-pint glass jars, bottoms up, on a counter near the oven. Also place three ramekins next to you.

3 You will bake three 6-inch round cookies on each half-sheet pan. Work with one pan at a time. Spoon 2 tablespoons of the batter at each end of the pan, about 3 inches from the sides of pan, and the last 2 tablespoons of batter between the other two portions. Using the back of the spoon, making a circular motion, spread the batter into a 3- to 4-inch round (figure 1). Using a small offset metal spatula, thinly smooth each round of batter to about 6 inches in diameter (figure 2). Do not spread the batter on the second pan yet.

4   Bake on the center rack until the cookies are completely golden, 7 to 10 minutes. Remove from the oven. Using a small offset metal spatula, one cookie at a time, remove the hot, pliable cookies from the pan. Turn each cookie bottom side up and place over a jar (figure 3). Quickly shape each cookie into a wavy cup (figure 4). Gently place a ramekin on top and press carefully to complete the shape (figures 5 and 6). If the cookies on the pan cool and become too firm to mold, return the pan to the oven for a minute or so to heat the cookies until pliable again. Remove the ramekin and let the tuile stand until cool. Repeat with the remaining batter, using a cool buttered and floured pan for each batch. With practice, you should be able to bake two pans at the same time. (The tuiles can be stored in a large airtight container at room temperature for 1 or 2 days.)

Piña Colada Sorbet

Makes about 1 quart

....

One of my bakers gave me this recipe and insisted that I try it. At first, I turned my nose up at this concoction made from two canned ingredients: pineapple juice and cream of coconut. It was love at first bite. Please give this icy treat a try. It is a great summer dessert when served with fresh tropical fruits. But for a truly indulgent experience, scoop into glasses, douse with a big splash of rum, and serve as a cocktail.

3 cups canned unsweetened pineapple juice

*1 cup canned sweetened cream of coconut
(not unsweetened coconut milk), whisked well*

2 tablespoons fresh lime juice

1   Place the pineapple juice, cream of coconut, and lime juice in a medium bowl and whisk to combine.

2   Transfer the mixture to an ice-cream maker and process according to the manufacturer's instructions. Pack the sorbet into a covered container and freeze for at least 4 hours before serving.

Chapter Ten

Spreadable Fruits

WHEN I WAS A YOUNG GIRL, MY FAVORITE AFTER-SCHOOL SNACK WAS JAM SWIRLED INTO SOUR CREAM. TODAY, EVEN THOUGH IT IS EASY to grab preserves off the shelf in my bakery, I still put up jars of luscious home-made jams at my weekend home on the East End of Long Island. My neighbor, farmer Bill Zaluski, saves the best of his harvest for me to simmer into preserves. In the summer, it is likely to be freshly picked raspberries, blackberries, strawberries, or peaches, and when the weather turns cool, apples. The reward is a constant supply of spreadable fruit to enjoy on toast, spoon over ice cream, or even savor straight from the jar. Preserve making is a very simple process. These recipes make reasonably sized batches to share with friends and family, or to hoard for yourself if you can't bear to part with them. In any case, try your hand at this time-honored procedure—you might be so pleased with your effort that you will consider making it into a career. That's what happened to me.

A LESSON ON JAMS AND PRESERVES

Preserves When preserving fruits into spreads, the goal is to capture the flavor of the fruit in a jar. I don't care how thick it is. In fact, you'll find that the fruit spreads in this chapter are definitely looser than other recipes you may have made over the years. I like a jam that's a bit runny, filling in the nooks and crannies of the toast or English muffin. As long as the spread hasn't crossed the line into a syrup, the flavor is more important than the thickness.

First let's define the differences among the types of fruit spreads. Jellies are made from fruit juice without any pieces of fruit. Preserves are chunks of fruit suspended in a fruit-based syrup. Jam is like preserves, but the fruit has been cooked almost until it loses its shape. Preserves and jams are my favorites because the fruit retains its identity.

How a fruit spread gels depends on the amount of pectin in the fruit. Pectin is a natural substance found in various quantities in different fruits. Some fruits (like apples and blueberries) have a lot of pectin, so spreads made from these fruits set up nicely As pectin is often concentrated in the seeds and skin of the fruit, some recipes cook them with the pulp to supply extra gelling power. Other fruits (like strawberries) are low in pectin, so most cooks think it's necessary to add commercial pectin to the preserves to get them to gel. I don't like commercial pectin. I can control gelling by the amount of lemon juice and sugar in the spread and by the length of cooking (which evaporates some of the liquid from the preserves, making it thicker and more likely to gel). Or, I add apple juice or other high-pectin fruits to the recipe to give the spread body, and provide another flavor dimension.

Getting Organized Making fruit spreads at home can be very satisfying—if you take the time to set up your kitchen. At different points in the process you will be handling hot utensils and food, and harried, disorganized cooks get burned more often than calm, organized ones.

If you are going to get into preserving, you should have the right utensils. The pleasures of canning will be enhanced with the proper tools.

A **heavy-bottomed nonreactive pot** (which means not made from untreated aluminum, which can react with the acids and give the preserves a metallic flavor) will let you cook the fruit and sugar without worrying about scorching too much. For the hot-pack-processing, get a **large canning pot** with a lid. These are usually made of a thin material so the water will come to a boil quickly. A **canning rack** is indispensable for getting jars in and out of the water bath. **Canning tongs** and a rubber-grip **jar holder** will come in handy. A wide-mouthed **canning funnel** is a clean way to get the spread into the jar.

Canning jars must be absolutely clean and have no nicks or cracks. There is no cutting corners when it comes to canning jars. You must purchase high-quality jars with new lids. Old supermarket jars with screw tops will not work (in fact, they'll probably break during processing).

Canning rings, used to secure the lids in place, are reusable. However, buy new rubber-coated **canning lids** for every time you preserve. The lids cannot be reused because heat shrinks the rubber and weakens the seal.

You'll also need thick **towels** to place the jars on for insulation during cooling—if the jars come in contact with a cold surface, they could crack.

The Process of Preserving Since preserving isn't an everyday procedure for most cooks, I'd like to outline the basic method. Remember that heat kills harmful bacteria, so it's important that the fruit is very hot and the jars are sterile.

Fill the canning pot at least half-full with water, cover, and bring to a boil over high heat. (Allow about 30 minutes or more for this procedure, as you are using a large quantity of water.) Bring a kettle of water to a boil just in case you need to add more water to the canning pot. Wash the jars, lids, and bands in hot soapy water, and rinse well. Dry the bands. If you wish, use a dishwasher. Jars that are piping hot and fresh out of the dishwasher don't need sterilizing in a hot-water bath. Do not put the lids in the dishwasher.

Cook the fruit and sugar as directed in each recipe, stirring occasionally to avoid scorching. Use a large metal spoon to skim off the foam.

While the fruit is cooking, sterilize the jars: Use canning tongs to immerse the jars in the boiling water. Add boiling water if needed to cover the jars by 1 inch. Place the lids in a saucepan and cover with hot tap water and bring to a simmer. Turn off the heat and let sit in the hot water until ready to use. The hot water softens the seal on the lip of the lid, creating a tighter seal.

Using the canning tongs, carefully remove the jars from the water. Invert the jars to remove any water and place right side up on a clean kitchen towel to drain. Spoon the hot fruit into the jars, leaving a ¼-inch gap from the top. (A canning funnel is very useful.) Wipe any spills from the edge of the jar with a hot, wet towel. Using a dinner knife, adjust the fruit in the jar to allow any air pockets to escape. Attach the hot, wet lids and bands, but do not screw on tightly—just twist the bands until you feel resistance.

Place the jars in the canning rack and lower into the water in the canning pot. If necessary, add enough boiling water to cover the jars by 1 inch. Return to a boil and process for 10 minutes at a slow boil. Low-acid fruits (apples and pears) should be processed for 20 minutes. Carefully follow the processing times given in each recipe.

Place a clean, thick kitchen towel on the work surface. Remove the rack with the jars from the pot. Using the tongs, transfer each jar to the towel and let cool completely, undisturbed, for at least 12 hours. You will know the jars are properly sealed if the lids are slightly concave in the centers. Also, when the lids are pressed in the centers, they should not make a clicking sound. If necessary, re-process or refrigerate them and serve within four weeks. Before storing, give the rings another turn to be sure they are tight. Hot-packed jars can be stored at room temperature for about one year. Once they are open, be sure to refrigerate them.

When serving, never place unclean spoons or butter knives back into the jar. This will create bacteria and your beautiful preserves will spoil.

Blackberry Jam

Makes 7 half-pints

Those of you who have berry bushes know that they are a summertime blessing, but really—how often can you put those berries on top of your cereal? Here's a great recipe to help you make use of the seemingly endless mountains of berries. It makes a lightly set purple-black jam bursting with berry flavor.

8 cups fresh blackberries, picked over and rinsed	*6 cups granulated sugar*
1 cup unsweetened apple juice	*¼ cup fresh lemon juice*

1 Bring the blackberries and apple juice to a simmer in a nonreactive large saucepan over medium heat. Stir in the sugar and lemon juice and bring to a boil. Reduce the heat to medium-low to maintain a steady simmer. Cook, skimming and stirring occasionally, until the juices thicken to a light-bodied syrup, about 25 minutes (figure 1).

2 Following the instructions in "A Lesson on Jams and Preserves" (pages 270 to 272), fill the jars (figure 2). Attach the lids (figure 3). Process the jars for 10 minutes. Place a kitchen towel on the work surface. Remove the rack with the jars from the pot. Using tongs, transfer the jars to the towel and cool completely.

Chunky Apple Preserves

Makes 6 half-pints

....

Here's one of my favorite recipes—a chunky, spiced apple spread that is good just as it is, or served next to grilled pork chops or chicken sausages, or spooned over griddlecakes. It is not dark brown, like a typical apple preserve, but a translucent light golden brown. Use the preserves as the filling for the Apple Turnovers on page 31.

BAKER'S NOTE: There is no "right" apple for preserves. Each variety has its own characteristics. Granny Smith, Jonagold, Golden Delicious, Empire, and Winesap are full of flavor and keep their shape when cooked. McIntosh apples will fall apart into a smooth puree, so if you want to use them, be sure to combine them with some of the harder apples or your preserves will be completely smooth. You may want to mix two or more of your favorites.

10 Granny Smith apples (about 4 pounds), peeled, cored, and cut into ½-inch cubes

1 cup unsweetened apple juice

3 tablespoons fresh lemon juice

½ teaspoon ground cinnamon

3 cups granulated sugar

1 Plumped Vanilla Bean (page 295)

1 Bring the apples, apple juice, lemon juice, and cinnamon to a simmer in a nonreactive large saucepan over medium heat, stirring often. Reduce the heat to medium-low and simmer, stirring often, until the apples are barely tender, about 10 minutes.

2 Stir in the sugar. Squeeze in the vanilla seeds. Split the bean lengthwise and add it to the mixture. Return to a simmer. Cook, stirring often, until the apples have broken down into a thick, chunky puree, about 25 minutes. Remove and discard the vanilla bean.

3 Following the instructions in "A Lesson on Jams and Preserves" (pages 270 to 272), fill the jars. Attach the lids. Process the jars for 20 minutes. Place a kitchen towel on the work surface. Remove the rack with the jars from the pot. Using tongs, transfer the jars to the towel and cool completely.

Billy's Blueberry Jam

Makes 7 half-pints

....

My husband, Bill, loves anything with blueberries in it. This jam is his favorite. When you pour it into the jars, it will seem loose and liquid, but don't be deceived—there is a lot of natural pectin in blueberries, and the jam will set as it cools. I've also included a raspberry variation that I love almost as much as the original.

8 cups fresh blueberries, picked over for green berries and stems, rinsed and drained

5½ cups granulated sugar

⅓ cup fresh lemon juice

1   Combine the blueberries, sugar, and lemon juice in a nonreactive large saucepan, and bring to a boil over medium heat, stirring often to dissolve the sugar.

2   Reduce the heat to medium-low to maintain a low boil. Cook, stirring often, until the juices thicken into a light-bodied syrup, 25 to 30 minutes. During the last few minutes, skim the foam from the surface of the jam.

3   Following the instructions in "A Lesson on Jams and Preserves" (pages 270 to 272), fill the jars. Attach the lids. Process the jars for 10 minutes. Place a kitchen towel on the work surface. Remove the rack with the jars from the pot. Using tongs, transfer the jars to the towel and cool completely.

Raspberry Jam: Substitute 8 cups fresh raspberries for the blueberries. Use 5 cups sugar and ¼ cup fresh lemon juice. Makes 6 half-pints.

Lemony Pear-Pineapple Preserves

Makes 8 half-pints

....

When winter arrives and local berries are long gone, there is always an abundance of pears in the market. I revived this old favorite from many years ago, fondly remembered by my friend Tracey Zabar. This very special preserve makes a wonderful topping for Vanilla Bean Ice Cream (page 250).

1 medium pineapple, peeled, cored, and cut into 1-inch pieces

6 to 8 ripe Bartlett pears (about 4 pounds), peeled, cored, and cut into ½-inch cubes

4 cups granulated sugar

⅓ cup fresh lemon juice

1 Plumped Vanilla Bean (page 295)

1. In a food processor fitted with the metal blade, chop the pineapple coarsely. Strain the juices into a nonreactive large saucepan. Reserve the pineapple pieces. Add the pears to the pineapple juices in the saucepan. Bring to a boil over medium heat, stirring often. Reduce the heat to medium-low and simmer until the pears are tender, about 15 minutes.

2. Add the reserved pineapple. Stir in the sugar and lemon juice. Squeeze in the vanilla seeds. Split the vanilla bean lengthwise, add it to the mixture, and return to a simmer. Cook, stirring often, until the pears are soft and chunky and the mixture is slightly thickened, about 25 minutes. Remove and discard the vanilla bean.

3. Following the instructions in "A Lesson on Jams and Preserves" (pages 270 to 272), fill the jars. Attach the lids. Process the jars for 20 minutes. Place a kitchen towel on the work surface. Remove the rack with the jars from the pot. Using tongs, transfer the jars to the towel and cool completely.

Strawberry-Peach Preserves

Makes 10 half-pints

....

These preserves have a healthy orange-pink blush and a deep fruit flavor. They are the perfect example of saving summer's tastes in a jar. For the best results, use thoroughly ripened (but not squishy or bruised) peaches and strawberries (without any white or green tips). I usually don't like to boil peaches to peel them, but as the fruit is going to be cooked anyway, I make an exception here.

4 pounds ripe peaches	*8 cups fresh strawberries, rinsed, hulled, and quartered lengthwise*
7 cups granulated sugar, divided	*½ cup fresh lemon juice*

1   Bring a large pot of water to a boil over high heat. In batches, add the peaches to the water and boil until the skins loosen, 30 to 60 seconds. Using a large skimmer or a slotted spoon, transfer the peaches to a large bowl filled with an ice bath. Peel and pit the peaches, and cut into 1-inch pieces.

2   Mix the peaches with 3½ cups of the sugar in a nonreactive large saucepan. Cook over medium-low heat, stirring occasionally, until the peaches soften and release their juices, and the sugar dissolves, 5 to 10 minutes.

3   Stir in the strawberries, the remaining 3½ cups sugar, and the lemon juice. Increase the heat to medium-high and bring to a boil, stirring often. Reduce the heat to medium-low to maintain a steady simmer. Cook, skimming and stirring often, until the liquid is thick and syrupy and the peaches are soft and chunky, about 40 minutes.

4   Following the instructions in "A Lesson on Jams and Preserves" (pages 270 to 272), fill the jars. Attach the lids. Process the jars for 10 minutes. Place a kitchen towel on the work surface. Remove the rack with the jars from the pot. Using tongs, transfer the jars to the towel and cool completely.

Cherry-Plum Preserves

Makes 7 half-pints

....

Two summertime favorites, sweet Bing cherries and ripe plums, are combined in this preserve. Use any plums you like, but be sure that they are good and ripe to supply the right amount of sweetness.

2 pounds Bing cherries, pitted

2 pounds ripe plums, pitted and cut into ½-inch cubes

½ cup fresh orange juice

3 cups granulated sugar

⅓ cup fresh lemon juice

1 Combine the cherries, plums, and orange juice in a nonreactive large saucepan. Bring to a boil over high heat, stirring often. Reduce the heat to medium-low and simmer, stirring often, until the fruit is tender, about 15 minutes.

2 Stir in the sugar and lemon juice and return to a simmer. Cook, stirring often, until the fruit has fallen apart into a thick, chunky puree, about 20 minutes.

3 Following the instructions in "A Lesson on Jams and Preserves" (pages 270 to 272), fill the jars. Attach the lids. Process the jars for 10 minutes. Place a kitchen towel on the work surface. Remove the rack with the jars from the pot. Using tongs, transfer the jars to the towel and cool completely.

Chapter Eleven

Frostings, Fillings, and Sweet Sauces

WE ALL KNOW THE PHRASE "THE ICING ON THE CAKE." IT IS USED WHEN SOMETHING NICE IS ADDED TO ANOTHER ITEM THAT IS ALREADY PRETTY good. That is true, but with many desserts, the icing is a full-fledged piece of the finished picture, not just a garnish. The same goes for fillings, sauces, and the other "sweet nothings" that, frankly, many desserts can't do without. Take the humble génoise cake. It must be moistened with syrup and layered with buttercream before it is goes through a Cinderella-like transformation into a multifaceted, gorgeous cake. Fill empty puffs of *pâte à choux* with ice cream and drizzle with butterscotch sauce, and you have created exceptional profiteroles.

Get to know these invaluable flourishes to the pastry maker's art. With practice, you can whip up any of them in a few minutes and have them ready to work in tandem with your baked creations.

Meringue Buttercream
Makes about 1 quart

....

Buttercream is an all-important component of layer cakes. Too many bakeries buy theirs ready made, and that stuff is far from the light, fluffy, buttery frosting that we make. There are buttercream recipes that use egg yolks, but the frosting ends up with a yellowish tinge that makes it less than versatile. I love this version, with a base of beaten egg whites and sugar, which gives the finished frosting a neutral coloring and satiny sheen. It is easy to add another flavor to this basic vanilla buttercream, and I've included a couple of my favorites on page 284.

BAKER'S NOTE: Temperature is the key to making perfect buttercream. The meringue must be heated to 160°F, then beaten until it is completely cooled. • Let the butter stand at room temperature until it has softened only slightly—it should have a somewhat plastic consistency so it can incorporate air when beaten into the meringue. • To ensure that the sugar dissolves into the egg whites, use superfine sugar. • After the butter has been added to the meringue, continue beating until the buttercream is truly fluffy.

1¼ pounds (5 sticks) unsalted butter, cut into tablespoons

5 large egg whites

1¼ cups superfine sugar

Seeds from 1 Plumped Vanilla Bean (page 295)

1 Let the butter stand at room temperature until slightly softened and malleable (it should not be soft or shiny), about 20 minutes.

2 Choose a saucepan that will snugly hold the bowl of a heavy-duty stand mixer. Add 1 inch of water to the saucepan (the bottom of the bowl should not touch the water). Bring the water to a boil over high heat, then reduce the heat so the water is at a simmer. Add the egg whites and sugar to the mixer bowl and whisk with a balloon whisk until the sugar dissolves.

3 Place the bowl over the water in the saucepan and stir constantly with a silicone spatula, frequently scraping down the sides of the pan, until the mixture is hot and opaque (an instant-read thermometer will read 160°F), about 5 minutes. Keep checking the temperature, being careful not to overcook the egg mixture. Attach the bowl to the mixer and fit with the whisk attachment. Whip with

the mixer on high speed until the meringue is cool (place your hand on the bottom of the bowl to judge the temperature) and forms stiff, shiny peaks, 5 to 7 minutes (figure 1). (If you use a handheld electric mixer, allow at least 10 minutes to beat the meringue until it is cool.)

4. Change the whisk to the paddle attachment. With the mixer on medium-high speed, beat in the butter, 1 tablespoon at a time, letting the first addition absorb into the buttercream before adding another (figure 2). After all of the butter has been added, squeeze in the vanilla seeds and continue beating until the buttercream is very light in texture and color, 3 to 5 minutes (figure 3). The buttercream can be made, covered, and stored at room temperature for up to 2 hours. Use a rubber spatula to stir the buttercream well before using.

Lemon-Rose Buttercream: I use this delicately scented buttercream for the Lemon-Raspberry Cake on page 159, and it is my favorite for wedding cakes. Beat 1½ tablespoons Lemon Curd (page 287) and ¾ teaspoon rose water (available at Indian and Mediterranean grocers) into the meringue buttercream.

Hazelnut Buttercream: This buttercream, used for the Hazelnut-Espresso Roulade on page 155, is made in a slightly smaller amount, as a roulade doesn't require as much frosting as a layer cake. Following the directions above, make the meringue buttercream with 4 large egg whites, 1 cup superfine sugar, and 1 pound (4 sticks) unsalted butter. Omit the vanilla seeds. Beat 2 teaspoons hazelnut liqueur, such as Frangelico, and 2 teaspoons brewed espresso (or ½ teaspoon espresso powder dissolved in 2 teaspoons boiling water), cooled, into the buttercream.

Mango Buttercream: This buttercream is used for the Coconut and Mango Cake (page 165). Beat 2 tablespoons mango liqueur into the finished meringue buttercream.

Pastry Cream

Makes about 1½ cups

....

Pastry cream (French bakers call it *crème patisserie*) is endlessly useful. Many professional bakers use it as a filling for their classic fruit tarts, and it is good for the home baker to know how to whip it together when he or she comes across perfect fruit at the market. Lightened with whipped cream to give it a looser, billowing texture, it shines in the Mille-Feuille with Summer Berries on page 167. It also is the base for my Banana Cream Pie on page 185, and in the *Pains aux Raisins* on page 43. Please try to use a vanilla bean here—its fragrance and flavor will make a world of difference.

BAKER'S NOTE: Common kitchen knowledge says that liquid containing eggs should not be boiled or the eggs will curdle. The cornstarch (some recipes use flour, but cornstarch has a less obtrusive flavor) in pastry cream insulates the egg yolks to keep them from curdling. In fact, you must be sure to bring the cream to a full boil or an enzymatic reaction in the yolks will make the cream thin in a matter of hours. So, if you've ever had thick pastry cream turn watery overnight, now you know the reason.

1½ cups whole milk

½ Plumped Vanilla Bean (page 295)

4 large egg yolks

⅓ cup plus 2 tablespoons granulated sugar

2 tablespoons cornstarch

1 Place a heatproof medium bowl with a medium-mesh wire sieve near the stove. Pour the milk into a heavy-bottomed medium saucepan. Squeeze in the vanilla seeds from the vanilla bean. Split the bean lengthwise and add to the saucepan. Bring the milk mixture to a simmer over medium heat.

2 Meanwhile, whisk the yolks and sugar together in another heatproof bowl until the mixture is pale yellow. Whisk in the cornstarch. Gradually whisk in the hot milk mixture. Pour the mixture back into the saucepan.

3 Whisk constantly over medium heat, being sure to reach into the corners of the saucepan, until the pastry cream comes to a full boil. Reduce the heat to low and simmer for 1 minute. Continue whisking until the cream begins to thicken, about 1 minute more. Strain through the sieve into the bowl. Discard the vanilla bean. Cover the pastry cream with plastic wrap pressed directly onto the surface of the cream. Pierce a few holes in the plastic with the tip of a sharp knife. Cool completely.

Lemon Curd

Makes about 2 cups

....

Smooth-as-silk lemon curd is a British favorite. It can be a little tricky to make, so I've provided plenty of hints in the recipe as added assurance. There are many uses for lemon curd beyond its traditional function as a spread on hot scones. Its sweet-tart flavor complements so many fruits, especially berries, and it makes a perfect tart filling or lemon mousse. Its puckery flavor is perfect for the Lemon Meringue Tartlets (page 195).

BAKER'S NOTE: When stirring the curd during cooking, a silicone spatula works better than a metal whisk, as the whisk froths the yolks and makes their thickness difficult to gauge. • When cooked egg whites set at a lower temperature than egg yolks, threads of whites will be visible before the curd reaches the right consistency. They will be strained out, along with the zest, creating a silky-smooth curd.

4 large lemons

10 large egg yolks

1 cup plus 2 tablespoons granulated sugar

8 tablespoons (1 stick) unsalted butter, at room temperature, cut into ½-inch cubes

1 Rinse the lemons under cold water and dry well. Using the small holes on a box grater or a Microplane zester, remove the yellow-colored zest from the lemons, being sure not to remove the bitter white pith. Cut and squeeze the lemons and strain the juice. You should have about ⅔ cup juice.

2 Place a heatproof medium bowl with a medium-mesh wire sieve near the stove. In a large heatproof bowl, whisk the yolks, sugar, lemon juice, and zest to combine. Place over a saucepan of simmering water. Using a silicone spatula, cook the curd, scraping down the sides of the bowl often, until it is opaque and thick enough to cling to the spatula, about 10 minutes. (A finger run through the curd on the spatula will cut a swath, and an instant-read thermometer inserted into the curd will read 185°F.)

3 Strain the mixture through the wire sieve into a medium bowl. (Using the spatula, stir the mixture to help it flow through the sieve and gently push the curd through the strainer. Don't force any solids into the bowl.) Gradually whisk in the butter, allowing each addition to incorporate before adding more. Press a piece of plastic wrap directly onto the curd, and pierce a few holes to allow the steam to escape. Cool completely, transfer to a covered container, and refrigerate for up to 3 days.

Butterscotch Sauce

Makes about 2 cups

....

I f it is gooey, creamy, or buttery, I love it. As this sauce has all three of these qualities, it has become one of my favorites to pour over ice cream or serve with other desserts, such as the Butter Pecan Profiteroles on page 258.

BAKER'S NOTE: One important thing to remember when caramelizing sugar is to be sure to cook it until it is the deep amber/copper color of an old penny. If the caramel isn't smoking with a distinct bitter aroma, it isn't ready, and the finished sauce will lack depth of flavor. And remember that caramel is extremely hot, so use extra caution when making it, and especially when adding the hot cream to the caramelized sugar.

1½ cups heavy cream	5 tablespoons unsalted butter, cut into tablespoons
1¼ cups granulated sugar	Seeds from ½ Plumped Vanilla Bean (page 295) or
¼ cup water	½ teaspoon pure vanilla extract

1 Place a heatproof medium bowl with a medium-mesh wire sieve near the stove. Heat the cream in a small saucepan over medium heat until steaming. Remove from the heat. Combine the sugar and water in a heavy-bottomed large saucepan. Cook over medium-high heat, stirring constantly, until the sugar is dissolved. Stop stirring and cook, occasionally swirling the saucepan by its handle instead of stirring with a spoon, until the caramel is a deep copper color and is smoking, 3 to 5 minutes. (The caramel will smoke for a while before it reaches the right color, so don't use the smoke as your only indicator. It should have a distinct, slightly sharp aroma that doesn't smell merely sweet.) Do not be alarmed if the syrup browns in one area before the entire mixture has turned copper color—just swirl the saucepan, and the browned area will combine with the clear syrup.

2 Add the butter to the caramel and let it melt. Carefully and gradually pour the hot cream into the caramel—it will bubble up. Whisk, being sure to get into the corners of the saucepan, until the bubbles have receded and the sauce is smooth. Strain the sauce through the wire sieve into the heatproof bowl. Stir in the vanilla. Let cool to room temperature. (The sauce can be made up to 1 day ahead, cooled, covered, and refrigerated. Reheat slightly in a double boiler over a very low heat, just until more fluid but not hot.)

Chocolate Sauce

Makes about 1 cup

There are times when a dessert—say, a simple cake—needs a little extra something. That's where this chocolate sauce comes in. Most chocolate sauces have a base of heavy cream, but that can make them too rich and spoil the overall balance of the dessert. This one uses brewed coffee, an ingredient that also enhances the chocolate, and just a touch of cream.

½ cup brewed coffee (not French or Italian roast)

2 tablespoons water

1 tablespoon superfine sugar

6 ounces semisweet or bittersweet chocolate (no more than 62 percent cacao), coarsely chopped

1 tablespoon heavy cream

¼ teaspoon pure vanilla extract

1. Combine the coffee, water, and sugar in a small saucepan. Bring to a boil over medium heat, stirring to dissolve the sugar. Remove the saucepan from the heat. Add the chocolate and let stand until the chocolate softens, about 3 minutes. Whisk until the chocolate is melted and smooth. Whisk in the cream and vanilla.

2. Transfer the sauce to a bowl. Let it sit until slightly thickened; it should be thick enough to nicely coat a wooden spoon. If it thickens too much, thin it with more brewed coffee as needed. (The sauce can be made up to 2 days ahead, and refrigerated in an airtight container.)

Raspberry Sauce

Makes about 1 cup

....

With its vibrant red hue, raspberry sauce is used often to brighten up a dessert that isn't so colorful. The easiest way to make raspberry sauce is to puree and strain uncooked berries. However, for this sauce, I find that the food processor or blender blade chops the tiny berry seeds and releases their bitterness. Instead, briefly cook the berries to soften them, then rub them through a sieve, which does the double job of pureeing and removing the seeds.

BAKER'S NOTE: Adjust the sweetness of the sauce with a little more sugar, if you wish. You can also use a teaspoon or two of raspberry liqueur, such as Chambord, or framboise eau-de-vie.

Two 6-ounce containers fresh raspberries

3 tablespoons superfine sugar

Seeds from ½ Plumped Vanilla Bean (page 295)

1   Combine the raspberries, sugar, and vanilla seeds in a nonreactive small saucepan. Cook over medium heat, stirring occasionally to dissolve the sugar, until the berries have given off some juices and they come to a boil.

2   Transfer to a fine-mesh wire sieve set over a bowl. To remove the raspberry seeds, use a silicone spatula and rub the berries and juices through the sieve. This will take some elbow grease and patience. Transfer the sauce to a covered container. (The sauce can be made up to 3 days ahead, covered, and refrigerated.)

Whipped Cream

Makes about 2 cups

....

Too often, whipped cream is considered an afterthought, no more than a dessert garnish. Actually, whipped cream is one of the most delectable ingredients in a baker's repertoire, and should be treated with respect. It is not difficult to make, but attention to detail will make all of the difference.

BAKER'S NOTE: If you can find it, use pasteurized (not ultra-pasteurized) heavy cream for the best flavor. • To help the cream firm up and keep its shape longer, the cream and utensils must be very cold. Place the bowl and whisk in the freezer for a few minutes before beating, and create an ice bath for the bowl during beating. This is important when the kitchen is hot. • Superfine sugar dissolves quickly in the cream, and the seeds of a plumped vanilla bean give superior flavor. • Finally, it is better to under-whip and settle for soft billows of whipped cream than run the risk of overbeating. A handheld electric mixer or a whisk works best for this amount of cream.

1 cup heavy cream, well chilled	*Seeds from ¼ Plumped Vanilla Bean (page 295) or*
3 tablespoons superfine sugar	*¼ teaspoon pure vanilla extract*

1   Place a medium bowl and beaters (or a whisk) in the freezer until very cold, 5 to 10 minutes.

2   Create an ice bath in a large bowl. Remove the medium bowl from the freezer and place in the ice bath. Add the heavy cream. Whip with a handheld mixer on high speed until the cream is lightly thickened and the beater leaves a trail on the surface. Gradually add the sugar and vanilla and beat just until soft peaks form. If using the cream to fill a pastry bag, beat just until stiff. (The whipped cream can be made a few hours ahead and stored in the refrigerator. Lightly whisk before serving.)

Simple Syrup

Makes about 1 1/3 cups

....

By itself, génoise is very plain sponge cake. In order to be complete, it needs to be soaked with syrup to give it moisture and extra flavor. Here is the recipe for the simple syrup that transforms génoise into cake. Even though each cake uses only a half-cup or so, simple syrup keeps for a couple of months, so make it in this quantity to refrigerate and have ready.

BAKER'S NOTE: Simple syrup is an ingredient in quite a few cocktails, so you might be glad that you have it on hand when you want a mint julep or whisky sour. It can also be used as a quick sweetener for fruit salad, and it dissolves much better than sugar in iced beverages.

1 cup granulated sugar ⋅ 1 cup water

Combine the sugar and water in a small saucepan. Bring to a boil over medium heat, stirring constantly. Stop stirring and boil for 1 minute. Cool completely. (The syrup can be stored in a covered container and refrigerated for up to 2 months.)

Apricot Glaze

Makes about ½ cup

....

This sweet-tart glaze gives a transparent shine to the surface of many pastries. It is a simply prepared mixture of apricot preserves thinned with a little water.

⅓ cup apricot preserves ⋅ 2 tablespoons water

Combine the preserves and water in a heavy-bottomed small saucepan. Bring to a boil over medium heat, stirring constantly. Reduce the heat to low and simmer for 1 minute. Strain through a medium-mesh wire sieve set over a small bowl and discard the solids in the sieve. Let cool slightly, but use while warm. (The glaze can be cooled and stored in a covered container for up to 1 month. Reheat and melt over low heat before using.)

Plumped Vanilla Beans

Makes 1 dozen

....

Early in my training, I developed a preference for the exotic flavor and aroma of vanilla beans. As good as vanilla extract can be, whenever possible I use vanilla beans. Plumping the beans in rum softens the inner seeds into a kind of pulp that is more pleasant to eat than crunchy seeds from an unsoaked bean. With a simple squeeze you can totally empty the bean and remove every last seed in seconds. There are times in the book when I really prefer plumped beans (stopping just short of insisting on them), but there are also recipes where I give an option for vanilla extract. Allow at least 2 weeks for the beans to plump in the rum.

BAKER'S NOTE: Look for a reliable source of vanilla beans and compare prices. Vanilla beans are never inexpensive, but if you buy them in bulk, the price will become more reasonable. • This recipe uses 12 vanilla beans. However, you can soak up to 3 dozen beans in the same amount of rum. The beans will last for up to 6 months in the rum, after which time they may get too soft. • You can substitute an equal amount of unsoaked vanilla bean for the plumped bean. Just split the bean in half lengthwise, and use the tip of a small sharp knife to scrape out the seeds. If directed to do so, add the emptied bean to infuse into the liquid in the recipe. • In some cases, 1 teaspoon of pure vanilla extract can be substituted for 1 vanilla bean. Vanilla extract has an alcohol base, and exposure to heat evaporates the alcohol and dissipates the flavor. (See page 7 for more information on vanilla beans and extract.) • Either dark or golden rum will do for soaking the vanilla beans. You must use liquor because the alcohol has a dual role as a preservative and flavor fixative. The rum will absorb some vanilla flavor, but it won't be nearly as strong as vanilla extract. Nonetheless, you can add it to whipped cream, pastry cream, apple desserts, or other recipes where rum and/or vanilla are common flavorings. • If you wish, turn the spent vanilla beans into Vanilla Dust (see page 296). Use the dust whenever you want a boost of vanilla flavor and aroma.

12 vanilla beans, preferably Madagascar or Bourbon • Dark or golden rum, as needed

1   Cut ⅛ inch off the bottom end of each vanilla bean. Stand the beans, cut ends down, in a large glass jar that is at least 12 inches tall. Pour in 2 inches of rum. Cover the jar and let stand until the beans are softened, at least 2 weeks. There is no need to turn the vanilla beans—just let them be.

2   To use a bean, remove one from the jar. Hold the cut end of the bean over the bowl containing the mixture that you want to flavor. Starting at the unsnipped end of the bean, squeeze down the length

of the bean to extrude the pulp. (This will remind you of squeezing the last bit of toothpaste from its tube.) If using the bean, split it lengthwise to release more flavor. When a recipe calls for less than a whole bean, return the unused part to the jar.

Vanilla Dust: Use this powder by the pinch in any recipe for an extra hint of vanilla. Start with emptied vanilla beans that have not been cooked in custards, sauces, or preserves. Stand the used vanilla beans in an open jar and leave until they are as dry as twigs and snap when bent; at least a week. Break into 1-inch pieces and pulverize in a clean coffee grinder until powdery. Store in a small airtight jar.

Sources

....

Amazon

www.amazon.com

A well-stocked supplier of baking goods, including my favorite Matfer nylon rolling pin, covered Pullman loaf pans, BeaterBlades, Frieling and Norpro glass-bottomed springform pans, Dexter pizza wheels, unrolled parchment paper, silicone baking mats, and more, including a full range of canning supplies.

Beanilla

P.O. Box 3111
Grand Rapids, Michigan 49501
(616) 855-5535
www.beanilla.com

Excellent selection of vanilla beans from around the world at good prices.

Bowery Kitchen

460 West 16th Street
New York, New York 10011
(212) 376-4982
www.bowerykitchens.com

A great source for cookware and bakeware, right across the hall from Sarabeth's in the Chelsea Market.

Creative Cookware

www.creativecookware.com

Another well-stocked online supplier of metal cake and entremet rings and general baking supplies.

Fante's

1006 South Ninth Street
Philadelphia, Pennsylvania 19147
(800) 443-2683 or (215) 922-5557
www.fantes.com

This cook's paradise sells salamanders for crème brûlée, ice-cream scoops of various sizes, ice-cream cone makers and molds, and countless other kitchenware items.

L'Epicerie

(866) 350-7575
www.lepicerie.com

Specialty edibles, including flavorings, chocolate pearls, bâtons, and pistoles.

J. B. Prince

36 East 31st Street
New York, New York 10019
(212) 683-3553 or (800) 473-0577
www.jbprince.com

Where New York's chefs love to shop, J. B. Prince carries the very best, including hard-to-find items like professional-grade plastic cookie cutters.

King Arthur Flour

135 Route 5 South
Norwich, Vermont 05055
(800) 827-6836
www.kingarthurflour.com

A top-notch flour manufacturer (their unbleached all-purpose, cake, and pastry flours are all excellent), King Arthur also sells a full line of baking equipment, both by catalog and online.

Pastry Sampler

1672 Main Street, Suite E, #159
Ramona, California 92065
(760) 440-9171
www.pastrysampler.com

One-stop shopping for the passionate baker, with everything from Ateco and Wilton pastry tips to cake boards, metal rings, and offset spatulas.

Sarabeth's Bakery

75 Ninth Avenue
New York, New York 10011
(212) 989-2424
www.sarabeth.com

Come by our store in Chelsea Market.

Sarabeth's Kitchen

(718) 589-2900
www.sarabeth.com

Use this Web site to order our Legendary Spreadable Fruits, gift boxes, and more; find the locations of Sarabeth's restaurants; or to reach us by phone.

Sur La Table

P.O. Box 840
Brownsburg, Indiana 46112
(800) 243-0852
www.surlatable.com

Their motto is "The Art and Soul of Cooking," and you are likely to find what you need for your baking, too, at one of their many stores, or online.

Whole Foods Markets

550 Bowie Street
Austin, Texas 78703
(512) 477-4455
www.wholefoods.com

These markets are a good place to buy bulk chocolates, vanilla beans, flours, and other essentials for people who love to bake.

Williams-Sonoma

3250 Van Ness Avenue
San Francisco, California 94109
(877) 812-6235
www.williams-sonoma.com

They carry a large variety of first-quality bakeware, cookware, and kitchen equipment.

Zabar's and Company

2245 Broadway
New York, New York 10024
(800) 697-6301 or (212) 496-1234
www.zabars.com

The granddaddy of food emporiums—visit their New York store or Web site for endless baking equipment and cookware.

Conversion Charts

All conversions are approximate

LIQUID CONVERSIONS

U.S.	METRIC
1 teaspoon	5 ml
1 tablespoon	15 ml
2 tablespoons	30 ml
3 tablespoons	45 ml
¼ cup	60 ml
⅓ cup	75 ml
⅓ cup plus 1 tablespoon	90 ml
⅓ cup plus 2 tablespoons	100 ml
½ cup	120 ml
⅔ cup	150 ml
¾ cup	180 ml
¾ cup plus 2 tablespoons	200 ml
1 cup	240 ml
1 cup plus 2 tablespoons	275 ml
1¼ cups	300 ml
1⅓ cups	325 ml
1½ cups	350 ml
1⅔ cups	375 ml
1¾ cups	400 ml
1¾ cups plus 2 tablespoons	450 ml
2 cups (1 pint)	475 ml
2½ cups	600 ml
3 cups	725 ml
4 cups (1 quart)	945 ml (1,000 ml = 1 liter)

WEIGHT CONVERSIONS

U.S./U.K.	METRIC
½ ounce	14 g
1 ounce	28 g
1½ ounces	43 g
2 ounces	57 g
2½ ounces	71 g
3 ounces	85 g
3½ ounces	100 g
4 ounces	113 g
5 ounces	142 g
6 ounces	170 g
7 ounces	200 g
8 ounces	227 g
9 ounces	255 g
10 ounces	284 g
11 ounces	312 g
12 ounces	340 g
13 ounces	368 g
14 ounces	400 g
15 ounces	425 g
1 pound	454 g

OVEN TEMPERATURES

°F	Gas Mark	°C
250	½	120
275	1	140
300	2	150
325	3	165
350	4	180
375	5	190
400	6	200
425	7	220
450	8	230
475	9	240
500	10	260
550	Broil	290

Index

....

At the Bakery

Marcelo Gonzalez
pastry chef

Jose Zaldivar
pastry sous chef

Juan E. Estevez
baker

Nancy Velazquez
baker

Leonel Aguírre
baker

Agustin Guzmán
assistant baker

Acknowledgments

For the past thirty years, I have been blessed to have been able to do what I love most, giving others pleasure through my baking—and I could not have done it alone.

There is no way to really thank my wonderful husband and business partner, Bill. He has been with me every step of the way in both my professional and personal lives. His patience and support during the long book process were immeasurable. Thank you, too, to my biggest fans, our children and grandchildren. Deepest thanks are especially due to my mother, Doré; daughter Jennifer; sister, Lynn; and brother Jeff, who worked with me over the years. Also, to my daughter Tina and brothers Mel and Jay for their constant encouragement.

Over the years, I have baked side by side with some incredible pastry chefs, and they have strongly influenced my personal approach to baking. I would especially like to thank my dear friends Michael and Wendy London, who inspired me to open my own bakery, and shared recipes and their expertise in the true spirit of friendship. I will always be grateful for the generosity of the talented Peggy Cullen, and tuile maker supreme Susan Rosenfeld. Others to whom I owe thanks include Vicki Wells, Nancy Heller, the late Craig Ruttman, and Dorie Greenspan.

This book would never have happened without the commitment of my bakery staff, who keep the bakery functioning at the highest level of professionalism. Pastry chef Marcelo Gonzalez has been with me since the very beginning—what would I do without him? Special thanks to pastry sous chef Jose Zaldivar. And appreciation goes to the bakers Jorge Vicente, Juan E. Estevez, Nancy Velazquez, Leonel Aguírre, and Agustin Guzmán, and to the porters, who help us keep our bakery clean. Kudos to our retail manager Jackie Grullón, Socorro Gomez, and Francisco Ponce, who make our customers happy each and every day. Special thanks also to Arlene Stein, our invaluable office manager and paperwork queen, as well as to our bookkeeper, Maria Latorre. Thanks to our drivers, George Barraza and Abdou Basse, who deliver our baked goods all over New York City.

Rick Rodgers and I started working on this book many years ago. Together, we spent endless months of testing and writing to get these recipes to be exact duplications of what you might eat at the bakery. We took on the challenge and surpassed my expectations. His knowledge and insights were invaluable to the project.

Thank you to Rizzoli's publisher, Charles Miers, who gave me the book of my dreams. My extraordinary editor, Sandy Gilbert, endlessly impressed me with her hard work and dedication to this project. Thanks also go to production director Maria Pia Gramaglia and director of publicity Pam Sommers. The beautiful book design is the work of my longtime graphic designer, the remarkable Louise Fili, and the meticulous design coordinator, Liney Li, who assisted her. This book has been simmering for many years, but it really never got off the ground until Tracey Zabar made the introduction to Rizzoli, and eventually became a very helpful member of the editing team.

I have long admired the amazing photography of Quentin Bacon, and it was a great privilege to work with him. Thanks also to his delightful assistant, Lauren Volo. Pamela Duncan Silver was our prop stylist.

A team of experts tended the manuscript after Sandy and Tracey worked their magic. Leda Scheintaub was the initial copy editor, Mary Goodbody did a very helpful subsequent read, Deborah Weiss Geline was our stellar copy editor/proofreader, and Marilyn Flaig was the indexer. Angela Miller, my agent, dealt with the many business aspects.

To all of the Sarabeth's customers who have enjoyed and frequented our bakery and restaurants over the many years, thank you.

Finally, I am eternally grateful to my Baba Ganapati, who true to his name, removed obstacles and cleared the path for this book.